The Dow Jones-Irwin
Guide to Franchises

The Dow Jones-Irwin
Guide to Franchises

Peter G. Norback   **Craig T. Norback**

Dow Jones-Irwin   Homewood, Illinois 60430

ISBN 0-87094-169-0
Library of Congress Catalog Card No. 78–55302

Printed in the United States of America

1 2 3 4 5 6 7 8 9 0 K 5 4 3 2 1 0 9 8

preface

At one time or another everyone thinks about going into "business for him- or herself." And since the turn of the 1970s, people have been doing more than just thinking about it.

Aspiring capitalists have set up shop in the darndest places selling the darndest things. Unfortunately, many of them go out of business almost before they get the front door open, because they are not aware of the pitfalls of operating a small business. They have cash flow problems, inadequate warehousing, not enough demand, not enough supply, taxes, laws, the list is endless.

Most of these people aren't experts. They just have an idea of freeing themselves from corporate life. If they thought a little, as you are doing now, they would realize that the best way to escape to a new life is not to start from scratch, but to buy a successful franchise. This means the risk of failure is low because of the franchisor's marketing track record and business acumen, both of which come with the package.

Until now, no single source book was available on the top franchises in the country. We list almost 500 franchises with detailed explanations on what the franchise is, how much capital is required, the type of financing available, if any, what training is provided, and what managerial assistance is offered during the life of the franchise contract. Also, we list an address, telephone number, and contact for each.

The book is organized by franchise category—Employment Service, Foods-Restaurants/Drive-ins/Carryouts, Motels-Hotels, Printing, and so on—but there is an alphabetical index of company names. This structure will allow you to investigate those franchises in an area which is of interest to you or you may look up a familiar company name.

Before contacting any franchise, we recommend you read the section titled "What Is Franchising?" This section is not intended to take the place of your consulting with your attorney or accountant, but it will provide you with the basics of franchising and what to expect.

If you have any questions about a specific franchise or franchising in general, contact the International Franchise Association, Education Department. The IFA is the only franchise association in the United States, and is the oldest and largest in the world. (See IFA section for address and telephone number.) They are most helpful and will be able to provide you with the information you need.

We have also included a section on the "U.S. Department of Commerce" (local names and numbers), and the "Small Business Administration." The latter can be contacted for financing if no other source is available to you. For those who wish to read more on the subject of franchising, we have compiled an extensive bibliography of general and technical books and other references.

Franchising can mean fun, freedom, and profits for you and your family, but before you take one penny out of savings, do what the International Franchise Association urges, "investigate before investing" in any franchise business.

November 1978

PETER G. NORBACK
CRAIG T. NORBACK

contents

section 1
The International Franchise Association, 1

section 2
The International Franchise Association Code of Ethics, 3

section 3
What Is Franchising? 7

section 4
Listing of Franchises, 35

section 5
U.S. Department of Commerce, 237

section 6
Small Business Administration, 243

section 7
Bibliography, 251

Index, 259

The International Franchise Association

7315 Wisconsin Avenue
Washington, D.C. 20014
(301) 652–6270

The International Franchise Association (IFA) is a trade association representing firms in a wide variety of industries who use the franchising method of distribution.

IFA was formed in 1960 by forward-looking franchise company executives who saw a need for an organization that would serve the interests of firms involved in franchising. Since its founding, the association has grown in numbers and stature to the point where it has become the spokesperson for responsible franchising.

Of primary importance to IFA is its effort to make membership connotative of the highest standards of business conduct. Membership applications are screened carefully and all members must pledge to adhere to a comprehensive Code of Ethics and the Ethical Advertising Code. It is IFA's intent that its trademark symbolize these standards.

The association shares the concern of its member companies that prospective franchisees or investors have at their disposal the maximum amount of information possible on which to base a business decision.

section

2

The International Franchise Association Code of Ethics

PREAMBLE

A Code of Ethics is a statement of the rules of good business conduct It is structured on the principles that the conduct of one person necessarily affects others; that the common good must always be a prime consideration in decisions made and action taken; and that no man should act in disregard of the rights of others.

This Code of Ethics recognizes:

That the relationship between a franchisor and his or her franchisees is necessarily comprehensive, covering a wide area of activities, and of mutual and reciprocal obligations and responsibilities.

That franchising is an economic technique of distribution and not an industry and therefore embraces many industries, each with its own unique attributes.

That the primary objective is to serve properly and effectively the ultimate user or consumer of the franchising company's products, goods, system, or services.

To assure the enhancement of mutual trust and confidence in the franchise relationship and in the franchise system of distribution, and being ever mindful of the public welfare, we, the members of the International Franchise Association, do hereby adopt and subscribe to this Code of Ethics.

THE CODE

I.   No member shall offer, sell, or promote the sale of any franchise, product or service by means of any explicit or implied representation which is likely to have a tendency to deceive or mislead prospective purchasers of such franchise, product, or service.

II. No member shall imitate the trademark, trade name, corporate name, slogan, or other mark of identification of another business in any manner or form that would have the tendency or capacity to mislead or deceive.

III. The pyramid or chain distribution system is inimical to prospective investors and to the franchise system of distribution and no member shall engage in any form of pyramid or chain distribution.

IV. An advertisement, considered in its totality, shall be free from ambiguity and, in whatever form presented, must be considered in its entirety and as it would be read and understood by those to whom directed.

V.   All advertisements shall comply, in letter and spirit, with all applicable rules, regulations, directives, guides and laws promulgated by any governmental body or agency having jurisdiction.

VI. An advertisement containing or making reference, directly or indirectly, to performance records, figures or data respecting income or earnings of franchisees shall be factual, and, if necessary to avoid deception, accurately qualified as to geographical area and time periods covered.

VII. An advertisement containing information or making reference to the investment requirements of a franchise shall be as detailed as necessary to avoid being misleading in any way and shall be specific with respect to whether the stated amount (s) is a partial or the full cost of the franchise, the items paid for by the stated amount (s), financing requirements and other related costs.

VIII. Full and accurate written disclosure of all information considered material to the franchise relationship shall be given to prospective franchisees a reasonable time prior to the execution of any binding document and members shall otherwise fully comply with Federal and state laws requiring advance disclosure of information to prospective franchisees.

IX. All matters material to the franchise relationship shall be contained in one or more written agreements, which shall clearly set forth the terms of the relationship and the respective rights and obligations of the parties.

X. A franchisor shall select and accept only those franchisees who, upon reasonable investigation, appear to possess the basic skills, education, personal qualities, and financial resources adequate to perform and fulfill the needs and requirements of the franchise. There shall be no discrimination based on race, color, religion, national origin or sex.

XI. The franchisor shall encourage and/or provide training designed to help franchisees improve their abilities to conduct their franchises.

XII. A franchisor shall provide reasonable guidance and supervision over the business activities of franchisees for the purpose of safeguarding the public interest and of maintaining the integrity of the entire franchise system for the benefit of all parties having an interest in it.

XIII. Fairness shall characterize all dealings between a franchisor and its franchisees. To the extent reasonably appropriate under the circumstances, a franchisor shall give notice to its franchisee of any contractual breach and grant reasonable time to remedy default.

XIV. A franchisor should be conveniently accessible and responsive to communications from franchisees, and provide a mechanism by which ideas may be exchanged and areas of concern discussed for the purpose of improving mutual understanding and reaffirming mutuality of interest.

XV. A franchisor shall make every effort to resolve complaints, grievances and disputes with its franchisees with good faith and good will through fair and reasonable direct communication and negotiation. Failing this, consideration should be given to media-on or arbitration.

section
3

What Is Franchising?[*]

* We would like to give our sincerest thanks to the International Franchise Association for allowing us to reprint *Investigate before Investing* by Jerome L. Fels and Lewis G. Rudnick and the IFA Code of Ethics; and too, for their guidance and assistance in putting this book together.

Franchising frequently and inaccurately is described as an industry or business. It is neither, but is a method of doing business, of marketing a product and/or service, which has been adopted and used in a wide variety of industries and businesses. Some of those businesses may have only one thing in common—a franchise system of distribution—and be very diverse in most other critical respects. There is no simple, single definition of franchising.

Franchise arrangements have been subdivided into two broad classes: (1) Product distribution arrangements in which the dealer is to some degree, but not entirely, identified with the manufacturer/supplier; (2) Entire business format franchising, in which there is complete identification of the dealer with the buyer. Some prefer a subdivision into three broad classes, namely:

a. Establishing a selective and limited distribution system for particular products (for example, automobiles, bicycles, gasoline, tires, appliances, cosmetics) to be distributed under the manufacturer's name and trademark;

b. Franchising of an entire retail business operation, including the license of a trade name, trademark, method, and format of doing business, sometimes called "pure," "comprehensive," or "entire business format" franchising (for example, fast-food restaurants and stores, motels, car rentals, personnel businesses, and schools, and so on).

c. Trademark and brand name licensing for processing plants, for example, soft drink bottlers, which combine some elements of (*a*) and (*b*).

Franchising has been defined, in part, in a prototype franchise disclosure law as "a contract or agreement either expressed or implied, whether oral or written, between two or more persons by which:

> *a.* A franchisee is granted the right to engage in the business of offering, selling or distributing goods or services under a marketing plan or system prescribed in substantial part by a franchisor; and
> *b.* The operation of the franchisee's business pursuant to such plan or system is substantially associated with the franchisor's trademark, service mark, trade name, logotype, advertising, or other commercial symbol designating the franchisor or its affiliate; . . .

Entire business format franchising provides for a contractually integrated system of marketing and distribution of goods, services, or both. Under such a system, a franchisor who has developed a product or service and a business format for his or her type of business, contracts with independent small businessleaders (franchisees) to give them the right and license to sell—and assists them to sell—the franchisor's types or brands of products and services to the public under its trademarks and service marks, and pursuant to its business format. The sound franchisor, whose system should be viable before starting to franchise, grants a franchisee a contractually limited use of a trademark, goodwill and know-how, including use of trade secrets and copyrights, access to systemwide promotion, standardized operating procedures, product and service research, and group purchasing power. The franchisor should train the franchisee in use of the know-how and in the establishment and operation of the business and should maintain and agree to maintain continuing assistance.

Franchises offer many of the advantages of an integrated chain organization to both franchisors and franchisees without some of its disadvantages, because they are created voluntarily by contract and not by central ownership. Moreover, aggregate marketing and distribution cost is divided between the franchisor and many franchisees, so that each may do for the benefit of all and the system what none might be able to afford to do acting alone. This system combines the efforts of an independent businessperson contributing some financing for the business, the motivation of a person who owns the business, and local management skills with those of an experienced strong "partner" who has a proven product or service and management and marketing know-how and standardized operating procedures. The relationship is continuing and cooperative.

In most arrangements, the "bundle of rights" granted to a franchisee requires in consideration some monetary contribution from the franchisee and some contractually imposed responsibilities and restraints to achieve the system standardization, uniformity, and quality required to meet customer expectations, and to preserve the chain image and goodwill.

PROTECT YOURSELF—WATCH FOR THE WARNING SIGNALS

Franchising has achieved an enormous growth. There has been much publicity about the franchise "boom." However, as the IFA has frequently noted, the well-earned and publicized success of the great majority has attracted the usual quota of those unprincipled and unqualified promoters who customarily attempt to ride on the coattails of the successful. Many publications, government agencies, local and national offices of the Better Business Bureaus, and others have attempted to check on companies selling franchises and to publish information about them. Fundamentally, however, protection of franchise prospects must rest with them and their professional advisers. The advisers must make proper investigation to evaluate the nature and characteristics of a particular operation, the costs to franchise, the availability of financing, the prospective returns, the training, experience, and work involved; and to compare these factors with the prospective competition.

EVALUATING THE OFFER

In addition to consulting your professional advisers, you and they should consider the following points and seek answers to the following questions.

The Franchise Business and the Prospective Franchisee

To properly evaluate a franchise offering, you must consider not only a specific franchisor, its reputation and business record, but the industry of which it is a part. Examine its system of franchising and its status in that industry and your own competence and motivations in relation to that industry, as elements in evaluating the offer from your viewpoint. Consider your decision to be one for a lifetime. Is the industry in a business area in which you are interested, in which you have some training or experience, or for which you have some aptitude?

Who Are You—What Are Your Qualifications?

A franchisor worth your confidence will want satisfactory answers to those questions and so should you. It is difficult to do, but you must evaluate yourself.

1. Have you carefully considered whether you are qualified for the franchise offered physically, by experience, education, learning capacity, temperament, and financial status?
2. If your interest is in food, should you be considering an automobile repair shop; if it is in things mechanical, such as automotive parts and repairs, should your target be food?
3. Are you anticipating, prepared for, and equipped for hard work as well as financial risk? If you intend to have only a passive or investor's role, have you determined at the outset whether the franchisor will accept this? If so, have you considered whether adequate employees will be available to you? Can you manage others? What has your personal history been in this regard? Is supervisory employee training available if your role is to be only that of a passive investor?
4. Do your advisers, family, and friends think you are adaptable, trainable, and generally qualified?

Most franchise contracts, especially in entire business system franchising, provide for controls reasonably necessary to protect all franchises, the system, and its image and goodwill; controls which require franchisees to maintain certain quality and uniformity standards. How do you react to such controls? Are you a "lone wolf?" Do you resent "authority" or restraints? Are you a "confirmed bachelor" who is on the verge of a "business marriage?" If so, franchising may not be for you.

What Is the Product or Service?—The Business Area?

Is the type of business and the type of franchise distribution you are considering the one for which you have an aptitude and strong motivations?[1]

If a product is involved, is it stable or seasonal, new or nearly obsolescent? Is it proven and is there a market for it generally and in the territory in which you will operate? Are you considering an outdoor swimming pool franchise for Alaska or a distressed urban area? Is the product untested, speculative, or a gimmick? How long has it been on the market? Is the product manufactured by the franchisor or a third party? How strong and reputable is the source? Check the reliability of delivery and availability.

Determine who controls product price to you and whether prices have been and are competitive. Is any suggested or projected selling price realistic in the light of competitive product conditions and anticipated returns?

What is the competition?

Are there governmental standards and regulations governing the product? Does it meet the standards? Are there government restrictions on use?

Are there product warranties or guarantees? Who makes them and who backs them? Are there arrangements for repair or replacement? At whose cost are repairs made, warranties honored? If the franchisor assumes warranty responsibility, what are the mechanics for and what is the franchisor's track record on warranty servicing?

Is there some product line diversification existing or planned? What new products, if any, are to be added? When?

Is the product patented? Is it protected by trademarks or copyrights? Does it involve formulas and trade secrets not available to others?

Do the product and the supplier enjoy good reputations?

After you have determined the product line, industry, or business area in which you are interested and for which you are suited by training, ability, temperament and desire, then begin investigating prospective franchisors.

---

[1] Many franchises offered are for service businesses. Some involve both products and services. For convenience, where the word "product" is used it shall include "service."

Who Is the Franchisor?

There are more than a thousand companies that distribute their products or services by franchising and there are directories which list them. If you receive a "kit" from a franchisor in response to any inquiry, read it carefully but do not limit yourself to this material alone. The purpose of your investigation should be to determine whether a franchising company is experienced, successful, strong financially and in management, and is reputable in its business area. Such characteristics are vital to any success you may hope to achieve. Moreover, if you will require financing and must find it yourself, the franchisor's reputation, credit rating, and track record (as well as its contract) may be vital considerations in your ability to obtain such financing.

The size of a franchisor should not be a controlling factor in your decision. A small company may meet the critical criteria set forth in this section. Many small companies are well managed and successful franchisors with very successful franchisees. Relatively few franchisors (including the most successful) are "big business" as the term is commonly understood in business, banking, and government circles. Moreover, the fact that a franchisor has conducted business and franchised only in one region or market area (state or metropolitan) does not mean that one should not consider operating under its franchise outside that region or area. Many franchisors who commenced business in one location or state have become regional or national.

One should consider whether the success achieved by a franchisor (and the franchisees) in one area may be an indication that the franchisor and franchisees will be similarly successful in another area if the merger conditions are similar, and if the franchisor can and will devote the capital and effort and select qualified franchisees who will devote the effort to duplicate and multiply any initial successes.

The Company—Generally

Determine whether the company is a public or private company; or whether it is a subsidiary of a larger company. If it is a subsidiary, the reputation, stability, and financial strength of both parent and subsidiary should be considered.

Investigate the franchisor and its officers and directors. Determine whether there is real business experience behind the company. How long has it been in business and how long has it been granting franchises?

Check the current financial condition of the franchisor. If it is publicly held, data is readily available. If it is a privately held company, the sources referred to in the sections dealing with "Aids to Investigation" and

"Regulation of the Offer and Sale of Franchises" can help you. In the section on "Franchise Laws" you will find a list of administrative agencies of fourteen states where such information may be obtained.

How many franchisees and company-owned outlets are there in "your" territory?

Is the franchisor a corporation, partnership, or proprietorship?

How long has the franchisor conducted business in its industry? How long has it granted franchises for the business? Has the company granted franchises in other lines of business; how long in each line; are they competitive or significantly different?

How many franchisees and company-owned outlets are claimed? Seek some verification.

Is the franchisor carefully checking your qualifications and otherwise indicating a long-term interest, or does the franchisor appear interested only in selling quickly for the initial fee? Are you being rushed or is mutual verification encouraged? Is adequate time offered to study the contract before signing?

Obtain a list of and contact other franchisees and learn about the operation from the inside. Verify that performance generally matches promises. Franchisees will not hide complaints.

Trademarks and Copyrights

Verify trademarks, trade names, and other commercial symbols and that they are the ones you think they are—not merely similar? Is the franchisor to do business under and be generally identified by the names and marks or is it only one of many company divisions to do so?

Is the trade name that of a well-known person? If so, is he or she active? What is the person's financial interest? Does he or she receive compensation for work or solely for use of the name? Does he or she have any equity interest? Is the person independently famous or is his fame attributable, in part, to his association with the franchisor? Is the franchise relying on the promotional value of such person's name or is the franchisor's use of it a relatively minor aspect of the franchisor's program? What is the duration, scope, and exclusivity in your business field of the license to use such a well-known person's name? What are the limitations on such use? Are the "well-known" person's business, profession, or activities sensitive or historically subject to serious impairment so that undue reliance on it may be dangerous? If the franchisor relies heavily on the promotional value of the name of an independently well-known person, careful analysis should be made of other elements of the franchisor's program.

All trademarks, service marks, copyrights, patents, logotypes, trade names, commercial symbols, and registrations (federal and state) should be specifically described.

Are there any agreements currently in effect which significantly limit the rights of the franchisor to use or license the use of such trademarks, service marks, trade names, logotypes, or other commercial symbols in any manner material to the franchise?

If a food service franchisor uses a "celebrity" name and/or likeness as its trade name and/or mark, is the franchisor's use limited to one or two products (e.g., fish and chips) and to one marketing system (takeout or in-facility service), and may the celebrity engage in other food businesses or franchise others to do so?

Are there any presently effective determinations of the Patent Office, a state trademark administrator or any court, or any pending interference, opposition, or cancellation proceeding or material litigation involving such trademarks, service marks, trade names, logotypes, or other commercial symbols and which are relevant to their use in the state in which you plan to conduct business?

Are any actual or potentially infringing uses known to the franchisor which could materially affect the franchisee's use of such trademarks, service marks, trade names, logotypes, or other commercial symbols in the state in which you plan to conduct business.

Patents and copyrights have a limited life by law. Determine the duration of any patents or copyrights that are material to the franchise and whether the franchisor may and intends to renew.

Management

Who are the principal officers, directors, partners, and management personnel?

What was the principal occupation of each during the preceding five-year period? What experience does each have in his or her field of management, in the business field, and in franchising?

Litigation

Have the franchisor or any of its principal officers, directors, partners, or management personnel been involved in litigation in the recent past?

1. Did any of them have any criminal or material civil actions (or a significant number of civil actions irrespective of materiality) pending against them alleging fraud, embezzlement, fraudulent conversion, restraint of trade, unfair or deceptive practices or misap-

propriation of property? If so, determine the current status of any pending action and get a summary of the opinion of counsel representing the franchisor in each such action as to its merits.

2. Were any of them convicted of a felony or have any of them been held liable in a civil action by final judgment if such felony or civil action involved fraud, embezzlement, fraudulent conversion, restraint of trade, unfair or deceptive practices, or misappropriation of property.

3. Are any of them subject to any currently effective restrictive court order relating to the franchise or under any federal or state securities, antitrust, trade regulation, or trade practice law as a result of a concluded or pending action or proceeding brought by a public agency?

4. Have any of such persons, during the preceding five-year period been adjudicated a bankrupt or reorganized due to insolvency or was any such person a principal officer or general partner of any company that has been adjudicated a bankrupt or reorganized due to insolvency.

Profit Projections

Most franchisors will submit profit projections with their "franchise kit" or promotions. You should seek them and you and your accountant should examine them carefully, particularly in the following respects:

a. Analyze the profit projections of the franchisor. Has your accountant made a projection based on other data available to him and compared it to the one submitted?

b. On what specific data is the franchisor's projection based—on the franchisees' experiences or on the operations of others, and over what period of time? Is verification available?

c. If the projection is based on actual past and current franchisees' experience, what was the area mix and character of the locations included in the computation? What time period was involved?

   Determine the locations, length of time in business, territory protection, management (franchisee or employee managed) and number of franchisees whose earnings were used in the projections.

d. Compare your projected profit (considering, if you are to be active in the business, reasonable compensation for yourself, if allowance is not provided in the franchisor's projection) with what you would earn for equal work elsewhere and from other investments you could acquire with the funds to be invested in the franchise. Verify these projections with other franchisees. They are a primary source for determining whether performance matches promise in this and in other areas. Get franchisee names and addresses from the franchisor and use such information to inquire and to make personal visits with those in your market area to the extent feasible.

e. If the projected returns are realized, will the results satisfy your needs economically and psychologically? Are you taking into account the history of new business ventures such as tough going for the first year or two and limited savings opportunities?

Franchise Cost—Initial Fees and Cash Requirements

Most franchises—especially entire business system franchises—require monetary contributions by franchisees consisting of some or all of the following: (1) an initial franchise or license fee; (2) training cost (tuition and/or room, board, and transportation) and on-site, start-up aid and promotion charges (some or all of which may be included in the initial franchise or license fee or may in whole or in part be separately stated) ; and (3) periodic royalties or service fees and an advertising contribution (usually payable monthly or weekly and based on a specified percentage of sales) . Sometimes there is a charge for centralized bookkeeping, accounting, and data processing services. There may also be initial payments for premises, equipment, supplies, and opening inventory, if acquired from franchisor. (If acquired from other approved sources, the payment for them is nonetheless part of your initial opening cost.) Get specific details on all cost items: amount, time of payment, financing arrangements.

Terms such as "initial cost," "initial fee," "total cost," and "royalties" should be specifically defined and made quite clear to you. The terms "cash required," "initial cash required," "investment," "down payment," and "equity investment" mean different things in different offerings.

"Initial fees" probably do not include any equipment or product inventory down payment.

Make certain your investigation is complete and your understanding clear in the following areas:

1. Initial license fee
   a. Is there one? How much is the total fee? Is it payable in a lump sum or in installments? If in installments, with or without interest? Is it refundable? Is it nonrecurring?
   b. If the initial license fees are not the same for each franchise concurrently granted, on what factors are the differences based?
   c. Does an initial license fee include compensation in full for any or all of the following? Use of the then current operation manual, training, and start-up aid, including personal on-site and promo-

tional assistance, at franchisor's cost? It does not in many cases. The understanding should be clear; the contract explicit.

2. **Continuing regular fees**

   a. Are there periodic royalties? How much are they? How determined? In business format franchising, generally, there is a periodic royalty (usually payable monthly or weekly) commonly based on a percentage of sales.

   b. How and when are sales and royalties reported and royalties paid?

   c. Royalties are not only payment for use of a trademark and trade name (and where available and applicable other commercial symbols, patents, or formulas) but may also constitute a fee for services to be performed by franchisors. If the periodic payment is in part a service fee, what ongoing services are you to receive from the franchisor? Are accounting services included or available? Are they computerized? Will updated merchandising services, operating manuals, and training be furnished without additional, or at nominal, cost?

3. **Other fees**

   What other fees and charges, if any, are payable (for example, advertising and promotion)?

4. **Total cost**

   Do not confuse "initial fees," "initial cash required," "initial investment," or "initial costs" with total costs. Initial cost or initial investment, may require computation and inclusion of some or all of the following, in addition to initial franchise or license fees and royalties, concerning which inquiry should be made:

   a. Are you required to purchase or rent business premises? Who finds the site? What is its cost to you as purchaser or lessor? How is it to be financed, if purchased?

   b. Does "initial" cost or investment include an "opening" inventory of products and supplies; a down payment on equipment and fixtures; a lease security payment; or all or part of the franchise fee? What amount is attributable to each such item?

   c. Don't confuse down payment or initial cost with ultimate cost. What are deferred balances? Who finances any deferred balances? At what interest? If the franchisor doesn't, is help in finding a source of financing offered? Have you received commitment for financing offered? Have you received commitment for financing before commiting yourself? May you seek competitive financing sources or is use of the franchisor or its designated source mandatory? (It should not be.)

   d. What, if any, are construction, remodeling and decorating costs, security deposits, if any, and initial equipment and inventory requirements costs?

e. In determining total costs, check every aspect of the deal. Do not overlook the cost of finding, buying or leasing, and improving and equipping a business location, obtaining zoning licenses for the operation at that location and the financing costs involved. In determining total opening costs do not overlook working capital and rent (where applicable), inventory, payroll, insurance, and your own promotions and salary during the first year. Know what your monthly debt service will be under your deferred payments financing.

Training and Start-up Aid

In most instances you will be assuming ownership responsibilities for the first time and will be entering a relatively new and unfamiliar field of business. You will require proper training in each area. Some franchise agreements will require training of some employees at the franchisor's training site or on your premises.

Successful and reputable franchisors treat the proper training of franchisees as a serious and essential responsibility. This is a critical area! The contract provisions relating to training should be reasonably specific.

You should determine all of the following:

a. Is experience or training required? If not, why not? If training is not mandatory, do new franchisees customarily enroll in the training program?

b. What are the nature, duration, and extent of training? What are the costs and who pays them? In assessing training costs, determine whether there is tuition; who pays room, board, and transportation. What is to be the location of the training facilities—the franchisor's home office training facility, an operating franchised business or company unit in your area, your own outlet, or more than one of these?

c. Is the training of any of your employees included in any training cost charge or allowance agreed upon? If employee training is not at the franchisor's training facility but at the franchisee's outlet, how much of the training will be done by franchisor's field representatives and to what extent are you to assist in training your employees?

d. Determine whether supplemental training will be available to cover routine supervisory employee turnover; whether it is required or permitted; at what cost; and who bears the cost. Is it included in the initial franchise or license fee, periodic service fee, or royalty?

e. Is there and will there be a continuing training program, not only to cover routine employee turnover but to keep you and your supervisory personnel "updated" periodically on management improvement and product and marketing changes? Is there a specific program? Will updating training be at a franchisor's facility or on your premises? Will there be personal training or seminars or mailed materials?

Will there be a charge? If so, what is the cost?

f. Determine whether there will be start-up assistance including assistance by franchisor personnel at the franchised outlet, immediately before and for a limited time after opening the unit, including supervision of equipment layouts, business operations, and start-up and preopening promotions. If it is not included in the initial franchise or license fee, what is the cost?

The franchise agreement should be specific and should clearly set forth all initial and continuing training obligations of the franchisor and franchisee.

Location, Territory and the Operating Facility

Is your proposed franchise for a specific business location in a particular territory? Is it confined to that one location?

As generally used, the terms "site," "location," or "facility" refer to the specific premises from which you are to conduct business. If a fixed location is a requirement of the system, the term "territory" is frequently used to describe the geographical area in which the site is to be located and which may be assigned to you as a protected or exclusive area.

Site location and the expertise with which it is selected may be a factor of critical importance in determining the success of the venture.

If the marketing system is based upon customers coming to your place of business, the feasibility of the proposed location and facility may be of overriding importance. In the vast majority of cases, the expertise in this area will be in franchisor's staff. The franchisor is most likely to have location standards and a profile of successful site criteria; techniques for measuring traffic counts, accessibility, traffic "quality," average income in the area and its character (single family, apartments, young/old families, and so on). Particular attention should be paid to the foregoing and to the following specific items:

Will the franchisor find and offer or specify the location and provide for facility construction? Will the franchisor arrange with a third party to build, finance, and lease to you or will a "tenantable" building be subleased by the franchisor to you? On what terms and within what time period? Will leases or subleases be for the same term as the franchise, including parallel renewal options? (They should be.)

Who is to find the site, negotiate the lease or purchase, build and equip the facility—you or the franchisor? Is any of this included in the initial franchise or license fee? If not, what is the charge? Who is to obtain financing?

If you are to lease from third parties directly and arrange for any required construction, what aid will you receive from the franchisor in site selection and how expert is the franchisor in this regard? If you are to find, lease the site, or lease or build the facility, be certain of site and facility availability and financing before you are committed.

Building plans and specifications for premises and layout may be an essential part of the system image. Are you to receive plans and specifications from franchisor if you or your lessor build? Is the cost included in the initial fee? Mutual responsibilities should be clearly stated in the franchise agreement and any preliminary agreements.

Be certain lease terms and renewals are coextensive with those of the franchise.

If a particular territory and site is specified, on what basis was it determined? Have you checked it with your advisers as to neighborhood character and quality, zoning, traffic hours and density, and surrounding business establishments, including competitive ones and the apparent activity in them? Have you checked other franchised outlets and franchisees, and compared their locations and yours in the light of the foregoing characteristics?

Is your franchise exclusive? Does the franchisor agree not to conduct business or have a company place of business in the territory assigned to you? Does the franchisor agree not to franchise others to do business in that territory?

Your lawyer should advise you as to legal limitations on the extent to which an "exclusive franchise" protects you. The terms "exclusive" or "protected" frequently only mean that the franchisor will not operate a facility and will not franchise others to do business from a location in the territory. A franchisor generally may not lawfully undertake to keep others from selling products in or transshipping into your territory from locations outside that territory. In the past many franchisors desired to grant more protection than they can now lawfully provide under current antitrust laws. If a contract purportedly provides "protection" for each franchisee's "exclusive territory" by prohibiting you and other franchises from selling outside of your respective territories it is probably unlawful.

A prescribed territory may be made your primary area of responsibility —the area in which you must concentrate your primary efforts and which you must not neglect because you are selling elsewhere.

Check this carefully with your lawyer.

If your area is not exclusive, determine the existence of any alleged company policy which has the practical effect of a limited exclusive. What is company policy and how faithfully and successfully is it implemented? Where are company and franchised outlets in other territories and yours; how many are there usually?

Keep in mind, you and other franchisees and the franchisor may not lawfully agree to or enforce, a territory division policy.

If the franchise is "exclusive," can your territory be altered with population increase? If so, on what prescribed formula is the alteration right based? Do you have a first refusal option as to any new additional franchise in the territory?

Can your territory be reduced or your exclusive modified if you fail to meet specified quotas or for other reasons.

If you do not have an "exclusive territory" and if the franchisor proposes to franchise an outlet at a new location closer to you than to any other franchisee, do you have a first refusal option to acquire a franchise for that outlet? Are the terms spelled out specifically?

May the franchisor or its parent or affiliate establish other franchises or company-owned outlets selling or leasing similar products or services under a different trade name or trademark?

Operating Practices, Assistance and Controls

Understand the franchise contract provisions relative to operating controls, practices and assistance before you sign the agreement. Neither the franchisor nor you will desire a relationship which is unhappy because of misunderstanding.

As indicated before, uniformity and standardization of product character and quality is an important characteristic of franchising. It is essential in preserving franchise identity and in continuing the value of trade names and trademarks in maintaining that identity. The contract will undoubtedly contain many control and restraint provisions concerning: facility appearance; equipment, fixtures, and furnishings; kind, quantity, quality, specifications, and layout (where the facility is important to the enterprise) ; product specifications control, availability, and standards (and frequent determination of sources of supply) ; advertising, promotion, and internal procedures controls.

Some items merit special attention.

What continuing management aid and assistance will you receive? Are they included in the service or royalty fee or is there some additional charge?

Must the franchisee participate personally in conducting the franchised business? If so, to what extent? Is such participation a policy matter or an express requirement of the contract? Did you compare projected net receipts from the franchise with your family needs and in doing so take the value of your time and loss of other employment into account?

What advertising and promotion will there be? At what level—national, regional, or local? Under whose direction and control? At whose expense and at what cost? What is the franchisor's past practice and record? What is the promise? What does the contract say? Check particularly the following?

Are there to be any advertising charges to you, over and above initial fees and continuing royalties. Are they specifically stated? Are they limited to a maximum percentage of sales? Is there an undertaking by the franchisor to expend on advertising and promotion not less than the aggregate franchisee advertising fees collected?

Will company stores be required to contribute to an advertising fund on the same basis?

Will advertising be local or in your market region or national? Is any percentage of each specified?

If the franchisor promises to spend not less than specified sums or percentages of sales on "advertising and promotion," what does the term include? Is the cost of the franchisor's advertising for additional franchisees included, or are included costs limited to advertising the system as a whole and the products being sold by franchisees?

Is the local advertising/promotion an extension of the national or regional program or is it solely at your expense? If it is partly or all at your expense, to what extent (if at all) is it mandatory? Determine whether your cost of local advertising is limited to your local agency, media, and printing costs and charges; if you will receive continuing aids from the franchisor in areas which reduce duplication and thus costs for all franchisees, such as artwork, mats, charts, photographs, standard copy with space for price and outlet identification inserts; and, if so, are they "camera ready" or not? Does franchisor distribute adaptable scripts, programs, or point of purchase or mail promotion materials? At what cost?

If you may use the name of a well-known person in your promotions are there extra charges for it? Are there limits on its use? Does the franchisor supply photographs and copy? If so, at whose expense?

What are the bookkeeping, accounting, and reporting requirements? Are the accounting system and report forms furnished? At whose expense and at what cost? If there is centralized, franchisor-maintained accounting and data processing, is it available or required and at whose expense and at what cost?

Are there quotas? Are they realistic? What are the penalties for not meeting them (for example, reduction of territory, loss of exclusive, or termination)?

Are facility business hours and days specified? Do you consider them practical in your area? (Many franchisors provide for such things in the operating manual.)

Does the contract specify what you must offer for sale or limit what you may sell?

What are the general provisions on equipment and premises maintenance, product/service quality and character controls? Are source controls provided for? Will you benefit from the franchisor's mass-purchasing power? Is that purchasing power merely available or is it mandatory that you purchase from the franchisor or designated suppliers some or all of the items you will need? Are prices to be fair and competitive? Ascertain in particular:

1. What goods, services, supplies, fixtures, equipment, inventory, or real estate are required to be purchased or leased from the franchisor or designated sources of supply, if any?
2. Whether, and if so, the means by which, the franchisor will or may derive income based on or as a result of any such required purchases or leases.
3. Whether prices to you are or must be competitive.
4. What goods, services, supplies, fixtures, equipment, inventory, or real estate, if any, are required to be purchased or leased in accordance with specifications of the franchisor from the franchisor or from suppliers approved by the franchisor? In what manner does the franchisor issue and modify specifications or grant and revoke approval of suppliers?
5. Will the franchisor or persons affiliated with the franchisor derive income from franchisee purchases made from the franchisor or from its approved suppliers?

You and your attorney should carefully examine the operating control policies and contract provisions of the franchisor. Be certain you understand them and understand the extent to which noncompliance may be grounds for termination. Do you agree with the controls, the objectives of such restraints, and the consequences of nonperformance? Do you readily accept the premise of the franchisor that its controls and specifications are required to assure the product quality, standardization, and uniformity necessary to protect all franchisees and the system integrity, image, and goodwill? Are you mentally and temperamentally attuned to accepting such direction from others? Answering that question should be one of the critical objectives of your exercise in "self-examination" at the outset.

Premises and Equipment Rehabilitation

Most franchise contracts require the franchisee to keep the business premises, equipment, and furnishings clean and in good repair and working condition. Many such agreements provide that:

a. If any item of equipment or furnishing becomes so depreciated as to require replacement for the proper and efficient operation of the business in accordance with the system, franchisee will replace the same with items then required by the then current manual and franchisor specifications.

b. Franchisor, from time to time, may require franchisee to effect such refurbishing of the business premises as the franchisor reasonably requires to maintain or improve the appearance and efficient operation of the business premises in accordance with uniformly applied standards. Such remodeling or refurbishing may include: replacement of depreciated, malfunctioning, or obsolete equipment and furnishings; redecorating; repair of the premises; repair and resurfacing of any parking area adjacent to the facility and a part of the franchisee's premises; and structural modifications and remodeling of the premises. There may be a limitation on the expenditures required of the franchisee expressed as a dollar amount or as a percentage of aggregate sales from start of the franchised term to the rehabilitation date or related to the amount of depreciation.

The franchise agreement should be explicit. You should make certain you understand these terms.

Assignment—Franchisee's Right to Sell

Can you sell the franchised business and assign the franchisee agreement to the buyer? Is the franchise assignable to your family or may it be sold by your estate on death or disability? There are limitations on assignment in virtually every franchise agreement.

Know and check the specific details of the contract and of the practice of your proposed franchisor. It should be uncommon for a franchisor to unreasonably refuse assignment to a qualified assignee.

What are the specific conditions to your right to assign the franchise contract?

If you require and must secure your own financing, check your lender's requirements in this area. In all probability your lender will require assignment of the franchise and facility lease as security, and assignment will be a condition in the loan commitment.

Check your lease. May you assign it to any permitted assignee of the franchise?

Give your lawyer an opportunity to examine the franchise contract, related leases, equipment purchase agreements, and financing documents before any are signed.

Term, Renewals and Termination

Most agreements will specify a term. Check this carefully. What are the renewal rights, if any?

What does the contract provide about termination? Are the defaults for which there may be a termination "good cause" in your opinion? Are you entitled to notice of default and reasonable time to cure the default? Does franchisor have any option to cancel the agreement other than for "good cause"?

What are the specific conditions and terms on which the franchisee may renew the contract?

Under what conditions and on what terms may the franchisee terminate the agreement, if at all?

If you must arrange your own financing, have you determined in advance if the term, renewal, and termination clauses are satisfactory to your proposed lender or facility or equipment lessor?

Does the franchisor have an option or a duty to buy any or all of your equipment, furnishings, inventory, or other assets in the event it terminates for good cause or elects not to renew on expiration of the term of the franchise, or if you elect not to renew? Do the terms differ depending on the reason for termination or nonrenewal? How?

What is the purchase price? Are there specific formulas to be followed or will there be impartial appraisal or arbitration?

If the franchisor has an option or duty to buy the assets of your business at the expiration of the term or upon termination, what are the purchase terms; how and by whom are the terms determined? Will there be independent appraisal? Will any effect be given to goodwill or franchisee's equity?

Determine what your obligations will be after termination of the relationship by the franchisor (by its refusal to renew on expiration of the term) including your obligations under facility or equipment purchase agreements or leases. Are the obligations different if the franchise agreement is terminated by the franchisee or is terminated for good cause by the franchisor?

Competition with Franchisor

Most contracts restrict all competing operations during the term of the franchise. They also may restrict any competing activity or business after the term for a limited area and for a limited period. They typically restrict and prohibit revealing trade secrets at any time. Check specific terms of the contract in this regard.

The Contract

Franchisors should expect and encourage you to read and understand the contract. Submit it to your attorney and accountant and discuss it with them. They will understand it. Be sure that you do and that they know your objectives.

Check the contract against your objectives and the representations made which attracted you. Are they specifically covered? Resolve misunderstandings in advance. Your contract governs your legal relationship.

Some sources suggest that prospective franchisees bargain for modification of provisions or for better terms. There may be areas for legitimate modification for good reasons where conditions vary. Your reasonable suggestions should not and will not be ignored. If a franchisor is entering a new area which is known to you, your suggestions, for example, about inventory and product-type requirements, operating hours or other modifications justified by special or local geographic, climatic, ethnic, religious, or local merchant association or trade customs, rules, or practices may be of value to all parties.

However, if a franchisor is sound and ethical, he or she will not bargain away major essential points of the system. If the franchisor is willing to do so, why were they included in the first place?

The quality and operating control sections should be structured to preserve product uniformity and quality and thus protect the business image, all franchisees, the system, and the public. If bargaining away of such controls were common, a franchisor could erode by bits and pieces the standardization and quality controls necessary to protect each franchisee and the public who rely on the franchisor's trade names and the entire system. There would remain no goodwill and no national or chain image worth your investment. What you have today could be bargained away tomorrow. If a franchisor will bargain away the quality and standardization controls in order to get your initial cash, you should look elsewhere for a franchise opportunity.

Aids to Investigation

To the extent that reference is made to costs in terms which may have different meanings in different offerings (e.g., "initial cash," "initial investment," "cash required," or "initial fee"), careful analysis is required before one can compare offerings.

You and your advisers may obtain additional aids from the Small Business Administration regional offices and national office (particularly the SBA Office of Management Assistance and its Small Business Administration Management Series publications); the Better Business Bureau local office in the area and the Council of Better Business Bureaus, Inc., 1150 17th St., N.W., Washington, D.C. 20036; Federal Trade Commission field offices and Bureau of Consumer Affairs, 6th St. and Pennsylvania Ave., N.W., Washington, D.C. 20580; and the local Chamber of Commerce in your area.

If a franchisor is publicly held, reports are available which will be of assistance to your accountant in analyzing company financial records and track record in its industry. University and public libraries will have reference works with much of the required information.

In addition, if the franchisor is a private company, seek a Dun & Bradstreet or other credit report; and check supplier, bank, and franchisee references, as well as local Better Business Bureau data on the company.

Regulation of the Offer and Sale of Franchises

There has been extensive development of state laws regulating the offer and sale of franchises, generally termed "franchise disclosure laws." These laws apply to many, but not all, business opportunities which are characterized as "franchises." For example, distributorships and dealerships that involve no more than the sale of goods by a supplier to a distributor or dealer generally are not covered by these laws, even though the distributorship or dealership may be termed a "franchise."

A state franchise law typically requires a franchisor to register the offer of its franchises within the state and to provide each prospective franchise purchaser with a disclosure statement (variously termed an "offering prospectus," "public offering prospectus," "disclosure statement," and "offering circular") containing information about the franchisor, the franchise being offered and the terms and conditions of the legal relationship into which the franchisee will enter. The agency which administers the state's franchise disclosure law typically reviews the franchisor's application to register franchises, the proposed disclosure statement, financial statements, franchise advertising materials, information about persons who will engage in the sale of its franchises, a copy of the franchise agreement, and all other agreements which the franchisee must sign to acquire the franchise.

The purposes of this review are to determine initially whether the franchisor has fully complied with all requirements of the law; whether the application, proposed disclosure statement and other documents contain all required information in a clear and understandable form; if there is any inconsistency between the proposed disclosure statement and the franchise agreement (or any other agreement) or any other materials or information filed by the franchisor; if franchise advertising materials contain any prohibited claims or representations; and if the franchise being offered or the method by which it is offered or sold is fraudulent, deceptive, unfair, or inequitable.

State franchise laws also typically authorize the administrative agency to determine whether a franchisor has demonstrated that adequate financial arrangements have been made to fulfill obligations to provide real estate, improvements, equipment, inventory, training, or other items to be included in the establishment and opening of the franchise business being offered. If the agency determines that the franchisor has insufficient financial resources, it can require the franchisor to escrow initial franchise fees and other amounts paid by franchisees until such obligations have been fulfilled. In lieu of an escrow of franchise fees and other funds, a franchisor typically has the option to post a surety bond.

Administrative agencies may deny or revoke the registration of the franchise offering on a variety of grounds, including the franchisor's failure or refusal to fully comply with the state's law; an incomplete or misleading disclosure statement; any false, fraudulent, or deceptive practice by the franchisor or any person acting on its behalf; or because the franchisor's financial condition would adversely affect its ability to perform its obligations to franchisees or the franchise or the method of its sale is fraudulent, deceptive, unfair or inequitable to the franchisee.

> You should not assume that the registration of a franchise or the preparation of a disclosure statement for use in your state means that the information in the franchisor's disclosure statement is complete, accurate, and free of excessive claims and misleading statements or that the ad-

ministrative agency of your state has made such a determination or has in any way approved the franchise. The resources and investigative staff of the state administrative agencies are limited and the agencies are not able to fully investigate all franchises offered in your state. Independent verification (e.g., by checking with existing franchisees) of the information contained in a disclosure statement is essential if you are to do a thorough job of investigating before you invest.

State franchise disclosure laws generally require the franchisor to provide the prospective franchisee with the information that this pamphlet recommends you obtain, including:

1. The identity of the franchisor and of its directors, principal officers, or general partners, their business backgrounds and certain criminal convictions, civil judgments, and administrative orders involving any of them.

2. The business and franchising experience of the franchisor, a description of the franchise offered and the goods, training programs, supervision, advertising, and other services to be provided by the franchisor.

3. The franchisor's trade names, trade or service marks, and other commercial symbols to be licensed to the franchisee and of any restrictions on or litigation involving the franchisor's and the franchisee's rights and obligations relative to such trade names and trade or service marks.

4. All initial and continuing fees that the franchisee will be required to pay, how fees are determined if not uniform, the extent to which fees are refundable, and an estimate of the total investment to be made by the franchisee.

5. The number of franchised and franchisor-owned outlets currently operating and the number of franchises proposed to be sold in the next year.

6. Whether the franchisee is required to purchase or lease goods or services from the franchisor or suppliers designated by the franchisor, and whether and the means by which the franchisor derives income from any such requirement.

7. Whether the franchisee is required to purchase goods or services in accordance with specifications of the franchisor or from suppliers approved by the franchisor and a description of any specification or approved supplier program.

8. The conditions under which the franchise may be terminated or renewal refused; the franchisee's rights and obligations upon expiration and termination; any option or right of first refusal that the franchisor has to acquire the franchise: a description of any

covenant not to compete to which franchisee will be subject; and the franchisee's right to assign and otherwise transfer the franchise.

9. A description of any financing offered by the franchisor, including any waiver of defenses contained in a note, contract, or other obligation of the franchisee and whether the franchisor has in the past assigned or expects to assign any obligation containing any such waiver.

10. Limitations on the goods or services that the franchisee may sell.

11. A description of the territorial protection which the franchisee will have.

12. Compensation paid to a public figure whose name is used in the franchise or who endorses the franchise.

13. The data and methods used by the franchisor in preparing any projected sales, expenses, or income of the franchised business.

14. Copies of the most recent balance sheet and profit and loss statement of the franchisor audited by an independent certified public accountant.

The laws give the administrative agencies broad discretion to require disclosure of additional information and the highlighting of alleged "risk factors" in the disclosure statement, discretion which is being used with increasing frequency, particularly as the agencies gain experience under their laws.

Disclosure statements and copies of the franchise agreement and all other agreements that the franchisee must sign to acquire the franchise must be given to the prospective franchisee from two to seven days (depending on the state's law) in advance of the signing of any agreement or payment of any money to the franchisor.

Each of the state franchise disclosure laws provides for civil and criminal penalties for fraud or misrepresentation in the offer and sale of franchises and for other violations of the law, and persons damaged by such violations are given a statutory right to sue the franchisor, its officers, and any other persons who commit any such violation. Fraud and misrepresentation are generally defined in these laws far more broadly than their traditional legal meaning.

Several of the state franchise disclosure laws do not require registration of the offer of franchises by large and experienced franchisors (the Oregon law does not contain a registration requirement for any franchisor) and other laws may provide exemptions from registration. If a franchisor representative or salesperson claims that the franchisor is exempt from registration in your state, verify this claim with the agency that administers your state's franchise disclosure law. However, each of the laws requires all franchisors to disclose information to prospective franchise purchasers and the civil and criminal penalties for fraud and misrepresentation and other violations of the law apply to all offers and sales of franchises within the jurisdiction of such laws. If your state has a franchise disclosure law, the franchisor must give you a disclosure statement in advance of accepting any payment from you or of having you sign any agreement.

Franchise Laws

To date, 14 states have enacted franchise laws. These states and the administrative agency of each which administers its laws (and from which information about franchisors may be obtained) follows:

California
    Mr. Willie R. Barnes
    Corporations Commissioner
    Department of Corporations
    600 South Commonwealth Avenue
    Los Angeles, CA   90005
    (213) 620–2720

    1025 P Street
    Sacramento, CA   98514
    (916) 445–7205

    1350 Front Street
    San Diego, CA   92101
    (714) 232–7341

    600 California Street
    San Francisco, CA   94108
    (415) 557–3787

Florida
    Mr. Bernard S. McLendon
    Consumer Counsel
    Assistant Attorney General
    Department of Legal Affairs
    The Capitol
    Tallahassee, FL   32304
    (904) 488–2719 and 488–4481

Hawaii
    Mr. Wayne Minami
    Mr. James Williams*
    Mr. Malcolm Greer*

Director of Regulatory Agencies
1010 Richards Street
Honolulu, HI   96813
(808) 548–4017

Indiana
    Mr. Raymond J. Hafsten, Jr.
    Mr. Richard Hodgin*
    Mr. Tom Hinshaw*
    Securities Commission
    102 State House
    Indianapolis, IN   46201
    (317) 633–6681

Illinois
    Mr. David Hart Wunder
    Mr. Donald Schierer*
    Securities Commissioner
    Office of the Secretary of State
    Securities Division
    Centennial Building, Room 296
    Springfield, IL   62756
    (217) 782–2256

    188 West Randolph, 16th Floor
    Chicago, Illinois
    (312) 793–3388

Michigan
    Mr. Hugh H. Makens, Director
    Mr. John Balasis*
    Mr. Judd Freeman*
    Department of Commerce

Securities Division
Corporations & Securities Bureau
5511 Enterprise Drive
Lansing, MI   48913
(517) 373–8074

Minnesota
Mr. John R. Larson
Mr. Robert R. Raines, Jr.*
Commissioner of Securities
Department of Commerce
Securities Division
5th Floor, Metro Square Building
Seventh and Roberts Streets
St. Paul, Minnesota   55101
(612) 296–5689

North Dakota
Mr. Robert Holt
Mr. Harold Kocher*
Securities Commissioner
State of North Dakota
Capitol Building
Bismarck, ND   58501
(701) 224–2910

Oregon
Mr. Frank J. Healy
Mr. Donald McCann*
Corporations Commissioner
Department of Commerce
Corporations Division
Commerce Building
Salem, OR   97310
(503) 378–4333

Rhode Island
Mr. Thomas J. Corrigan
Securities Examiner
Department of Business Regulation
Securities Section
169 Weybosset Street

Providence, RI   02903
(401) 277–2405

South Dakota
Mr. John Meyer, Director
Securities Division
Department of Commerce and
   Consumer Affairs
State Capitol
Pierre, SD   57501
(605) 224–3241

Virginia
Mr. Lewis W. Brothers, Jr.
State Corporations Commission
Division of Securities and Retail
   Franchising
1300 Travelers Building
Richmond, VA   23219
(804) 770–7751

Washington
Mr. Eugene G. Olsen
Mr. Robert Kline*
Securities Administrator
Business & Professions
   Administration
Securities Division
P.O. Box 648
Olympia, WA   98548
(206) 753–6928

Wisconsin
Mr. Jeffrey B. Bartell
Mr. James R. Conohan*
Commissioner of Securities
Office of the Commissioner
   of Securities
448 West Washington Avenue
Madison, WI   53701
(608) 266–3414 (Franchising)
(608) 266–3431 (Main Office)

* Individuals with specific responsibilities for franchising.

The Federal Trade Commission first issued its proposed trade regulation rules on franchising in 1971 and held extensive hearings on the proposed rule in February of 1972. A revised proposed rule still is pending before the commission, and further action is expected in the future, with possibly the issuance of the rule in final form in 1978. The trade regulation rule would require franchisors to make essentially the same advance disclosure to prospective franchisees as is required by the state franchise disclosure laws. It would apply to offers and sales of franchises anywhere in the United States.

Several states have enacted legislation limiting the right of a franchisor to terminate or refuse to renew a franchise (Delaware, Connecticut, Hawaii, New Jersey, Wisconsin, and Washington). Laws of this type have been held invalid with respect to franchise relationships that commenced before the effective date of the law and have been challenged as unconstitutional even as to their effect on franchise relationships entered into subsequent to the law becoming effective.

Franchising has entered the age of full disclosure. The regulation of the offer and sale of franchises which the states have enacted should not be expected to be an ironclad guarantee. It will not protect all prospective franchisees from purchasing a misrepresented or unsound franchise or from all potential problems of the franchise relationship. But it will have a strong remedial effect on these problems. All prospective franchisees should take full advantage of the information available on franchisors and their franchises as a result of these laws. Even if your state has not enacted a franchise disclosure law, franchisors offering franchises in your state may have registered and/or prepared disclosure statements to meet the requirements of the laws of one or more other states. Inquire if this is the case, and if so, ask for a copy of such disclosure statement. It should provide you with a good starting point for obtaining the information which this pamphlet recommends that you secure and carefully consider before you purchase a franchise.

section 4

Listing of Franchises

*AAMCO AUTOMATIC TRANSMISSIONS, INC.
408 East Fourth Street
Bridgeport, PA 19405
(215) 277–4000
Contact: Ron Smythe

BUSINESS: Recondition and rebuild automatic transmissions for all cars.

FRANCHISES: 675 in 48 states and Canada.

FOUNDED: 1958.

REQUIRED CAPITAL: $26,000.

FINANCIAL ASSISTANCE: A total investment of $69,000 is required to open a franchise. A total of $57,000 is required in a secondary market. Company can arrange financing for one half of total requirement, if franchisee has good credit references. Franchisee has the option to arrange own outside financing.

TRAINING: A comprehensive six-week course is provided at the company headquarters. In addition, field training is offered at the opening of the operation to launch that franchisee properly.

MANAGERIAL ASSISTANCE: A consulting and operation division continually works with each center on a weekly basis to ensure proper day-by-day operation. Also, monthly area meetings are held.

ABC MOBILE SYSTEMS
9420 Telstar Avenue
El Monte, CA 91731
(213) 579–7260
Contact: Joseph V. Mavila

BUSINESS: Specially designed mobile vans providing brake service at service stations and automotive repair shops.

FRANCHISES: 140 in 36 states.

FOUNDED: 1962.

REQUIRED CAPITAL: $8,000.

FINANCIAL ASSISTANCE: $8,000 plus $4,000 working capital required for one-truck franchise. Balance of $30,000 total investment can be financed.

TRAINING: Initial training at home office for two weeks, with additional two weeks' training in franchisee's area.

MANAGERIAL ASSISTANCE: Managerial and technical assistance provided throughout length of franchise which includes bulletins, advertising (national), management aids, training manuals, clinics, and bookkeeping system. The managerial staff visits franchisees through personal visitations and telephone contact monthly. National conventions and regional seminars are held.

AID AUTO STORES, INC.
1150 Metropolitan
Brooklyn, NY 11237
(212) 381–0909
Contact: Alan Koller

* Asterisk denotes franchisor is a member of the International Franchise Association.

BUSINESS: Retail sales of automotive parts, tools, and accessories.
FRANCHISES: 74 in New York, New Jersey, Connecticut, and Florida.
FOUNDED: 1954.
REQUIRED CAPITAL: $40,000.
FINANCIAL ASSISTANCE: None.
TRAINING: Thirty-day minimum. Continual assistance after initial training.
MANAGERIAL ASSISTANCE: Supervisor visits stores on a periodic basis to help franchisees maintain a stable business, and to inform them of new products and procedures.

ATV-AUTO, TRUCK AND VAN
300 Bethpage-Spagnoli Road
Melville, NY 11746
(516) 271–8130
Contact: Jerry Frgio

BUSINESS: Retails major brand automotive parts, accessories, high-performance equipment, van supplies, and off-road equipment and supplies.
FRANCHISES: 3 in New York.
FOUNDED: 1974.
REQUIRED CAPITAL: $100,000 for inventory, equipment, signs, fixtures, working capital, and fees.
FINANCIAL ASSISTANCE: Franchisee receives complete assistance in obtaining necessary financing from appropriate lending agencies.
TRAINING: Two weeks of headquarters and company-operated store, plus two weeks in franchisee's store. The complete training program is aimed at providing the franchisee with all the tools and knowledge needed to run the business.
MANAGERIAL ASSISTANCE: Franchisee receives assistance and guidance on a permanent basis. Visits average two per month and are intended to help the franchisee with any matter concerning the business.

AUTOMATION EQUIPMENT, INC.
P.O. Box 3208
Tulsa, OK 74101
(918) 582–0035
Contact: Orville Strout

BUSINESS: Conveyorized automatic car washers, self-service car washers, and automatic and manual truck washers.
FRANCHISES: 65 in 11 states.
FOUNDED: 1971.
REQUIRED CAPITAL: $5,000 to $60,000.
FINANCIAL ASSISTANCE: None.
TRAINING: On-the-job training ranging from three to seven days.
MANAGERIAL ASSISTANCE: Usually handled by phone and as long as company parts and detergents are used exclusively.

BERNARDI BROS., INC.
101 South 38th Street
Harrisburg, PA 17111
(717) 564–7300
Contact: C. G. Geiger

BUSINESS: Automatic conveyorized car wash, automatic brush car wash, and self-service car washes.
FRANCHISES: Over 5,000 throughout the United States and abroad.
FOUNDED: 1946.
REQUIRED CAPITAL: $10,000 to $60,000.
FINANCIAL ASSISTANCE: Some assistance available through individual distributors. In addition, factory finance plan is available.
TRAINING: Service school held each month at the factory.
MANAGERIAL ASSISTANCE: None. Local distributor expertise available. Assistance of Bernardi marketing personnel furnished as requested.

BOU-FARO COMPANY
274 Broadway
Pawtucket, RI 02861
(401) 724–8180
Contact: Carmine DeCristoforo

BUSINESS: Auto transmission repair center.
FRANCHISES: 38 in Rhode Island, Massachusetts, Pennsylvania, and New Hampshire.
FOUNDED: 1970.
REQUIRED CAPITAL: $39,500.
FINANCIAL ASSISTANCE: $24,500 for a total of $39,500.
TRAINING: Approximately four weeks.
MANAGERIAL ASSISTANCE: A full range of assistance is available on a year-round basis.

CAR-MATIC SYSTEM
Division of Vail Spring Works, Inc.
P.O. Box 12466
Norfolk, VA 23502
(804) 627–2979
Contact: W. W. Vail

BUSINESS: Distributorship and a retail outlet.
FRANCHISES: 61 in six states.
FOUNDED: 1919.
REQUIRED CAPITAL: Distributors must have $35,968. Retail outlets must have $15,840.
FINANCIAL ASSISTANCE: Complete overall financing plans are available to qualified applicants.

TRAINING: Four weeks, management and sales training, plus setup and assistance in field operations.

MANAGERIAL ASSISTANCE: Initial training of four weeks, and continual consultation services available when and if needed.

CAR-X SERVICE SYSTEMS, INC.
444 N. Michigan Avenue
Chicago, IL 60611
(312) 836–1500
Contact: Harold Krieger

BUSINESS: Sale and installation of automotive exhaust systems, shock absorbers, brakes, and other automotive products and services.

FRANCHISES: 60 in 10 states.

FOUNDED: 1973.

REQUIRED CAPITAL: $82,000.

FINANCIAL ASSISTANCE: Company assists in obtaining financing up to $40,000.

TRAINING: The training program consists of a comprehensive three-week program, expandable to suit the needs of the individual franchisee. The course encompasses operations, finance, accounting, marketing, and human resource management in its broadest classification.

MANAGERIAL ASSISTANCE: Managerial assistance is provided in addition to ongoing field supervision in both the business management and technical areas.

COLLEX, INC.
512 Pennsylvania Avenue
Fort Washington, PA 19034
(215) 542–9393
Contact: Bryan L. Cosden

BUSINESS: Collision repair.

FRANCHISES: 42 in 11 states.

FOUNDED: 1972.

REQUIRED CAPITAL: $18,000 minimum for Collex Center and $75,000 minimum for area directorship.

FINANCIAL ASSISTANCE: Minimum total investment of $100,000 is needed for one Collex Center, plus $8,000 to $10,000 working capital. This includes a license fee of $18,000. The balance may be financed if the licensee has adequate net worth and good references. The licensee has the option to arrange for the financing.

TRAINING: Two to four weeks at the Collex headquarters, plus two to four weeks in licensee's center, with additional on-the-job training after center opening. Training covers all aspects of operation: advertising, marketing, promotion, accounting, customer relations, insurance, and production control. Additional training provided for area directors.

MANAGERIAL ASSISTANCE: Collex provides ongoing management services for the term of the franchise. Local assistance is provided through field directors and area directors by periodic visitations to each center. Home office assistance also available at all times.

COOK MACHINERY COMPANY
4301 South Fitzhugh Avenue
Dallas, TX 75226
(214) 421–2135
Contact: Thomas Guerrero

BUSINESS: Car wash.
FRANCHISES: 750 in the United States and Canada.
FOUNDED: 1961.
REQUIRED CAPITAL: $5,000 to $10,000.
FINANCIAL ASSISTANCE: Financing and leasing available for qualified applicants.
TRAINING: On-the-job training by local distributors.
MANAGERIAL ASSISTANCE: Managerial and technical assistance provided by local distributors.

*COTTMAN TRANSMISSION SYSTEMS, INC.
575 Virginia Drive
Fort Washington, PA 19034
(215) 643–5885
Contact: Richard O. Silva

BUSINESS: Repair, service, and remanufacture of automatic transmissions.
FRANCHISES: 155 in the United States and Canada.
FOUNDED: 1962.
REQUIRED CAPITAL: $22,500 to $48,000.
FINANCIAL ASSISTANCE: Partial financing available, usually through lending institutions.
TRAINING: Three weeks' training at the company office and additional two weeks' training at operator's location for management and technicians who need assistance in proper techniques of remanufacturing.
MANAGERIAL ASSISTANCE: The company continually works with each operator on all phases of operation, sales, management, employee relations, remanufacturing techniques, and so on.

DELKO TRANSMISSIONS TRUCK, INC.
270 Fourth Avenue
Brooklyn, NY 11215
(212) 624–4033
Contact: Licensing Manager

BUSINESS: Install and service automatic transmissions.
FRANCHISES: 11 in New York.
FOUNDED: 1966.
REQUIRED CAPITAL: $28,000.
FINANCIAL ASSISTANCE: None.
TRAINING: Two weeks of intense training in sales and services.
MANAGERIAL ASSISTANCE: Periodic training in all phases of the business is provided franchisees.

DRIVE LINE SERVICE, INC.
P.O. Box 782
704 Houston Street
West Sacramento, CA 95691
(716) 371–3332
Contact: Byron K. Scoggan

BUSINESS: Drive shaft service, repair, remanufacture, modification, and balancing.
FRANCHISES: 26 in 12 states.
FOUNDED: 1971.
REQUIRED CAPITAL: Approximately $40,000 for equipment and franchise, plus $20,000 for operating capital.
FINANCIAL ASSISTANCE: No financial assistance is currently offered.
TRAINING: The franchise includes a minimum of two weeks' training for the franchisee and one other person. All expenses except living and travel are borne by franchisor. Training is conducted at the West Sacramento, California, shop location.
MANAGERIAL ASSISTANCE: Franchisor maintains a staff qualified to provide assistance over the duration of the franchise agreement in all matters of management, technical assistance, and promotion. Usual problems and solutions are passed throughout the organization by regularly scheduled communications, monthly newsletters, and conferences.

ENDRUST CORPORATION
1725 Washington Road
Pittsburgh, PA 15241
(412) 363–4889
Contact: Bill Griser

BUSINESS: Provide automotive rustproofing for owners and operators of body shops, new and used car dealers, tire dealers, and gasoline service stations.
FRANCHISES: 497 in eight states.
FOUNDED: 1969.
REQUIRED CAPITAL: 6,500, subject to increase when due to market conditions.
FINANCIAL ASSISTANCE: None.
TRAINING: Training at Cleveland Training Center at company expense, excluding transportation. Two days is generally suggested, although in most cases if trainees are experienced body men, they gain sufficient expertise in one day.
MANAGERIAL ASSISTANCE: All that is required by trainee.

ENERGY SAVING INTERNATIONAL, INC.
115 West Green Street
Perry, FL 32347
(904) 584–7025
Contact: P. Andy Bowin

BUSINESS: Selling an auto product which helps to reduce emission pollutions.
FRANCHISES: 6 in Michigan, Indiana, Ohio, and Kentucky.
FOUNDED: 1974.

REQUIRED CAPITAL: $5,000 minimum.

FINANCIAL ASSISTANCE: A total investment of $10,000 is required for inventory of equipment with Kemco Corporation financing one half of the needed amount to applicants with a good credit rating.

TRAINING: A two-week school is provided for all new franchisees, with a refresher course following at 12-month intervals. Constant field supervision will be provided and needed literature, brochures, and selling aids are furnished free of charge.

MANAGERIAL ASSISTANCE: Company testing laboratory will be able to assist if and when an unusual problem occurs that cannot be corrected in the field. All company products carry a 30-day written money back guarantee, with a lifetime replacement warranty. A complete turnkey operation is available if desired by the franchisee; i.e., the company furnishes the complete operation ready for the franchisee to open for business.

THE FIRESTONE TIRE AND RUBBER COMPANY
1200 Firestone Parkway
Akron, OH 44317
(216) 379–7000
Contact: W. F. Tierney

BUSINESS: Selling tires, auto and home supplies, and automotive services.

FRANCHISES: Over 60,000 direct and associate dealers operating through the United States and Canada.

FOUNDED: 1900.

REQUIRED CAPITAL: $35,000 or more; varies as to locations, business, equipment, and inventory.

FINANCIAL ASSISTANCE: Counsel sales and credit personnel and assist franchisee to obtain necessary financing through local sources or through company's assistance programs.

TRAINING: Home office and field personnel are available at all times to train the dealer and employees in all phases of sales and business management. Films, self-training programs, on-the-job training programs, and so on, are constantly being revised and updated to keep dealer informed on all aspects of the business.

MANAGERIAL ASSISTANCE: Home office and local sales personnel are available to give assistance on any matter requested, including all phases of retail selling.

GAIL INDUSTRIES
621 4th Avenue Southeast
P.O. Box 1864
Cedar Rapids, IA 52406
(319) 366–6241
Contact: Joe W. Aossey

BUSINESS: Sales and distribution of automotive cleaning products, chemicals, and equipment for self-service and retail center car cleaning.

FRANCHISES: 120 in 49 states and worldwide.

FOUNDED: 1962.

REQUIRED CAPITAL: About $15,000.
FINANCIAL ASSISTANCE: Financing available for qualified applicants.
TRAINING: Complete training is provided.
MANAGERIAL ASSISTANCE: Continuous management assistance on an advisory level.

B. F. GOODRICH TIRE COMPANY
500 South Main Street
Akron, OH 44318
(216) 379–2000
Contact: Terry J. Bordelon

BUSINESS: Sell and service tires and related automotive service merchandise.
FRANCHISES: Thousands of direct dealers and associate dealers throughout the United States.
FOUNDED: 1870.
REQUIRED CAPITAL: Varies as to market, style of business, projected volume, and so on.
FINANCIAL ASSISTANCE: Assistance is provided to help franchisee obtain required financing through local source and/or franchisor's assistance programs. Required financing is dependent upon market potential, requirements, and projected profitability.
TRAINING: Training on a continuous basis is provided by the company covering product knowledge, servicing techniques, and business management.
MANAGERIAL ASSISTANCE: See "Training" above.

THE GOODYEAR TIRE AND RUBBER COMPANY
1144 E. Market Street
Akron, OH 44316
(216) 794–2121
Contact: A. Piquette

BUSINESS: Sale of tires, tire and automotive service, and other car and home-related merchandise.
FRANCHISES: Approximately 6,000 independent Goodyear dealers including 270 Tire Center franchisees throughout the United States.
FOUNDED: 1898. Tire Center franchise program has operated since 1968.
REQUIRED CAPITAL: Varies for regular Goodyear dealership. $35,000 minimum required for Tire Center.
FINANCIAL ASSISTANCE: Lease real estate; equipment and fixtures, long-term note line as needed and justified; and open account credit as needed and justified.
TRAINING: Formal three months' training plus continued on-the-job training.
MANAGERIAL ASSISTANCE: Business counsel and data processing provided on a continuing and permanent basis. Program also includes local, cooperative advertising to tie in with national advertising; display and point-of-sale advertising; identification and fixture assistance; monthly and quarterly marketing and merchandising programs; and complete sales training programs.

INSTA-TUNE, INC.
17755 Sky Park East
Irvine, CA 92714
(714) 540–7744
Contact: Ralph D. Brown

BUSINESS: Automotive tune-ups.

FRANCHISES: 81 in 13 states.

FOUNDED: 1974.

REQUIRED CAPITAL: $45,000.

FINANCIAL ASSISTANCE: Minimum cash investment $25,000 with financial assistance is available.

TRAINING: Technical training on equipment and on-the-job training are initially provided, followed by continuous field training and counseling.

MANAGERIAL ASSISTANCE: Operations manuals are provided. Licensee receives constant assistance and periodic dealer meetings are held to discuss al aspects of operations of a center.

INTERSTATE AUTOMATIC TRANSMISSION CO., INC.
29200 Vassar Avenue, Suite 501
Livonia, MI 48152
(800) 521–6087
(313) 478–9206 (in Michigan)
Contact: Donald Stewart

BUSINESS: Repair and replace all types of standard and automatic transmissions.

FRANCHISES: 115 in 16 states.

FOUNDED: 1973.

REQUIRED CAPITAL: $28,500.

FINANCIAL ASSISTANCE: A total investment of $54,000, excluding working capital, is required. Because of the amount of equipment involved in an Interstate Transmission Center and depending upon the individual licensee's credit standing local financing can usually be arranged in the amount of $28,000.

TRAINING: Two weeks of intensive management and in-shop training is provided at the corporate headquarters. Additional on-site training is given during the opening period.

MANAGERIAL ASSISTANCE: Interstate Transmission provides constant operational support in both management and technical services. Field operation managers visit each center on a periodic basis and each week each licensee submits a report on individual Interstate Transmissions Center's operation which is reviewed by the home office.

KING BEAR ENTERPRISES INC.
40 New York Avenue '
Westbury, NY 11590
(516) 997–3600
Contact: A. Blaker

BUSINESS: Automotive repairs.
FRANCHISES: 21 in New York and New Jersey.
FOUNDED: 1973.
REQUIRED CAPITAL: $35,000 to $40,000.
FINANCIAL ASSISTANCE: Limited financing available.
TRAINING: In shop training for two weeks, plus full management training in home office. Additional training provided in franchisee's shop.
MANAGERIAL ASSISTANCE: See "Training" above.

KWIK KAR WASH
11351 Anaheim Drive
Dallas, TX 75229
(214) 243–3521
Contact: Ray Ellis

BUSINESS: 24-hour self-service car wash.
FRANCHISES: 1,556 in 44 states.
FOUNDED: 1964.
REQUIRED CAPITAL: $15,000 minimum.
FINANCIAL ASSISTANCE: A typical four-stall installation requires an investment of approximately $60,000 excluding land cost which may be leased. A down payment of $15,000 is normal with balance financed for 60 months.
TRAINING: Training provided one to two days on-site at time of opening.
MANAGERIAL ASSISTANCE: Managerial assistance, large parts inventory, manuals, promotional business management, and complete service department with radio dispatched trucks.

*LEE MYLES ASSOCIATES CORPORATION
325 Sylvan Avenue
Englewood Cliffs, NJ 07632
(212) 386–0100
Contact: Sam Eisner or Charles George

BUSINESS: Transmission repair.
FRANCHISES: 100 in six states and Puerto Rico.
FOUNDED: 1948.
REQUIRED CAPITAL: $27,000.
FINANCIAL ASSISTANCE: Partial financing is available to qualified applicants.
TRAINING: Three-week training course, consisting of two weeks at parent company classroom and actual shopwork, plus one week in franchisee's own operation. Staff of experienced field consultants provides continuing guidance and assistance at all times thereafter.
MANAGERIAL ASSISTANCE: A divisional field consultant works with each franchise dealer to promote success with updated marketing formulas, technical information, and sales training.

*MAACO ENTERPRISES, INC.
381 Brooks Road
King of Prussia, PA 19406
(215) 265–6606
Contact: George E. Gardner

BUSINESS: Auto painting and body work.
FRANCHISES: 251 open. 71 other franchises sold.
FOUNDED: 1972.
REQUIRED CAPITAL: $99,500 ($35,000 cash).
FINANCIAL ASSISTANCE: None.
TRAINING: Complete training program for four weeks in class plus three weeks in area store.
MANAGERIAL ASSISTANCE: Continuous as long as the franchise is in operation.

MacCLEEN'S, INC.
14831 Snow Road
Brook Park, OH 44142
(216) 676–5650
Contact: David Butts

BUSINESS: Automatic car wash.
FRANCHISES: 54 in ten states.
FOUNDED: 1966.
REQUIRED CAPITAL: $19,600.
FINANCIAL ASSISTANCE: Commercial banking and American Leasing, Inc.
TRAINING: On location and at existing operations if desired.
MANAGERIAL ASSISTANCE: Assistance by store manager and company engineer.

MALCO PRODUCTS, INC.
361 Fairview Avenue
Barberton, OH 44203
(216) 753–0361
Contact: J. Ginley

BUSINESS: Sell line of automotive chemicals to service station.
FRANCHISES: 430 in the United States.
FOUNDED: 1953.
REQUIRED CAPITAL: $3,000 for inventory investment only.
FINANCIAL ASSISTANCE: None.
TRAINING: Thorough field and product training by regional sales manager in the distributor's sales area. Periodically during the year the regional sales manager provides the distributor and salespeople with special training.
MANAGERIAL ASSISTANCE: Distributor sales meetings are held twice a year for further training. Complete managerial assistance provided through company personnel and field representatives.

*MEINEKE DISCOUNT MUFFLER SHOPS, INC.
6330 West Loop South, Suite 103
Bellaire, TX 77401
(713) 661-0414
Contact: Al Hirsh, Director of Franchise Sales

BUSINESS: Install automotive exhaust systems and shock absorbers.
FRANCHISES: 85 in 16 states.
FOUNDED: 1972.
REQUIRED CAPITAL: $44,306 investment for inventory, equipment, signs, furniture, fixtures, estimated lease, and utility deposits.
FINANCIAL ASSISTANCE: Up to $21,510 to qualified applicants.
TRAINING: Three weeks' schooling and on-the-job training at Houston headquarters. In addition, Meineke provides continuous field supervision and group operational meetings.
MANAGERIAL ASSISTANCE: *Meineke Discount Muffler Operations Manual* provides clear and concise reference for every phase of the business. Home office staff analysis of weekly reports is provided on a continuous basis.

*MIDAS-INTERNATIONAL CORP.
222 South Riverside Plaza
Chicago, IL 60606
(312) 648-5600
Contact: William Strahan

BUSINESS: Install automotive exhaust system, brakes, shock absorbers, and front-end alignment.
FRANCHISES: 1,023 in 50 states, Canada, and Puerto Rico.
FOUNDED: 1956.
REQUIRED CAPITAL: $90,000-$100,000 investment for inventory, equipment, sign, furniture, fixtures, fees, and working capital.
FINANCIAL ASSISTANCE: Franchise receives complete assistance in obtaining necessary financing from appropriate lending agencies with which Midas has working arrangements.
TRAINING: Both a dealer orientation program and on-the-job training programs are initially provided, followed by continuous in-the-shop counseling and periodic dealer seminar-type meetings on all aspects of shop operations. Provide formal training program at National Training Center, Palatine, Illinois.
MANAGERIAL ASSISTANCE: A shop operator's manual is provided along with a record-keeping and accounting manual. Training received from regional directors covers all aspects of management, marketing, and sales.

MIRACLE AUTO PAINTING
Division of Multiple Allied Services, Inc.
P.O. Box 5026
San Mateo, CA 94402
(415) 349-6741
Contact: James L. Fowler

BUSINESS: Body repair work and auto painting.

FRANCHISES: 41 in California, the Pacific Northwest and Texas.

FOUNDED: 1953.

REQUIRED CAPITAL: $15,000 minimum.

FINANCIAL ASSISTANCE: The franchisee usually needs a minimum of $60,000 to establish the business on a profitable basis. A substantial amount of this capital can usually be financed. Miracle will assist the franchisee in obtaining financing.

TRAINING: A four-week training course is scheduled for new franchisees. Two weeks of the training is at a "Miracle" location and two weeks at the franchisee's location. Training covers systems and procedures for production painting and bodywork as well as sales and business procedures.

MANAGERIAL ASSISTANCE: Miracle provides continuing consultation not only for production techniques and procedures, but also for sales and business management, accounting and record keeping, and employee recruiting and training.

NATIONAL AUTO GLASS COMPANY, INC.
3434 West 6th Street
Los Angeles, CA 90020
(213) 385–2221
Contact: Murray Lavender

BUSINESS: Auto glass installation.

FRANCHISES: 175 in nine western states.

FOUNDED: 1956.

REQUIRED CAPITAL: $10,000 to $15,000.

FINANCIAL ASSISTANCE: None.

TRAINING: None.

MANAGERIAL ASSISTANCE: Ongoing program, primarily through field representatives and management.

NATIONAL AUTO SERVICE CENTERS
Division of National Automotive Industries, Inc.
1751 Ensley Avenue
Clearwater, FL 33516
(813) 581–8747
Contact: Albert Hurwitz

BUSINESS: Automotive repair.

FRANCHISES: 9 in Florida.

FOUNDED: 1972.

REQUIRED CAPITAL: $45,000.

FINANCIAL ASSISTANCE: Will arrange financing for $42,500 which represents 47 percent of selling price of the franchise.

TRAINING: Minimum of two weeks' classroom training and practical application of skills with equipment. Minimum of two weeks on-the-job training under supervision. Training includes business methods, bookkeeping, purchasing, salesmanship, marketing, service and repair procedures, and equipment operation. A 400-page operations manual is provided.

MANAGERIAL ASSISTANCE: The company handles advertising, holds field seminars, refresher courses, updating in new operation, and is available to cover trouble areas in operation.

NATIONAL TIRE WHOLESALE, INC.
6320 Augusta Drive
Suite 1500
Springfield, VA 22150
(703) 451–3322
Contact: Kyle Christopher Mudd

BUSINESS: Retailing tires. Franchisee does not need prior tire sales.

FRANCHISES: 28 in 10 states.

FOUNDED: 1973.

REQUIRED CAPITAL: $15,000 franchise and training fee plus inventory fee of $50,000.

FINANCIAL ASSISTANCE: Assistance available from National Tire Wholesale, Inc., the parent corporation, depending on size of building and market to be serviced.

TRAINING: Trainees are carefully schooled in selling techniques at home office. Special store bulletins, catalog sheets, manuals, inventory sheets, cost sheets, plus in-house advertising agency are available.

MANAGERIAL ASSISTANCE: Franchise stores are operated in the same manner as company-owned stores with a coordinator available at all times.

OTASCO
11333 East Pine
P.O. Box 885
Tulsa, OK 74102
(918) 437–7171
Contact: Robert E. Shireman

BUSINESS: Retailing of home and auto supplies, sporting goods, and major appliances.

FRANCHISES: 416 in 13 states.

FOUNDED: 1934.

REQUIRED CAPITAL: $35,000 minimum.

FINANCIAL ASSISTANCE: Financing of fixtures, floor planning of major appliances, financing of retail paper, dating terms on seasonal merchandise.

TRAINING: Two weeks minimum in company-operated store.

MANAGERIAL ASSISTANCE: Field representative in the store on the average of one day per month. Merchandise shows and sales seminars twice yearly. Regional sales meeting conducted two to three times per year. Operating manual, forms, advertising assistance (co-op), and bookkeeping system are also provided.

*PAINTMASTER AUTO/TRUCK PAINT CENTERS
Subsidiary of Paintmaster Systems Corporation
1110 Highland Building
Pittsburgh, PA 15206
(412) 362–4440
Contact: Alfred H. Wagman

BUSINESS: Painting automobiles, trucks, tractors, trailers, and boats.
FRANCHISES: 28 in 14 states, Puerto Rico, Guam, and Canada.
FOUNDED: 1966.
REQUIRED CAPITAL: Varies with type of equipment package ordered. The minimum cash required is $50,000.
FINANCIAL ASSISTANCE: Qualified applicants can receive up to 25 percent of the total cost with a five-year repayment period.
TRAINING: Management training is for four weeks. All other employees are trained on-site prior to and after the opening. Usual training period is two weeks.
MANAGERIAL ASSISTANCE: A continual program is always in effect. Also advertising aids and new paint formulas are available.

PARTS, INC.
Subsidiary of Parts Industries Corp.
601 South Dudley Street
Memphis, TN 38104
(901) 523–7711
Contact: John J. Tucker

BUSINESS: Wholesaling automotive parts, supplies, equipment, and accessories.
FRANCHISES: 785 in 38 states.
FOUNDED: 1958.
REQUIRED CAPITAL: Varies on basis of inventory investment but generally about $10,000 to $15,000. Total $40,000 to $50,000 investment.
FINANCIAL ASSISTANCE: Arranged if franchisee has outside collateral or will operate in a state where Uniform Commercial Code is applicable.
TRAINING: General management, to include bookkeeping and accounting system, operations manual, advertising and merchandising programs, market surveys, and product and technical clinics.
MANAGERIAL ASSISTANCE: Maintain daily contact through field representatives and/or through WATS telephone calls to assist jobber in any phase of the business and to supplement written operating manuals, bookkeeping and accounting system manuals, cost books, and catalog services. Financial ratios and expense control are designated to improve the jobber's sales, profits, and return on investment.

PENN JERSEY AUTO STORES, INC.
9901 Blue Grass Road
Philadelphia, PA 19114
(215) 671–9900
Contact: J. L. Rounds

BUSINESS: Home and auto store.
FRANCHISES: 99 in five states and District of Columbia.
FOUNDED: 1949.
REQUIRED CAPITAL: Total price—turnkey $55,000.
FINANCIAL ASSISTANCE: Financing by bank in area.
TRAINING: Extensive on-the-job training.
MANAGERIAL ASSISTANCE: Accounting guidance and district sales managers' visitation on regularly scheduled basis.

*POLY-OLEUM CORPORATION
16135 Harper Avenue
Detroit, MI 48224
(313) 882–4600
Contact: William C. McKay

BUSINESS: Auto-truck rustproofing.
FRANCHISES: 32 in 3 states and Canada.
FOUNDED: 1963.
REQUIRED CAPITAL: $15,000 to $25,000.
FINANCIAL ASSISTANCE: None.
TRAINING: One-week training in technical application of products and sales training course at company's home office.
MANAGERIAL ASSISTANCE: Company representative will spend one week with new franchisee to provide additional training in the field at new location and will make sales calls and train under actual working conditions.

RAYCO
Division of FDI, Inc.
3250 West Market Street
Akron, OH 44313
(216) 867–5900
Contact: Gerald Rosenfield

BUSINESS: Installation and service for tires, exhaust systems, shock absorbers, seat covers, convertible tops, auto interior upholstery, brakes, front end, audio equipment, and accessories.
FRANCHISES: 100 in the United States.
FOUNDED: 1945.
REQUIRED CAPITAL: $25,000 to $80,000. Two programs available to serve individual needs and finances.
FINANCIAL ASSISTANCE: Assistance in arranging equipment financing.
TRAINING: Complete on-the-job training program in phases of operation.
MANAGERIAL ASSISTANCE: Complete program of field supervision, in-store assistance, home office guidance, and personnel procurement.

ROBO-WASH, INC.
2330 Burlington
North Kansas City, MO 64116
(816) 842–4686
Contact: Braxton P. Jones

BUSINESS: Car wash.

FRANCHISES: 1,436 locations in the United States plus Canada, Europe, and the Far East.

FOUNDED: 1964.

REQUIRED CAPITAL: Minimum of $17,000 and up, depending upon building, location, and equipment requirements.

FINANCIAL ASSISTANCE: None.

TRAINING: Five days' training conducted at company office training school, and two to five days on-site technical training at time of initial hookup.

MANAGERIAL ASSISTANCE: Company provides national and regional parts inventory, tuition free training school, standard operating manuals and procedures (technical, promotional, and business management), periodic regional seminars (technical, management, and promotional), standard bookkeeping system, frequent technical and management bulletins. Also provided are a dealer-oriented company magazine and 24-hour emergency answering service.

SERVICE CENTER
High Performance Auto Parts
11034 South La Cienega Boulevard
Inglewood, CA 90304
(213) 649–2100
Contact: Sheldon Konblett

BUSINESS: Retailing auto parts, accessories, and marine equipment.

FRANCHISES: 35 in five states including Hawaii.

FOUNDED: 1963.

REQUIRED CAPITAL: $30,000.

FINANCIAL ASSISTANCE: None.

TRAINING: Complete two weeks' training period which will take place at company warehouse, offices, and retail stores.

MANAGERIAL ASSISTANCE: The company assists the franchise stores in inventory control and merchandising.

*TUFF-KOTE DINOL, INC.
P.O. Box 306
Warren, MI 48090
(313) 776–5000
Contact: Director of Franchising

BUSINESS: Automotive rustproofing.

FRANCHISES: 175 in 28 states; 3,500 in 48 countries.

FOUNDED: 1964.

REQUIRED CAPITAL: $35,000–$55,000.

FINANCIAL ASSISTANCE: None.

TRAINING: The International Training Center offers a two-week, comprehensive curriculum which includes both technical and management training. The latest in training innovations are used to assist the student in the application of the subject matter.

MANAGERIAL ASSISTANCE: The company offers assistance through two field service staffs and through quality control departments to help the franchisees in their own territories.

*WESTERN AUTO SUPPLY COMPANY
2107 Grand Avenue
Kansas City, MO 64108
(816) 421–6700
Contact: R. T. Renfro

BUSINESS: Retailing of automotive parts, hardware, sporting goods, tools and wheel goods, appliances, televisions, radios and other electronics, housewares, paint, toys, and furniture.

FRANCHISES: Over 3,900 in 48 states, Bahama Islands, Virgin Islands, and British West Indies.

FOUNDED: 1935.

REQUIRED CAPITAL: $40,000 and up depending on market selected.

FINANCIAL ASSISTANCE: Financing available on store fixtures. Floor planning of major items and deferred terms on some seasonal merchandise offered. Financing of retail customer installment sales also offered. Other financial assistance extended depending on personal financial statements on prospects.

TRAINING: Two-week training course in modern electronically equipped training facility prior to opening store provides instruction in store operation, display, bookkeeping, product information, advertising, and credit management. Company personnel continues to offer training, counseling and sales meetings after formalized training school is completed.

MANAGERIAL ASSISTANCE: Dealer contacted periodically in store by company personnel, such as territory sales manager and territory credit manager, offering counseling on sales, credit, and store operation.

WHITE STORES, INC.
3910 Call Field Road
Wichita Falls, TX 76308
(817) 692–3410
Contact: Weldon Herring

BUSINESS: Retailing of tires, batteries, automotive parts and accessories, TV, stereo and other electronics, housewares, sporting goods, tools, and summer goods.

FRANCHISES: 516 in 17 states.

FOUNDED: 1934.

REQUIRED CAPITAL: $40,000 minimum.

FINANCIAL ASSISTANCE: Floor planning of major appliances, datings on seasonal merchandise and financing of fixtures is available to franchisee. Amounts will vary depending on the size of operation and the franchisee's financial statement.

TRAINING: One-week school in home office. In-store training by field representative with a continuous callback program for the purpose of training and advising dealer. There are also periodic sales clinics.

MANAGERIAL ASSISTANCE: Continuous in-store training by field representative.

*ZIEBART RUSTPROOFING COMPANY
1290 East Maple Road
Troy, MI 48084
(313) 588–4100
Contact: Ted Nuoffer

BUSINESS: Rustproofing autos and trucks.

FRANCHISES: 650 plus in 31 states and 28 countries.

FOUNDED: 1963.

REQUIRED CAPITAL: Total project including operating capital averages $30,000 to $50,000.

FINANCIAL ASSISTANCE: None.

TRAINING: Ziebart provides ten days of intensive technical and marketing training at the home office in Troy, Michigan. This is followed with technical assistance in setting up the dealership and marketing assistance in preparing proper ads and announcements.

MANAGERIAL ASSISTANCE: Technical and marketing assistance through the technical department and the marketing department. A district sales manager calls once each month to check performance, makes sales calls with dealers, as well as reviewing procedure and advising on marketing strategy. Special training and technical help are available to dealers at all times in addition to annual seminars.

AJAX RENT A CAR COMPANY
8816 West Olympic Boulevard
Beverly Hills, CA 90211
(213) 272–0411
Contact: Jerry Kenney or Harvey Bibicoff

BUSINESS: Automobile and truck rental.

FRANCHISES: 66 in United States, 15 in Austria.

FOUNDED: 1969.

REQUIRED CAPITAL: From $25,000 to $100,000 depending on size of territory.

FINANCIAL ASSISTANCE: None.

TRAINING: Two weeks at the system's headquarters. Complete procedure manual provided.

MANAGERIAL ASSISTANCE: Accounting assistance available as well as continuous guidance regarding the acquisition and disposition of fleets. Periodic visits from district manager to keep franchisee aware of new development in the industry.

*BUDGET RENT A CAR CORPORATION OF AMERICA
35 East Wacker Drive
Chicago, IL 60601
(312) 641–0424
Contact: David J. Reid

BUSINESS: Automobile renting.
FRANCHISES: 1,100 in all states, Canada, and worldwide.
FOUNDED: 1960.
REQUIRED CAPITAL: $30,000 with $100,000 balance sheet.
FINANCIAL ASSISTANCE: None.
TRAINING: Two weeks on-the-job training.
MANAGERIAL ASSISTANCE: During the term of the franchise, Budget has full management team available to assist with financial, franchise, operations, promotion, advertising, and insurance problems.

DOLLAR RENT-A-CAR-SYSTEMS, INC.
6141 West Century Boulevard
Los Angeles, CA 90045
(213) 776–8100
Contact: E. Woody Francis

BUSINESS: Automobile and truck rental.
FRANCHISES: Over 300 in the United States, Canada, Puerto Rico, Haiti, and Mexico.
FOUNDED: 1966.
REQUIRED CAPITAL: Approximately $100,000.
FINANCIAL ASSISTANCE: Occasionally assist in financing.
TRAINING: Standardized accounting system set up. Operational training by franchisor's representative at site.
MANAGERIAL ASSISTANCE: Assistance in site selection. Standardized freestanding building. Nationwide advertising campaign and reservations service.

ECONO-CAR INTERNATIONAL, INC.
4930 West 77th Street
Edina, MN 55435
(612) 944–5287
Contact: Licensing Manager

BUSINESS: Automobile rental.
FRANCHISES: 165 in 40 states, District of Columbia, Canada, and Virgin Islands.

* Asterisk denotes franchisor is a member of the International Franchise Association.

FOUNDED: 1961.

REQUIRED CAPITAL: $5,000 minimum depending upon size of franchised area, and good credit rating.

FINANCIAL ASSISTANCE: Some financial assistance on initial franchise fee.

TRAINING: On-site training at established Econo-Car operation. Complete procedures manual provided.

MANAGERIAL ASSISTANCE: Opening kit of all necessary materials and initial operating supplies. National advertising, and sales and reservation system. Home office personnel available at all times for consultation.

HERTZ CORPORATION
660 Madison Avenue
New York, NY 10021
(212) 986–2121
Contact: Licensing Manager

BUSINESS: Automobile and truck rental.

FRANCHISES: 917 in 48 states.

FOUNDED: 1928.

REQUIRED CAPITAL: Varies according to franchise location.

FINANCIAL ASSISTANCE: None.

TRAINING: Zone system manager trains new franchisee before operation opens with Hertz Starter Kit (kit includes all forms needed to run a location). Visits by system manager on a periodic basis. Manager rental representative training classes are provided. Manuals and guides for running a location issued. Corporate training class available to franchisees. Annual business meeting.

MANAGERIAL ASSISTANCE: Accounting and operational guides are provided to run the franchise. Visits by zone system manager to act as a liaison between the corporate and licensee locations. All forms and training classes provided as needed. Yearly training and business meetings. Contact provided directly to corporate management for all areas of rental business (e.g., insurance, advertising, accounting, and so on).

PAYLESS CAR RENTAL SYSTEM, INC.
West 903 Comstock Court
Spokane, WA 99203
(509) 624–4238
Contact: L. E. Netterstrom

BUSINESS: Automobile rental.

FRANCHISES: 85 in 24 states, Canada and Morocco.

FOUNDED: 1971.

REQUIRED CAPITAL: Franchisee will require a credit line to finance rental fleet plus $4,000 minimum for a franchise in a city with a population of 200,000.

FINANCIAL ASSISTANCE: The $4,000 investment pays for the franchise fee, training, all supplies and forms during first year of operation, insurance deposit, signs (interior and exterior), and accounting system. A portion of the franchise fee may be financed. Payless will assist the franchisee in obtaining a credit line from local banks, GMAC, Ford Motor Credit, and so on.

TRAINING: Payless furnishes guidance in establishing, operating, and promoting the business of renting automobiles, with respect to: the institution and maintenance of office management systems and business operating procedures; the institution of a continuing sales campaign and securing a vehicle rental location and office.

MANAGERIAL ASSISTANCE: Franchisees are allowed to call the Payless National Headquarters collect with regard to technical problems, reservation handling, insurance questions, and supply or advertising needs. A monthly newsletter and operation manual changes are mailed to all franchisees.

THRIFTY RENT-A-CAR SYSTEM
2400 North Sheridan Road
Tulsa, OK 74151
(918) 838–3335
Contact: Cecil R. Davis

BUSINESS: Automobile rental.
FRANCHISES: 360 plus locations in all 50 states, Canada, Scotland, England, and Guatemala.
FOUNDED: 1958.
REQUIRED CAPITAL: $25,000 to $50,000.
FINANICAL ASSISTANCE: Franchisor assists licensee in setting up lines of credit.
TRAINING: On-the-job training one week in company-owned operation, plus one week in licensee operation.
MANAGERIAL ASSISTANCE: Continuing management and technical assistance.

THE BARBERS, HAIRSTYLING FOR MEN AND WOMEN, INC.
130 South 10th Street
Minneapolis, MN 55403
(612) 339–0385
Contact: Licensing Manager

BUSINESS: Men's and women's hairstyling shop.
FRANCHISES: 45 in 12 states.
FOUNDED: 1963.
REQUIRED CAPITAL: $25,000 to $40,000.
FINANCIAL ASSISTANCE: Available to qualified applicants.
TRAINING: One-week management and technical training with quarterly seminars and weekly newsletters to management. Must be licensed barber or hairdresser.
MANAGERIAL ASSISTANCE: Business management, including advertising, public relations, accounting and record keeping, training in hairstyling and all related services.

EDIE ADAMS' CUT & CURL
125 South Service Road
Long Island Expressway
Jericho, NY 11753
(516) 334–8400
Contact: Don von Liebermann

BUSINESS: Beauty salons.
FRANCHISES: 345 in 38 states.
FOUNDED: 1955.
REQUIRED CAPITAL: $15,000.
FINANCIAL ASSISTANCE: Up to $15,000 financing to qualified applicants.
TRAINING: Approximately ten days in-salon training. Preopening training in franchisee's salon and complete supply of manuals.
MANAGERIAL ASSISTANCE: Home office, technical, seminars, new techniques, and managerial procedures.

HARPER METHOD INCORPORATED
1657 Broadway
New York, NY 10019
(212) 582–2254
Contact: Philip E. Jakeway

BUSINESS: Beauty salon.
FRANCHISES: 86 in 26 states.
FOUNDED: 1892.
REQUIRED CAPITAL: $1,200 to $35,000.
FINANCIAL ASSISTANCE: Franchisor has no special financing plan other than the usual credit terms based on the franchisee's credit standing. Arrangements are available for franchisee to lease the initial equipment and where qualified, inventory may be acquired by a series of notes extending over 12 months in equal monthly payments.
TRAINING: Depending on location of franchisee, the initial training may be given in one of the company's schools or may be given by a teacher who visits the franchisee's salon. Initial training requires about a week of intensive work with occasional refresher courses.
MANAGERIAL ASSISTANCE: In addition to area seminars and refresher courses, Harper Method personnel periodically are available for training within an individual franchised salon.

MAGIC MIRROR BEAUTY SALONS, INC.
341 North Maple Drive
Beverly Hills, CA 90210
(213) 274–9311
Contact: Dale Scott

BUSINESS: Beauty salon.
FRANCHISES: 30 in California, New Jersey, and New Zealand.

FOUNDED: 1949.
REQUIRED CAPITAL: $10,000 to $15,000.
FINANCIAL ASSISTANCE: Help with locating financing.
TRAINING: Two weeks at the company headquarters. One week at franchisee's shop covering management and operation.
MANAGERIAL ASSISTANCE: Continuous training. Counselor visits every three months providing assistance in accounting, operations, and advertising brand name merchandise. Franchisee may buy supplies from other suppliers.

ROFFLER INDUSTRIES, INC.
400 Chess Street
Coraopolis, PA 15108
(412) 771–4333
Contact: Sharon Gilcrest

BUSINESS: Sells men's cosmetics and hairstyling and hair care preparations to barbers.
FRANCHISES: Approximately 7,000 in all states.
FOUNDED: 1968.
REQUIRED CAPITAL: $495 to cover franchise fee, equipment, and inventory.
FINANCIAL ASSISTANCE: None.
TRAINING: Local and national seminars in hairstyling trends. Refresher clinics are an integral part of the seminars. Seminars include education in additional services such as hairpiece fitting, cleaning, and coloring; hair and scalp treatments; facials, hair coloring, and hair straightening.
MANAGERIAL ASSISTANCE: Franchisor and its area dealers periodically conduct training seminars.

WINSLOW MANUFACTURING, INC.
1800 West 4th Avenue
Hialeah, FL 33010
(305) 885–4642
Contact: Harry Perrin

BUSINESS: Sell or lease products to beauty salons.
FRANCHISES: 100 throughout the United States.
FOUNDED: 1959.
REQUIRED CAPITAL: $6,000 for inventory. No fees or royalties.
FINANCIAL ASSISTANCE: Company is prepared to establish a 30-day open account for the distributor, amount to be determined by financial standing of distributor. Company is also prepared to grant longer term financing for equipment through conditional sales contracts. This requires a 10 percent down payment with payouts ranging up to 24 months. Company has granted credit to individual distributors in amounts ranging up to $25,000.
TRAINING: Company gives a five-day intensive training course at company's expense at headquarters in Hialeah, Florida. Follow-up training will be given from time to time by company personnel in the home territory of the distributor. Also manuals are provided.

MANAGERIAL ASSISTANCE: Mailings are made by the company for each distributor to all beauty salons in distributor's area. This is done at the company's expense. The company stays in touch with its distributors by phone at least once a month. Also, newsletters are published once a month where sales ideas are expounded and technical problems are discussed. Company also advertises extensively on a national basis through full-page ads in the major trade magazines such as *American Hairdresser, Modern Beauty Shop,* and others. Company also participates in coop local advertising. Company furthermore assists by supplying booth decorations and advertising material for local cosmetology shows or conventions. Company supplies literature.

ARMICO BUSINESS SERVICES
1710 South Amphlett Boulevard
San Mateo, CA 94402
(415) 692–1450
Contact: Gerald Weiss

BUSINESS: Computerized accounting business systems distributorship and management for small- to large-sized businesses with annual volumes up to $15,000,000.
FRANCHISES: 14 in eight states.
FOUNDED: 1968.
REQUIRED CAPITAL: $15,000 to $95,000.
FINANCIAL ASSISTANCE: The franchise fee is payable in a lump sum or installments. The company requires the leasing or purchasing of optional computer equipment; i.e., Remote Data Entry Terminal Model 40D2, $3,950; Model 102, $8,950; Serial Line Terminal Model 102, $8,950; printer, Model 102A, $3,950; System VM/16 computer, $31,950 to $79,950.
TRAINING: The company has an intensive three-day–160-hour training program. Technical and management instruction and on-the-job training is under the direction of licensed accountants and business consultants. Business development training is under the direction of marketing personnel with ten years of sales experience.
MANAGERIAL ASSISTANCE: A highly competent accounting, marketing, programming, and telecommunications staff stands ready to provide individualized help to franchisees. Part of this continuing support from the home office includes review of input and output data, client program support, and job performance evaluation. National and regional business conferences and technical clinics are held annually covering general operations.

AUDIT CONTROLS, INC.
45 Emerson Plaza East
Emerson, NJ 07630
(201) 265–3330
Contact: Arieh Douer

BUSINESS: A series of collection letters to be used in collecting overdue accounts.
FRANCHISES: 750 in 50 states.

FOUNDED: 1960.

REQUIRED CAPITAL: $150 plus postage.

FINANCIAL ASSISTANCE: None.

TRAINING. Detailed instructions mailed to each franchisee.

MANAGERIAL ASSISTANCE: Advisory assistance for the duration of the franchise of one year and renewals.

BINEX-AUTOMATED BUSINESS SYSTEMS, INC.
1787 Tribute Road
Sacramento, CA 95815
(916) 920–8806
Contact: Walter G. Heidig

BUSINESS Computerized services to small- and medium-sized businesses.

FRANCHISES: 52 in 20 states and Canada.

FOUNDED: 1966.

REQUIRED CAPITAL: $7,500. The fee covers training, manuals, and start-up supplies.

FINANCIAL ASSISTANCE: None.

TRAINING: Home study course, one to two weeks' home office and one week on the job. Franchisees may return for further training as needed. Complete operations manuals, technical manuals, and promotion manuals are provided.

MANAGERIAL ASSISTANCE: Support is provided on a continuing basis. Newsletters are sent out covering a variety of subjects including business operation, marketing, taxes, and so on. New programs and services are developed, documented, and made available regularly to all franchisees. Periodic regional meetings provide upgrading and review.

H & R BLOCK, INC.
4410 Main Street
Kansas City, MO 64111
(816) 753–6900
Contact: William T. Ross

BUSINESS: Preparation of individual income tax returns.

FRANCHISES: Over 7,573 offices throughout the United States, Canada and ten foreign countries. About 3,909 offices are franchised with the balance operated by the parent company.

FOUNDED: 1946.

REQUIRED CAPITAL: $1,000 to $1,500.

FINANCIAL ASSISTANCE: None.

TRAINING: Each year a training program is held in November for all new managers. Prior to tax season, a training program for all employees is conducted in major centers. Each summer a meeting is held for all managers for three days to discuss all phases of the operation and new developments and ideas.

MANAGERIAL ASSISTANCE: Any and all assistance required or needed.

BUSINESS CONSULTANT OF AMERCIA
Subsidiary of Horizons of America
P.O. Box 4098
Waterbury, CT 06714
(203) 574–0302
Contact: Greg Nolan

BUSINESS: Advisory services for small- and medium-sized business operations.

FRANCHISES: 9 in ten states and Canada.

FOUNDED: 1973.

REQUIRED CAPITAL: $7,500 plus $6,000 working capital.

FINANCIAL ASSISTANCE: Assistance with bank/government financing. Financing available from franchisor; 50 percent, five years, 10 percent rate of interest, upon rejection from reputable lending institutions, secured by promissory note.

TRAINING: Seven-week intensive training at company headquarters, followed by one-month cassette courses packaged by franchisor and other professional organizations. Continuing franchisor advisory newsletters and tapes.

MANAGERIAL ASSISTANCE: First-year, nonfee technical and advisory services at discretion of franchisee. Continued services on an as needed free basis. Additional memberships arranged in professional associations.

BUSINESS EXCHANGE, INC.
4716 Vineland Avenue
North Hollywood, CA 91602
(213) 877–2161
Contact: Marvin J. McConnell

BUSINESS: Barter service plan for business owners that allows business owners to trade their products (at retail) for the things that they need from the other participating dealers rather than paying cash.

FRANCHISES: 40 in 14 states.

FOUNDED: 1961.

REQUIRED CAPITAL: $19,900.

FINANCIAL ASSISTANCE: All of the accounting and administrative expenses are borne by the company. The company further finances all sales commission advances made to sales representatives in franchisee area to permit continued expansion by franchisee.

TRAINING: Complete training program provided at home office with actual field work as well as theory. If requested by franchisee, training and development of the program in franchisee area are also provided by the company.

MANAGERIAL ASSISTANCE: The company provides continuous management assistance and co-works with licensee on a continuous basis. Company provides a national directory three times yearly, and monthly newspaper for all members.

COMMERCIAL SERVICES COMPANY
2699 Lee Road—Suite 150
Winter Park, FL 32789
(305) 647–1113
Contact: James G. Sherwood

BUSINESS: Bookkeeping, accounting, and tax service to small- and medium-sized businesses.

FRANCHISES: 13 in six states.

FOUNDED: 1959.

REQUIRED CAPITAL: $18,000.

FINANCIAL ASSISTANCE: The company will finance $9,000 which is paid out of earnings (at 10 percent of cash receipts and includes principal and interest).

TRAINING: Training in all phases of operation is conducted by the company in Orlando, Florida. Sessions are one week or longer as required. A procedures manual is provided containing operating instructions. General guidance continues indefinitely.

MANAGERIAL ASSISTANCE: The company provides immediate backup assistance on all business matters, technical or managerial. Franchisee almost always receives a response within the same day to any general or specific question.

*COMPREHENSIVE ACCOUNTING SERVICE COMPANY
2111 Comprehensive Drive
Aurora, IL 60505
(312) 898–1234
Contact: John J. Keefer

BUSINESS: Independent accountants are provided a monthly computerized bookkeeping, accounting, and tax service appropriate for small- and medium-sized businesses.

FRANCHISES: 105 in 11 states.

FOUNDED: 1965.

REQUIRED CAPITAL: $20,000.

FINANCIAL ASSISTANCE: Partial or full financing consisting of notes collateralized by the franchisee's practice. Credit extended to franchisee may exceed $300,000 in certain cases.

TRAINING: Each new franchisee is required to complete a six-week training course, both in the classroom at the company headquarters and on-the-job training in the office of a franchisee.

MANAGERIAL ASSISTANCE: The company provides on an ongoing basis a personal consultant and a data processing consultant. Each consultant is available by phone or in person. Also provided are detailed production procedures and methods, plus sales aids for use in obtaining accounts: audiovisual projector, two professionally prepared filmstrips explaining services to prospective clients, a prospective client presentation manual, sample computerized financial statements, and various sales brochures. Monthly seminars provide continuing education and interchange of ideas.

*COMPREHENSIVE BUSINESS SERVICE COMPANY
2111 Comprehensive Drive
Aurora, IL 60505
(312) 898–1234
Contact: John J. Keefer

BUSINESS: Independent accountants are provided a monthly computerized bookkeeping, accounting, and tax service appropriate for small-and medium-sized businesses.

* Asterisk denotes franchisor is a member of the International Franchise Association.

FRANCHISES: 51 in 23 states.
FOUNDED: 1975.
REQUIRED CAPITAL: $20,000.
FINANCIAL ASSISTANCE: Financial assistance is available.
TRAINING: The franchisee is required to take a four-week course after sufficient home study preparation in COMPREHENSIVE® (CBS) production methods has been completed. Training at the company headquarters is divided equally between administration and marketing.
MANAGERIAL ASSISTANCE: The company provides a list of at least 2,000 prospects in the franchisee's area. COMPREHENSIVE® provides on an ongoing basis a management consultant, a marketing consultant, and a data processing consultant. Each consultant is available by phone or in person. Also provided are detailed production procedures and methods, plus sales aids for use in obtaining accounts: audiovisual projector, two professionally prepared filmstrips explaining the COMPREHENSIVE® services to prospective clients, a prospective client presentation manual, sample computerized financial statements, and various sales brochures. Also monthly seminars provide continuing education and interchange of ideas.

COMPUTER CAPITAL CORPORATION
6922 Hollywood Boulevard
Los Angeles, CA 90028
(213) 463-4841
Contact: Leonard H. vander Bie

BUSINESS: Investment counseling.
FRANCHISES: 36 in 20 states.
FOUNDED: 1969.
REQUIRED CAPITAL: $18,000 (nonexclusive territory).
FINANCIAL ASSISTANCE: None.
TRAINING: Initial training, approximately three days, then continuing day-to-day training while practicing financial consulting.
MANAGERIAL ASSISTANCE: Continuing on an ongoing basis for the ten-year agreement.

CONTACTS INFLUENTIAL
516 S.E. Morrison—10th Floor
Portland, OR 97214
(503) 236-2141
Contact: Matt J. Dutton

BUSINESS: Computerized business directories and select mailing lists.
FRANCHISES: 19 in 9 states and Canada.
FOUNDED: 1961.
REQUIRED CAPITAL: $3,000 for franchise fee. Approximately $20,000 for operating capital.
FINANCIAL ASSISTANCE: None.

TRAINING: Approximately two weeks in the field, plus any backup as needed or requested.

MANAGERIAL ASSISTANCE: Constant contact is kept with franchisees. All technical or computer assistance is taken care of by company.

CREDIT SERVICE COMPANY
101 Miles Building
2025 Canal Street
New Orleans, LA 70112
(504) 822–4881
Contact: E. G. Edwards

BUSINESS: Medical-dental-hospital collection service.

FRANCHISES: 64 in 27 states and Canada.

FOUNDED: Franchising since 1962.

REQUIRED CAPITAL: $2,350.

FINANCIAL ASSISTANCE: The required $2,350 covers everything except the initial supply of stationery, and this can be obtained by the franchisee at an additional cost of about $200. The franchisee pays 3 percent royalty, based on gross profit before taxes, during the first three years of operation, and this is then reduced to 1.5 percent thereafter.

TRAINING: A comprehensive two-week training course in New Orleans with round trip rail or air transportation (continental United States) meals and first-class accommodations included in the $2,350. A procedures manual is supplied, with copies of all forms, letters, and operational details. Further assistance is provided on a continuing basis at no added cost. There is no inventory to purchase and a typewriter is the only equipment needed.

MANAGERIAL ASSISTANCE: Monthly reports are required in order to determine areas in which the franchisee may require assistance. Newsletters are issued bimonthly in order to keep franchisee informed on matters of mutual interest.

*E-Z KEEP SYSTEMS
Division of Edwin K. Williams & Company
5324 Ekwill Street
Santa Barbara, CA 93111
(805) 964–4768
Contact: Duane B. Walsh

BUSINESS: Management counseling and record keeping for all types of businesses.

FRANCHISES: 198 in the United States.

FOUNDED: 1972.

REQUIRED CAPITAL: $5,000 to $25,000.

FINANCIAL ASSISTANCE: Limited financing.

TRAINING: Individual, seminar, on-the-job training.

MANAGERIAL ASSISTANCE: Ongoing year after year, seminars, conventions, and assistance by regional manager.

FEDDER COMPUTER SYSTEMS
Division of Financial Computer Corporation
412 West Redwood Street
Baltimore, MD 21201
(301) 837–9510
Contact: David E. Fedder, President

BUSINESS: Marketing of computers and related data processing equipment and services.
FRANCHISES: 15 in United States, Canada, and India.
FOUNDED: 1973.
REQUIRED CAPITAL: $25,000.
FINANCIAL ASSISTANCE: Equipment and receivables financing.
TRAINING: Marketing, computer installation and operation training for approximately three weeks, depending on prior experience.
MANAGERIAL ASSISTANCE: Varies depending on needs of franchisee. The company provides ongoing assistance in advertising, marketing, sales training, and related areas. Training and assistance is also offered in the areas of computer programs and technical support.

*GENERAL BUSINESS SERVICES, INC.
51 Monroe Street
Rockville, MD 20850
(301) 424–1646
Contact: R. F. Turner

BUSINESS: Business counseling, financial management, and tax services for the small independent business.
FRANCHISES: Over 1,000 in the United States.
FOUNDED: 1962.
REQUIRED CAPITAL: $15,000 for area directors; $10,000 for associate directors.
FINANCIAL ASSISTANCE: None.
TRAINING: All selected franchisees are appointed area or associate directors and receive without additional expense: (1) a four-volume operations manual containing all operating instructions, company policies, and procedures; (2) Basic Training Institute and Advanced Training Institute in Rockville, Md.: (3) individual field training; and (4) continuous training and individual guidance through permanently assigned regional directors.
MANAGERIAL ASSISTANCE: A complete and detailed franchise development program for new franchisees is provided.

*GETTING TO KNOW YOU INTERNATIONAL, LTD.
49 Watermill Lane
Great Neck, NY 11022
(516) 829–8210
Contact: Richard F. Wynn

BUSINESS: A newcomer Welcome Service for retail merchants and homeowner services companies.

FRANCHISES: 37 in 12 states.

FOUNDED: 1962.

REQUIRED CAPITAL: $25,000 minimum.

FINANCIAL ASSISTANCE: The franchise fee of $15,000 covers presentation materials, home office, and field training, basic area marketing survey and procedures. In addition, at least $10,000 operating capital is required for the first 8 to 12 months of operation, or until cash receipts are sufficiently established to defray expenses. An automobile is also needed. The franchisor will assist the franchisee in making inventory purchases after six months.

TRAINING: Initially, one week of orientation procedures and sales techniques at company headquarters, followed by one week of sales and marketing procedures in the franchisee's territory. Later, the franchisee receives additional training in renewal procedures prior to renewal sales.

MANAGERIAL ASSISTANCE: Franchisee receives total and constant assistance from the company in many forms, including marketing, production, and distribution. Complete operations manuals are provided, plus regular supplements. The company maintains a market research program and advertising program and makes regular and frequent contact with all franchisees.

INCOTAX SYSTEMS, INC.
223 Datura Street
West Palm Beach, FL 33401
(305) 655–4024
Contact: Richard Vowdrok

BUSINESS: Tax service system for small- and medium-sized businesses.

FRANCHISES: 14 in six states.

FOUNDED: 1967.

REQUIRED CAPITAL: $15,000 to $30,000.

FINANCIAL ASSISTANCE: None.

TRAINING: Complete management and tax preparation training for both owners and managers is conducted by the company. All previous owners and managers must receive refresher training once a year. Both training sessions are for one week conducted at regional sites.

MANAGERIAL ASSISTANCE: Continuous company inspection and management training is conducted. The company consultation and management suggestions are made to all franchisees. Complete procedural manuals and forms are furnished franchisees as well as monthly news bulletins.

MARCOIN, INC.
1924 Cliff Valley Way, N.E.
Atlanta, GA 30329
(404) 325–1200
Contact: J. T. Rhodes

BUSINESS: Business counseling and management services primarily for small businesses.

FRANCHISES: 180 licensee offices plus 20 company-owned branches in 41 states.

FOUNDED: 1952.

REQUIRED CAPITAL: Initial franchise and training fees vary according to potential and population. Total capital needs including working capital will range from $10,000 to $20,000.

FINANCIAL ASSISTANCE: Financing plan available in exceptional cases or will assist the applicant to arrange outside financing.

TRAINING: Four to five weeks' training in existing franchisee offices plus installation and follow-up. Formal training program also available.

MANAGERIAL ASSISTANCE: Regional supervisors and managers provide close and continued follow-up to ensure success. Complete management and operations manuals provided for each company program. Business counseling available if desired.

MEDI-FAX, INC.
1821 Summit Road
Cincinnati, OH 45237
(513) 948–8607
Contact: Kathleen Ruth

BUSINESS: Computerized accounts receivable management service for medical and retail professions.

FRANCHISES: 3 in three states.

FOUNDED: 1968.

REQUIRED CAPITAL: Minimum $5,500.

FINANCIAL ASSISTANCE: Will help local financing.

TRAINING: Four-day training session by psychologist and member of staff. Management people always available for consultation and to render varied types of assistance.

MANAGERIAL ASSISTANCE: Training manual provided, detail of program available in book form with proper indexing available to clients.

MUZAK
888 Seventh Avenue
New York, NY 10019
(212) 247–3333
Contact: Kirk G. Anderson

BUSINESS: Music programs for businesses of all kinds. Sound systems and related communication systems included as lease or sale to customers.

FRANCHISES: Approximately 300 in the United States plus 25 countries.

FOUNDED: 1934.

REQUIRED CAPITAL: Varies according to franchise.

FINANCIAL ASSISTANCE: None.

TRAINING: Orientation sessions held regularly in New York City. Continuing sales training sessions at various sites around United States.

MANAGERIAL ASSISTANCE: Field visits by company staff provide evaluations, assistance, and progress reports. National advertising, sales brochures, equipment specification sheets, and so on provided at all times.

NATIONAL HOMEOWNERS SERVICE ASSOCIATION, INC.
317 Plaza Building
Pensacola, FL 32505
(904) 432–9834
Contact: W. F. Johns

BUSINESS: Service club that is based on fair practices and better treatment of consumers.
FRANCHISES: 6 in Florida, Massachusetts, and Alabama.
FOUNDED: 1974.
REQUIRED CAPITAL: $4,000.
FINANCIAL ASSISTANCE: None.
TRAINING: Training will consist of a closely regulated 21 days of office and field training, one week to be in company headquarters with two additional weeks to be provided in the franchisee's chapter office. All training under supervision of well-trained, full-time company employees.
MANAGERIAL ASSISTANCE: The company provides management assistance in such areas as bookkeeping, advertising, operations manuals forms, service to members, service dealer relations, and member relations.

NATIONWIDE INCOME TAX SERVICE COMPANY
14507 West Warren
Dearborn, MI 48126
(313) 584–7640
Contact: Carl Gilbert

BUSINESS: Preparation of state and federal income tax returns for individuals.
FRANCHISES: 7 in three states.
FOUNDED: 1966.
REQUIRED CAPITAL: Dependent upon number of offices to be opened.
FINANCIAL ASSISTANCE: Assistance is available.
TRAINING: Five-day training period in company headquarters in all phases of income tax preparation and in the systems and procedures developed by the company.
MANAGERIAL ASSISTANCE: The company performs a market analysis that assists franchisee in selecting sites most suitable for business; provides personal guidance for personnel recruitment, selection and training of employees; office layout and design counseling; designs advertising and promotional materials and determines media and ad schedules; and maintains continuous liaison with franchisee through mail and telephone.

RELIABLE BUSINESS SYSTEMS, INC.
555 Commonwealth Avenue
Newton, MA 02159
(617) 964–6030
Contact: M. Michael Licker

BUSINESS: Federal and state tax return preparation.
FRANCHISES: 7 in eight states.

FOUNDED: 1955.

REQUIRED CAPITAL: $8,950.

FINANCIAL ASSISTANCE: None. However the company will, in certain situations where franchisee is above average, finance $2,000 of the capital.

TRAINING: One week in the field training by another experienced distributor and further training at the company headquarters if needed.

MANAGERIAL ASSISTANCE: Continuous flow of new material, also consultation available on an unlimited and continuous basis. Close contact with distributor maintained. Additional help by company accounting tax staff regarding tax matters when needed.

SAFEGUARD BUSINESS SYSTEMS
470 Maryland Drive
Fort Washington, PA 19030
(215) 643–4811
Contact: Richard V. Hemlin

BUSINESS: Bookkeeping and record-keeping systems.

FRANCHISES: 450 in the United States, Canada, and Puerto Rico.

FOUNDED: 1956.

REQUIRED CAPITAL: No franchise fee required.

FINANCIAL ASSISTANCE: The company carries the accounts receivable and inventory, thus reducing working capital requirements.

TRAINING: Eighty hours of initial training. Provision is also made for continual field follow-up.

MANAGERIAL ASSISTANCE: Operation and sales manuals furnished. Company provides advertising and promotional material on a national basis, together with both a cooperative and a corporate direct mail program.

STILLMAN & DOLAN, INC.
P.O. Box 125
Glenolden, PA 19036
(215) 461–7000
Contact: Joseph P. Dolan

BUSINESS: Sales representative for telecommunications consulting firm.

FRANCHISES: 3 in Massachusetts, Pennsylvania, Delaware, and New Jersey.

FOUNDED: 1966.

REQUIRED CAPITAL: $10,000.

FINANCIAL ASSISTANCE: Franchise fees are $15,000 to $20,000. Up to one third of this fee will be deferred for qualified applicants.

TRAINING: One week of intensive training at company headquarters and one week in field. A very close and highly supportive association with company personnel continues for the life of the franchise agreement.

MANAGERIAL ASSISTANCE: Periodic training in all phases of the business is provided to franchisee.

*SUCCESS MOTIVATION INSTITUTE, INC.
500 Lake Wood Drive
Waco, TX 76710
(817) 776–1230
Contact: R. J. Buchta

BUSINESS: Sale of specialized management, sales, and personal development programs to individuals, companies, governments, and other organizations.
FRANCHISES: 1,077 in 50 states and 23 foreign countries.
FOUNDED: 1960.
REQUIRED CAPITAL: $10,950.
FINANCIAL ASSISTANCE: Financial assistance provided.
TRAINING: Complete distributorship training program in printed and recorded form furnished with initial investment. Sales training and sales management seminars available monthly. Field sales training also available in most areas without cost to distributors.
MANAGERIAL ASSISTANCE: Continuous sales consultant provided by the company in distributors through use of monthly mailings, companyowned WATS lines, and prompt response to mail communications.

*SYSTEMEDICS, INC.
Princeton Air Research Park
P.O. Box 2000
Princeton, NJ 08540
(609) 924–9767
Contact: William P. Krause

BUSINESS: Computerized accounts receivable management system and related systems for the medical and health care delivery fields.
FRANCHISES: 61 in 40 states.
FOUNDED: 1964.
REQUIRED CAPITAL: $10,000 to $15,000.
FINANCIAL ASSISTANCE: Possible to finance part of purchase through company. No other form of financial assistance.
TRAINING: A five-day course at company headquarters or regional office.
MANAGERIAL ASSISTANCE: Company provides continuing assistance and field support to all franchisees who desire this assistance.

TAX MAN, INC.
639 Massachusetts Avenue
Cambridge, MA 02139
(617) 868–1374
Contact: Robert G. Murray

BUSINESS: Preparation of individual income tax returns.
FRANCHISES: 7 in New Hampshire and Massachusetts.

FOUNDED: 1967.
REQUIRED CAPITAL: $2,500 minimum.
FINANCIAL ASSISTANCE: Advertising support.
TRAINING: Eight weeks tax preparation training. One-week tax office management training.
MANAGERIAL ASSISTANCE: Complete tax advice, management assistance, site selection, advertising and marketing program.

TAX OFFICES OF AMERICA
Box 4098
Waterville, CT 06714
(203) 574–0302
Contact: Gregg Nolan

BUSINESS: Income tax preparation for individuals and small businesses.
FRANCHISES: 8 in the United States.
FOUNDED: 1966.
REQUIRED CAPITAL: Approximately $7,500.
FINANCIAL ASSISTANCE: Financing arranged through Horizons of America, Inc.
TRAINING: About one-week training provided at company headquarters, one week at franchisee's location plus a mail-order course. If available in franchisee's area, the company pays all expenses to a special training course set up by a nationally known organization.
MANAGERIAL ASSISTANCE: The company staff is always available for counseling.

*TELECHECK SERVICES, INC.
49 South Hotel Street
Suite 314
Honolulu, HI 96813
(808) 524–0925
Contact: Robert J. Baer

BUSINESS: Personal check verification for retailers, banks, and so on.
FRANCHISES: 31 in 28 states and the District of Columbia.
FOUNDED: 1972.
REQUIRED CAPITAL: $150,000 minimum with $32,500 for franchise fee.
FINANCIAL ASSISTANCE: The company will help to find investors.
TRAINING: A visit to an operating location is a prerequisite for signing an agreement. Franchisee receives on-location training in marketing, operations techniques, and data base construction. Trained representatives spend 7 out of the 12 preopening weeks with the franchisee.
MANAGERIAL ASSISTANCE: Regular visits are made to all franchises. A management information system provides statistics monthly to aid franchises in measuring their successes and identifying weak areas.

WHITEHILL SYSTEMS
Division of Small Business Advisors, Inc.
527 Madison Avenue
New York, NY 10022
(212) 758–4971
Contact: G. D. Jones

BUSINESS: Small business accounting service.

FRANCHISES: Franchises in 48 states.

FOUNDED: 1974.

REQUIRED CAPITAL: $14,500, includes training, cost of starting inventory, supply of sales and promotional literature, initial direct mail campaign. A $10,000 life insurance policy premium (paid for the first year).

FINANCIAL ASSISTANCE: Limited.

TRAINING: Six days' training in all phases of the system and selling methods at company office at company expense. Five days' field training in franchisee's territory, with experienced representative, at company expense.

MANAGERIAL ASSISTANCE: Retraining program and continuous assistance as needed.

*EDWIN K. WILLIAMS & COMPANY
P.O. Box 6406
Santa Barbara, CA 93111
(805) 964–4768
Contact: Gene H. Loepphe, Vice President, Field Operations

BUSINESS: Financial counseling and bookkeeping services for the oil industry and small businesses.

FRANCHISES: 260 in the United States.

FOUNDED: 1935.

REQUIRED CAPITAL: $8,000 to $25,000.

FINANCIAL ASSISTANCE: Limited financing.

TRAINING: Individual, seminars, and on-the-job training.

MANAGERIAL ASSISTANCE: Periodic training in all phases of the business is provided franchisees.

CAMPGROUNDS

*JELLYSTONE CAMPGROUNDS LTD.
236 Michigan Street
Sturgeon Bay, WI 54235
(414) 743–6586
Contact: C. C. Chouinard

BUSINESS: Economy family motor inns, camp resorts, miniature golf courses, and snack shops.

* Asterisk denotes franchisor is a member of the International Franchise Association.

FRANCHISES: 52 in 26 states and Canada.
FOUNDED: 1969.
REQUIRED CAPITAL: $75,000 to $100,000.
FINANCIAL ASSISTANCE: None, other than assistance in financing presentations.
TRAINING: Manager training.
MANAGERIAL ASSISTANCE: Engineering and construction planning and perpetual management service and advice.

KAMP DAKOTA, INC.
220 Bartling Building
Brookings, SD 57006
(605) 692–6515
Contact: M. L. Thorne

BUSINESS: Campgrounds for camping and trailering vacationers.
FRANCHISES: 36 nationwide.
FOUNDED: 1964.
REQUIRED CAPITAL: $50,000 and up.
FINANCIAL ASSISTANCE: Assistance in preparation and presentation of loan requests to potential financiers.
TRAINING: Training is provided at each campground as required.
MANAGERIAL ASSISTANCE: Managerial assistance is offered to franchisees on a continuous basis. Also, the company provides franchisees with complete engineering and construction planning for their particular campgrounds.

*KAMPGROUNDS OF AMERICA, INC.
P.O. Box 30558
Billings, MT 59114
(406) 248–7444
Contact: Harold Lloyd

BUSINESS: Campgrounds for recreational vehicles.
FRANCHISES: 850 in the United States and Canada.
FOUNDED: 1964.
REQUIRED CAPITAL: $55,000 minimum.
FINANCIAL ASSISTANCE: Company assists in obtaining financing, preparing prospectus, developing operating projections, and meeting with potential lenders.
TRAINING: The company provides formal classroom training in campground development and operations for franchisee and their personnel. Each school (development and operations) lasts three days; in addition, several seminars are conducted throughout the year.
MANAGERIAL ASSISTANCE: The company provides formal classroom training and continual management services for the life of the franchise in such areas as development, general operations, advertising, and merchandising. Also, complete manuals of development, operations, and supply catalogs are provided. Each campground is visited regularly to ensure conformance with standards and to

assist franchisee in solving problems. The company publishes an annual *Kampground Directory* semiannually and sponsors an annual meeting of franchisees.

SAFARI CAMPGROUNDS
Division of United Safari International, Inc.
1111 Northshore Drive
Knoxville, TN 37919
(615) 584–8536
Contact: Dave Collins

BUSINESS: Camping and recreational facilities.
FRANCHISES: 125 in 37 states and Canada.
FOUNDED: 1966.
REQUIRED CAPITAL: $50,000 to $100,000. Depends upon location and other considerations. In some cases cash needs could be less than above.
FINANCIAL ASSISTANCE: A comprehensive feasibility study and financial plan are prepared by the company and presented to franchisee's lending agency.
TRAINING: Real estate, zoning, and financial planning school of one- to two-day duration. Seminar covering construction, advertising, operating, and accounting procedures involved in campground management, lasting approximately one week.
MANAGEMENT ASSISTANCE: Consultation regarding acceptable site criteria and selection. On-site construction assistance, including custom campground layout and building plans. Ongoing consultation on all facets of campground operations. Frequent inspection visits to ensure chainwide adherence to quality standards. Maintenance of national reservations systems and national directory published annually. National advertising in all industry media. Regional camp owner association for cooperative advertising, and national annual convention.

CHILDRENS STORES/FURNITURE/PRODUCTS

BABY-TENDA CORPORATION
909 State Line
Kansas City, MO 64101
(816) 421–4250
Contact: David Jungerman

BUSINESS: A line of safety equipment for infants and children sold direct.
FRANCHISES: 64 throughout the United States.
FOUNDED: 1937.
REQUIRED CAPITAL: $8,000 to $12,000.
FINANCIAL ASSISTANCE: None.
TRAINING: Three weeks of intensive training in the franchisee's own territory.
MANAGERIAL ASSISTANCE: Regular help is available for franchisees.

*ATHLETE'S FOOT MARKETING ASSOCIATES, INC.
725 Liberty Avenue
Pittsburgh, PA 15222
(412) 471–5451
Contact: Mark R. Lando or Ross Glichman

BUSINESS: Athletic footwear and related soft goods.

FRANCHISES: 215 in 45 states.

FOUNDED: 1971.

REQUIRED CAPITAL: $7,500 for franchise fee plus approximately $65,000 inventory investment.

FINANCIAL ASSISTANCE: No financing provided by the company. However, the company does provide a package to present to investment institutions. Company does have lease program for furniture and fixtures.

TRAINING: Short, intensive-training program provided by the company prepares franchisee for complete operation of store. Written manual also furnished.

MANAGERIAL ASSISTANCE: Assistance in lease negotiations and site selection. Complete merchandise selection. Ongoing advertising and promotion suggestions.

FORMAL WEAR SERVICE
639 VFW Parkway
Chestnut Hill, MA 02167
(617) 325–7970
Contact: Murray and Jay Kuritsky

BUSINESS: Sale and rental of men's formal clothes.

FRANCHISES: 32 in Massachusetts, New Hampshire, New York, and Connecticut.

FOUNDED: 1940.

REQUIRED CAPITAL: $2,500 minimum for stock.

FINANCIAL ASSISTANCE: Formal Wear Service will finance if applicant has good credit rating.

TRAINING: Two weeks in-store training. Complete training course in all aspects of formal rental business to all franchisees plus a 60-page book *Can a Nice Guy Succeed in Formals?*

MANAGERIAL ASSISTANCE: The company provides bookkeeping, inventory control, and national and local cooperative advertising.

*GINGISS INTERNATIONAL, INC.
180 North LaSalle Street
Chicago, IL 60601
(312) 236–2333
Contact: Joel Gingiss

BUSINESS: Specialists in the sale and rental of men's formal clothes.

FRANCHISES: 116 in 24 states.

* Asterisk denotes franchisor is a member of the International Franchise Association.

FOUNDED: 1968.

REQUIRED CAPITAL: $40,000 to $55,000.

FINANCIAL ASSISTANCE: The company, through external sources, arranges and guarantees $45,000 financing for inventory and equipment.

TRAINING: Two-week comprehensive training at company headquarters approximately one month before center's opening. One-week on-site training during initial opening week. Also regular visits by training directors and various department heads.

MANAGERIAL ASSISTANCE: The company provides regular visits by field training directors, a comprehensive instruction manual, periodic bulletins, and telephone assistance as required.

HEEL 'N TOE, INC.
5225 Monroe Place
Hyattsville, MD 20781
(301) 277–1382
Contact: Michael C. Passas

BUSINESS: Partly self-service women's retail shoe chain.

FRANCHISES: 17 in four states and the District of Columbia.

FOUNDED: 1966.

REQUIRED CAPITAL: $7,500.

FINANCIAL ASSISTANCE: The company provides the complete shoe inventory on consignment. Inventories are not paid for until merchandise is sold. The required capital also provides working capital and for the initial purchase of accessories.

TRAINING: Intensive one-week training period at company headquarters. Additional training as needed in the franchisee's new store.

MANAGERIAL ASSISTANCE: The company provides continuous management services for the life of the franchise in such areas as advertising, bookkeeping, merchandising, and inventory control. All stores are visited by a district manager on a regular schedule.

JILENE, INC.
808 State Street
Santa Barbara, CA 93101
(805) 963–2815
Contact: Jim Klobucher

BUSINESS: A women's wear specialty store called "Kimo's Polynesian Shop."

FRANCHISES: 12 in California and 1 in Florida.

FOUNDED: 1969.

REQUIRED CAPITAL: $30,000 and up depending on size of store.

FINANCIAL ASSISTANCE: None.

TRAINING: Two weeks' training provided in franchisee's store. Training covers all general aspects of a retail women's wear store operation. A complete operations manual is provided.

MANAGERIAL ASSISTANCE: After initial two-week training period, the company is always available for consultation by letter or telephone for the duration of the franchise contract.

JUST PANTS
310 South Michigan Avenue
Chicago, IL 60604
(312) 435–8700
Contact: Alvin I. Greenberg

BUSINESS: Store sells jeans, slacks, tops, and accessories primarily to teenagers, college aged people and young men and women.
FRANCHISES: 54 in 26 states.
FOUNDED: 1969.
REQUIRED CAPITAL: Street store or strip center ($35,000). Regional Mall ($85,000).
FINANCIAL ASSISTANCE: None.
TRAINING: The company provides a training program consisting of two weeks or more of "on-the-job training" in two or more operating stores. The franchisee is responsible for the travel and living expenses and the compensation of the manager while he or she is enrolled in the training program.
MANAGERIAL ASSISTANCE: Operating assistance will include advice and guidance with respect to: (1) buying pants and other merchandise; (2) additional products authorized for sale in the stores; (3) hiring and training of employees; (4) formulating and implementing advertising and promotional programs; (5) pricing and special sales; and (6) the establishment and maintenance of administrative, bookkeeping, accounting, inventory control, and general operating procedures. Further, the company will advise the franchisee from time to time of operating problems of the store disclosed by financial statements submitted to or inspections made by the company. No separate charge is made to the franchisee for such operating assistance.

*KNAPP SHOE COMPANY
One Knapp Centre
Brockton, MA 02401
(617) 588–9000
Contact: Walter E. Cullen

BUSINESS: Retail shoe store.
FRANCHISES: 22 in 14 states.
FOUNDED: 1919.
REQUIRED CAPITAL: $28,000.
FINANCIAL ASSISTANCE: None.
TRAINING: Two-week retail selling at a company-owned store.
MANAGERIAL ASSISTANCE: Continual ongoing supervision and advice in such areas as merchandising, inventory control, and store operations for the life of the franchise. Also, the company furnishes manuals for store operations.

*LADY MADONNA MANAGEMENT CORP.
36 East 31st Street
New York, NY 10016
(212) 685-4555
Contact: Ronald Sommers

BUSINESS: Manufacture, wholesale, and retail women's maternity apparel.
FRANCHISES: 70 in 31 states.
FOUNDED: 1970.
REQUIRED CAPITAL: $25,000 to $35,000.
FINANCIAL ASSISTANCE: Normal inventory terms (8/10 E.O.M.). Licensee has option to arrange own outside financing.
TRAINING: Intensified training program beginning with one-week period in New York and continuing with two-week, in-store training by supervisor beginning with the store opening. Continuous field supervision.
MANAGERIAL ASSISTANCE: Continuous merchandising guidance, buying service, all advertising material, forms, and systems, and continuous field supervision of retail operations.

MODE O'DAY COMPANY
2130 North Hollywood Way
Burbank, CA 91505
(213) 843-4340
Contact: Mills Whitney

BUSINESS: Ladies' apparel specialty stores.
FRANCHISES: 657 in 32 states.
FOUNDED: 1936.
REQUIRED CAPITAL: Capital is required for store fixtures and leasehold improvements. Average store ranges from $8,000 to $9,000. Merchandise is placed on consignment.
FINANCIAL ASSISTANCE: Limited.
TRAINING: Training is provided by company personnel.
MANAGERIAL ASSISTANCE: Field supervisors work very closely with store owners to develop maximum sales.

MODERN BRIDAL SHOPPES, INC.
600 Route 130 North
Cinnaminson, NJ 08077
(609) 786-0300
Contact: Seymour Fine

BUSINESS: Retail sales of bridal apparel and cocktail formal wear.
FRANCHISES: 64 in 31 states.
FOUNDED: 1958.
REQUIRED CAPITAL: $12,000 to $35,000.
FINANCIAL ASSISTANCE: Guidance offered in obtaining loan through financial institutions.

TRAINING: Three weeks total training. One-week training at company-owned operation. Two weeks' training in the field.

MANAGERIAL ASSISTANCE: Complete manual of operations, field supervisor assistance, national seminar, and continuous buying service.

PAULINE'S SPORTSWEAR, INC.
3525 Eastham Drive
Culver City, CA 90230
(213) 559-4511
Contact: Richard W. Nagel

BUSINESS: Ladies' sportswear stores in which most items are under $8.

FRANCHISES: 170 in 29 states and Canada.

FOUNDED: 1961.

REQUIRED CAPITAL: $7,500 plus fixtures.

FINANCIAL ASSISTANCE: None.

TRAINING: Training is informal.

MANAGERIAL ASSISTANCE: The company provides management advice with respect to merchandising, display, advertising, and inventory. This advice and counsel is usually in the form of continuing personal and telephone contact.

*RED WING SHOE COMPANY
419–427 Bush Street
Red Wing, MN 55066
(612) 388-8211
Contact: Andrew J. Faecke

BUSINESS: Men's shoe store.

FRANCHISES: 188 in 31 states.

FOUNDED: 1905.

REQUIRED CAPITAL: $55,000.

FINANCIAL ASSISTANCE: None.

TRAINING: Trained in existing stores for five weeks, plus monthly supervision thereafter.

MANAGERIAL ASSISTANCE: Continuous counseling in all aspects of business such as budgeting, advertising, stock control, and promotions.

SALLY WALLACE BRIDES SHOP, INC.
232 Amherst Street
East Orange, NJ 07018
(201) 673-5501
Contact: John Van Drill

BUSINESS: Bride shop and bridal service.

FRANCHISES: 30 in 14 states.

FOUNDED: 1955.

REQUIRED CAPITAL: $30,000.

FINANCIAL ASSISTANCE: A total investment of $30,000 is needed for a complete turnkey operation including inventory and $5,000 operating fund backup. The company will finance 30 percent if applicant has good credit reference.

TRAINING: Three-week mandatory training course in one of company-owned stores. Trainer spends one week with franchisee to open new shop. Six months' follow-through by trainer with close supervision via written reports and telephone.

MANAGERIAL ASSISTANCE: Consultant buyer and merchandise manager supervision on a weekly basis, checking sales, money, inventory, and cost controls. Field personnel available as needed, to visit shops and assist in solving problems. Buying service supplied as part of franchise agreement.

CONSTRUCTION/REMODELING—MATERIALS/SERVICES

*A-TECH, INC.
2631 North Meade Street
P.O. Box 1954
Appleton, WI 54911
(414) 733-7324
Contact: Richard G. Anderson

BUSINESS: A service which locates and outlines internal water penetration areas of built-up roofs.

FRANCHISES: 34 in the United States and Canada.

FOUNDED: 1974.

REQUIRED CAPITAL: $4,500 (initial) ; $5,000 (delayed).

FINANCIAL ASSISTANCE: None.

TRAINING: Five days sales and technical training given in franchisee's territory. Additional training is offered as needed.

MANAGERIAL ASSISTANCE: The company expects franchisees to have business experience and to be able to operate and manage a business. This is a major condition in the selection of franchisees. All other technical training is furnished including complete manuals giving step-by-step instructions for proper operation of the technical aspects of the business.

DICKER STACK-SACK INTERNATIONAL
6211 Northwest Highway
Dallas, TX 75201
(214) 361-5488
Contact: Edward T. Dicker

BUSINESS: Process for construction.

FRANCHISES: 10 in New Mexico, Arkansas, Texas, and Idaho.

FOUNDED: 1967.

REQUIRED CAPITAL: $20,000 for equipment. Franchisee fee based on population of area desired.

FINANCIAL ASSISTANCE: Will finance franchise fee.

TRAINING: On-the-site training, length (average ten days to two weeks) determined according to structure (s) being constructed.

MANAGERIAL ASSISTANCE: Assistance for the duration of franchise agreement.

* Asterisk denotes franchisor is a member of the International Franchise Association.

ELDORADO STONE CORPORATION
P.O. Box 125
Kirkland, WA 98033
(206) 883–1991
Contact: John E. Bennett

BUSINESS: Simulated stone and brick building products.
FRANCHISES: 18 in 12 states and Canada.
FOUNDED: 1969.
REQUIRED CAPITAL: $25,000.
FINANCIAL ASSISTANCE: None.
TRAINING: The company provides one week of training in an established manufacturing plant, one week in franchisee's plant, and continuous supervision thereafter.
MANAGERIAL ASSISTANCE: The company provides continuous managerial assistance and sponsors annual meetings of franchisees.

GENERAL ENERGY DEVICES, INC.
1753 Ensley Avenue
Clearwater, FL 33516
(813) 586–3585
Contact: Clyde Bouse

BUSINESS: Solar heating equipment.
FRANCHISES: 241 in the United States.
FOUNDED: 1975.
REQUIRED CAPITAL: $18,750 for distributorship, $6,250 for dealership, 85 percent of cost for product inventory.
FINANCIAL ASSISTANCE: None.
TRAINING: Distributorrs are carefully schooled in product knowledge, installation, and selling techniques at company manufacturing and office facilities. Continuing program of assistance is provided by field personnel.
MANAGERIAL ASSISTANCE: Field representatives, merchandising shows and sales seminars, plus both regional and national meetings. In addition, the company provides operations manuals, forms, research and development, advertising and promotion on a national level, co-op advertising, and technical assistance.

HOMEWOOD INDUSTRIES, INC.
17641 South Ashland Avenue
Homewood, IL 60430
(312) 799–6800
Contact: Thomas W. Clark

BUSINESS: Renovating of existing kitchen cabinets.
FRANCHISES: 60 in 25 states.
FOUNDED: 1951.
REQUIRED CAPITAL: $20,000 working capital.
FINANCIAL ASSISTANCE: None.

TRAINING: One-week initial training course. Company representative provides continuous training and counseling.

MANAGERIAL ASSISTANCE: Provided by company representatives on a continuous basis.

MASONRY SYSTEMS INTERNATIONAL, INC.
600 South Cherry
Denver, CO 80222
(303) 320–5800
Contact: Paul W. Powers

BUSINESS: Masonry panels.

FRANCHISES: 6 in nine states.

FOUNDED: 1970.

REQUIRED CAPITAL: $70,000 to $200,000 depending on size of start-up plant.

FINANCIAL ASSISTANCE: None.

TRAINING: Intensive, 20-day training provided with purchase of franchise. Then further manufacturing and marketing assistance and training available on billable basis.

MANAGERIAL ASSISTANCE: Comprehensive assistance in all aspects of business.

*NEW ENGLAND LOG HOMES, INC.
2301 State Street
P.O. Box 5056
Hamden, CT 06518
(203) 562–9981
Contact: Vito Vizziello

BUSINESS: Manufacture precut, hand-peeled log homes from pine timber. The franchisee is required to erect a model home which serves as an office. This is provided at dealer's cost.

FRANCHISES: 63 in the United States.

FOUNDED: 1970.

REQUIRED CAPITAL: $75,000.

FINANCIAL ASSISTANCE: None.

TRAINING: Variable, depending on the individual's background. A yearly sales meeting is designed to inform the franchisee of the latest changes in the log homes, sales methods, and so on.

MANAGERIAL ASSISTANCE: Variable, depending on the individual's background.

PAUL W. DAVIS SYSTEMS, INC.
3515 St. Augustine Road
Jacksonville, FL 32207
(904) 396–1662
Contact: Paul W. Davis

BUSINESS: Repair of fire, water, and windstorm damage and home and commercial improvements.

FRANCHISES: 18 in Florida, North Carolina, Alabama, and Tennessee.

FOUNDED: 1968.

REQUIRED CAPITAL: The franchisee needs $20,000 to begin, depending on the size of the chosen area. The company puts up the franchise for 50 percent stock interest in the franchise.

FINANCIAL ASSISTANCE: The company assists in obtaining bank financing for accounts receivable and guarantees payment along with the investor.

TRAINING: Before the selection of an area, an initial survey is made. Franchisee trains in an existing franchise for two weeks and then a company representative works one week in new franchise area to open and solicit business. The representative then works with franchisee in the area for 13 days the first quarter, 6 days the second quarter, and a minimum of 3 days each quarter thereafter. The company assists in all recruiting, hiring, and training.

MANAGERIAL ASSISTANCE: Managerial and technical assistance continues throughout the life of the franchise for accounting, sales, management, cost controls, labor supply, and expansion.

PENEPRIME INTERNATIONAL, INC.
1840 Water Street
Box 2604
Waterloo, IA 50705
(319) 236–3636
Contact: Licensing Manager

BUSINESS: Specialty asphalt products for maintaining roofs and roads.

FRANCHISES: 16 in 14 states.

FOUNDED: 1972.

REQUIRED CAPITAL: Minimum equipment plus working capital amounting to $25,000.

FINANCIAL ASSISTANCE: Construction equipment leasing program.

TRAINING: On-the-job training in franchisee's territory. Peneprime will sell and install early projects for franchisee.

MANAGERIAL ASSISTANCE: Periodic field training visits; also national and field seminars.

PERMA-STONE COMPANY
2495 Bancroft Street
Columbus, OH 43211
(614) 475–9220
Contact: Jerry L. Martin

BUSINESS: Sell stone products to homeowners.

FRANCHISES: 32 in ten states.

FOUNDED: 1929.

REQUIRED CAPITAL: $10,000 minimum.

FINANCIAL ASSISTANCE: None.

TRAINING: Initial technical training provided to employees, and sales school available to franchisee and sales force.

MANAGERIAL ASSISTANCE: See "Training" above.

THE PERMENTRY COMPANY
37 Water Street
West Haven, CT 06516
(203) 934–9818
Contact: John K. Newton

BUSINESS: Leases steel molds which will precast in one piece outside basement stairwell entrances.
FRANCHISES: 46 in 15 states and 7 in Canada.
FOUNDED: 1960.
REQUIRED CAPITAL: Under $10,000.
FINANCIAL ASSISTANCE: None.
TRAINING: On-the-job training is made available. A complete "how to" manual is supplied.
MANAGERIAL ASSISTANCE: See "Training" above.

PORCELAIN PATCH & GLAZE COMPANY OF AMERICA
140 Watertown Street
Watertown, MA 02172
(617) 924–9100
Contact: Philip J. Gleason

BUSINESS: Refinishing, spraying, glazing, spot-blending and patching of porcelain and enamel finishes of all kinds.
FRANCHISES: 21 in 17 states.
FOUNDED: 1938.
REQUIRED CAPITAL: $2,000.
FINANCIAL ASSISTANCE: $1,000 down to franchisee with good credit.
TRAINING: Ten days at company headquarters.
MANAGERIAL ASSISTANCE: Periodic visits and direct mail advertising.

PORCELITE ENTERPRISES, INC.
14650 Southlawn Lane
Rockville, MD 20850
(301) 340–6933
Contact: H. D. Berardi

BUSINESS: Repair and refinish porcelain plumbing fixtures such as bathtubs, kitchen sinks, wash basins, and appliances.
FRANCHISES: 50 in 20 states.
FOUNDED: 1963.
REQUIRED CAPITAL: $7,500.
FINANCIAL ASSISTANCE: $2,500 is financed with acceptable credit.
TRAINING: Intensive five-day training session covering all aspects of porcelain repair.
MANAGERIAL ASSISTANCE: See "Training" above.

RUS-TIQUE BRIK INTERNATIONAL
North Highway 66
Miami, OK 74354
(918) 542–3334
Contact: George A. Mayer

BUSINESS: Manufacture of bricks.
FRANCHISES: 28 in 22 states.
FOUNDED: 1958.
REQUIRED CAPITAL: $250,000 and up.
FINANCIAL ASSISTANCE: Financing of lease equipment available.
TRAINING: One week minimum for operational instruction, and as necessary.
MANAGERIAL ASSISTANCE: The company provides periodic visits by representatives, a comprehensive instructional manual, bulletins, and telephone assistance as required.

SHAWNEE STEPS OF AMERICA, INC.
250 Tolland Street
East Hartford, CT 06108
(203) 289–6077
Contact: Michael N. Serigenese

BUSINESS: Manufacture, sell, and install concrete precast steps for the homeowner and building trades.
FRANCHISES: 13 in ten states and Canada.
FOUNDED: 1950.
REQUIRED CAPITAL: $15,000 to $25,000.
FINANCIAL ASSISTANCE: Chattel mortgage, lease arrangements, and up to one-third company assistance.
TRAINING: Training in all three departments, sales, manufacturing, and installation. Normal 30 days of training or whatever is necessary for each franchisee.
MANAGERIAL ASSISTANCE: Assistance available during life of agreement at company's pilot plant after normal assistance has been provided at no cost.

SURFA-SHIELD CORPORATION
2929 Eskridge Road
Fairfax, VA 22031
(703) 280–4600
Contact: W. F. Zartman

BUSINESS: Providing homeowners with exterior improvements such as roofing, storm doors and windows, replacement windows, aluminum siding, custom aluminum trim cover, patios, enclosures, and carports.
FRANCHISES: 28 in 14 states.
FOUNDED: 1957.
REQUIRED CAPITAL: $7,500 minimum.
FINANCIAL ASSISTANCE: None.
TRAINING: Intensive one-week training at company headquarters training facility

for key management personnel. An additional week of training at the franchisee's location, including management, sales, and construction personnel. Periodically scheduled visits to franchisee's location at various intervals by company personnel. In addition, the company conducts institutes and seminars on a regional basis throughout each year. "How to" manuals covering all phases of operation are provided.

MANAGERIAL ASSISTANCE: The company maintains a reporting system with each franchisee and provides assistance in the areas of sales, record keeping, administration, construction, advertising, cost controls, inventory controls, and cash flow. Field supervisors are available in all areas covered to provide assistance. In addition, the company offers regional seminars in marketing, sales advertising and construction, as well as quarterly managers' meetings and an annual national sales training convention for all salespeople and management.

TIMBERLODGE, INC.
1309 Swift Avenue
North Kansas City, MO 64116
(816) 471–6175
Contact: J. F. Pritchard

BUSINESS: Designing, manufacturing, and selling precut redwood homes and commercial buildings.

FRANCHISES: 55 in all 24 states.

FOUNDED: 1958.

REQUIRED CAPITAL: $25,000.

FINANCIAL ASSISTANCE: None.

TRAINING: Company sends trained personnel to franchisee's place of business to help erect first home and to aid in getting the new franchisee started.

MANAGERIAL ASSISTANCE: See "Training" above.

ZELL-AIRE CORPORATION
410 Orrton Avenue
Reading, PA 19603
(215) 376–5401
Contact: M. W. Zellers

BUSINESS: Introduce and promote electric heating by working along with the local electrical utility.

FRANCHISES: 20 in 15 states.

FOUNDED: 1966.

REQUIRED CAPITAL: $5,000 for inventory, $5,000 for rent, telephone, and so on.

FINANCIAL ASSISTANCE: Investment is for inventory only.

TRAINING: Three days' training at company headquarters or other designated location when applicable. Several additional days at franchisee's location.

MANAGERIAL ASSISTANCE: Periodic supervision to assist franchisee in promoting business volume. Generally, supervisor spends two to three days monthly with each franchisee.

CARE/SENTRY DRUG CENTERS
901 Southern Avenue, S.E.
Washington, DC 20032
(301) 630–4500
Contact: Harrison Leach

BUSINESS: Full-line retail drugstore, offering professional pharmacy services, health care products, and selective sundries.
FRANCHISES: 134 in 14 states.
FOUNDED: 1969.
REQUIRED CAPITAL: Varies, depending on program—up to $40,000.
FINANCIAL ASSISTANCE: Securing of lease and assistance in financing fixtures and inventory up to 80 percent.
TRAINING: Intensive training at company headquarters and in the field.
MANAGERIAL ASSISTANCE: Complete supervision of operations, accounting, advertising, purchasing, selection of personnel, store setups, and promotional activities.

MEDICINE SHOPPES INTERNATIONAL, INC.
100 Progress Parkway
Maryland Heights, MO 63043
(314) 878–0050
Contact: Edwin F. Prizer

BUSINESS: Retail sales of pharmaceuticals and medicines.
FRANCHISES: 250 in 46 states.
FOUNDED: 1971.
REQUIRED CAPITAL: $27,000 which includes fee, fixtures, opening inventory plus working capital.
FINANCIAL ASSISTANCE: None.
TRAINING: Five-day training seminar at company headquarters. Two days or longer for store opening assistance.
MANAGERIAL ASSISTANCE: Continuous training program for marketing and store operations. The company furnishes bookkeeping and marketing services and financial and operational analysis on a monthly basis. Also, the company provides assistance in site selection, lease negotiation, store layout, fixturing, personnel selection, and purchasing procedures.

REXALL DRUG COMPANY
3901 North Kings Highway Boulevard
St. Louis, MO 63115
(314) 679–7222
Contact: Harold R. Beatty

BUSINESS: Retail sales of pharmaceuticals, medicines, health and beauty aids, and vitamins to existing retail stores.

FRANCHISES: 10,000 in the United States, District of Columbia, and Guam.

FOUNDED: 1903.

REQUIRED CAPITAL: No franchise fee.

FINANCIAL ASSISTANCE: Conditional opening Rexall merchandise order payment program; promotional and seasonal merchandise dating terms; identification payment plan, equipment lease, or sales contract from associated service.

TRAINING: Retail sales training aids and retail sales personnel store meetings.

MANAGERIAL ASSISTANCE: Assistance from field regional sales managers and sales representatives.

SYD SIMONS COSMETICS, INC.
2 East Oak Street
Chicago, IL 60611
(312) 943-2333
Contact: Jerome Weitzel

BUSINESS: Sales of cosmetics and related services.

FRANCHISES: 5 in Illinois and Kansas.

FOUNDED: 1973.

REQUIRED CAPITAL: Approximately $30,000.

FINANCIAL ASSISTANCE: Company will assist franchisee in obtaining local financing.

TRAINING: Sixty-day training period in makeup and skin care as well as studio operations and business procedures at the company home office. Additional on-site training conducted periodically.

MANAGERIAL ASSISTANCE: Company provides continual managerial, legal, financial, and promotional guidance in accordance with the needs of the franchisee.

UNION PRESCRIPTION CENTERS, INC.
105 West Michigan Street
Milwaukee, WI 53203
(414) 271-4011
Contact: Albert P. Frank

BUSINESS: Retail pharmacies.

FRANCHISES: 132 in ten states.

FOUNDED: 1968.

REQUIRED CAPITAL: Approximately $34,000.

FINANCIAL ASSISTANCE: The company provides financial assistance to meet the needs of the franchisee.

TRAINING: Training in the operating and management of a retail pharmacy is provided. The duration is up to one week depending upon the background and experience of the franchisee.

MANAGERIAL ASSISTANCE: Managerial and technical assistance is provided to franchisee as requested by the franchisee or deemed necessary by the company.

AMERICAN PRE-SCHOOLS, INC.
160 Newport Center Drive
Newport Beach, CA 92660
(714) 640–7260
Contact: Jack Perry

BUSINESS: Preschool and child care center.
FRANCHISES: 7 in Arizona and California.
FOUNDED: 1968.
REQUIRED CAPITAL: $25,000.
FINANCIAL ASSISTANCE: The company will finance $10,000 of the $25,000 investment for franchisees with good credit.
TRAINING: One-week training at company headquarters plus additional training by company personnel in franchisee's own center.
MANAGERIAL ASSISTANCE: Continual assistance by company in all areas necessary for successful operation of high-quality professional preschool and child care center.

*BARBIZON SCHOOLS OF MODELING
689 Fifth Avenue
New York, NY 10022
(212) 371–4300
Contact: B. Wolff

BUSINESS: Modeling and personal development schools for teenage girls, homemakers, and career girls.
FRANCHISES: 70 throughout the United States.
FOUNDED: 1939.
REQUIRED CAPITAL: $25,000 to $50,000.
FINANCIAL ASSISTANCE: Franchisee can finance 50 percent of franchise fee with the company. Total franchise fee is $19,500 to $35,000.
TRAINING: Intensive three-week training program for franchisee and director at company headquarters. Extensive on-site field visits at franchisee's location by company staff during first six months. Periodic staff visits and conferences at company headquarters thereafter.
MANAGERIAL ASSISTANCE: In addition to the initial training indicated above, the company makes available staff visits as required, on a continuing basis; annual meetings of franchisees, new advertising programs, sales aids, new programs, brochures, direct mail pieces, and so on.

BUTLER LEARNING SYSTEMS
1325 West Dorothy Lane
Dayton, OH 45409
(513) 298–7463
Contact: Don Butler

BUSINESS: Audiovisual training program for salesmen, saleswomen, supervisors, and all workers.

* Asterisk denotes franchisor is a member of the International Franchise Association.

FRANCHISES: 21 in 12 states and Canada.
FOUNDED: 1959.
REQUIRED CAPITAL: $5,000.
FINANCIAL ASSISTANCE: None.
TRAINING: Training in using and selling training packages and holding seminars.
MANAGERIAL ASSISTANCE: Continual management assistance.

DOOTSON DRIVING SCHOOLS
9417 Las Tunas
Temple City, CA 91780
(213) 447–2603
Contact: Richard F. Dootson

BUSINESS: Driver education.
FRANCHISES: 7 in California.
FOUNDED: 1952.
REQUIRED CAPITAL: $20,000.
FINANCIAL ASSISTANCE: 100 percent automobile financing and equipment financing.
TRAINING: Two-week, 80-hour course given at company headquarters.
MANAGERIAL ASSISTANCE: Periodic training in all phases of the business is provided franchisee.

INTERNATIONAL TRAVEL TRAINING COURSES, INC.
936 North Michigan Avenue
Chicago, IL 60611
(312) 368–8860
Contact: Evelyn Echols

BUSINESS: Train students to be travel agents.
FRANCHISES: 2 in District of Columbia and California.
FOUNDED: 1962.
REQUIRED CAPITAL: $35,000. This capital is required for operating costs, including advertising, rent, furniture, and so on, for a three-month period prior to opening of the first class. Cost of the franchise is $50,000, which is paid to the company from gross receipts over a two-year period. Franchisee also pays the company 10 percent of the gross for the first five years and 5 percent of the gross thereafter. Contract renewable at option of either party every five years.
FINANCIAL ASSISTANCE: Providing the franchisee has good credit references, the company will help with the initial $20,000 cost. Franchisees also have the option of arranging their own outside financing.
TRAINING: Intensive six-week mandatory training is scheduled for all new franchisees at the company headquarters. During this time franchisee is trained in sales and marketing and also audits classes in session. New personnel are also offered the opportunity for this type of training.
MANAGERIAL ASSISTANCE: The company provides continual management service for the life of the franchise in the areas of marketing, advertising, and sales. All training materials are purchased through the company at a very low

cost. Executive personnel from the company spend a minimum of three weeks in the franchisee's area prior to the opening of the first class. They then visit each franchisee ten days per year to assist in interviewing, selling, and marketing. There is one meeting each year at the company headquarters.

JOHN ROBERT POWERS FINISHING & MODELING SCHOOL
9 Newbury Street
Boston, MA 02116
(617) 267–8781
Contact: Barbara Tyler, Executive Vice President

BUSINESS: A school for women of all ages which offers finishing, self-improvement and modeling courses. Also, there is an executive grooming and modeling course for men.
FRANCHISES: 60 in 26 states, Guam, and Greece.
FOUNDED: 1923.
REQUIRED CAPITAL: $25,000.
FINANCIAL ASSISTANCE: None.
TRAINING: Three weeks of teaching and administrative training plus annual seminars.
MANAGERIAL ASSISTANCE: The company provides managerial and technical assistance during the life of the franchise by visiting field personnel. Accounting assistance is provided by company personnel.

LEISURE LEARNING CENTERS, INC.
50 Greenwich Avenue
Greenwich, CT 06830
(203) 661–2777
Contact: Richard Bendett

BUSINESS: A combination store and learning center. One section contains a variety of audiovisuel teaching machines and programmed materials used to teach people such subjects as touch typing, foreign languages, shorthand, speed-reading, flying, art, plus a whole variety of math and reading courses for children. Also, within each store there are sections of merchandise which contain educational toys, books, records, tapes, adult mental games, puzzles, memorizing aids, science kits, and craft items.
FRANCHISES: 4 in Connecticut, North Carolina, Maryland, and Texas.
FOUNDED: 1972.
REQUIRED CAPITAL: Minimum total investment $55,000 plus leasehold improvement cost, and working capital. Distributorships also available from $5,000.
FINANCIAL ASSISTANCE: Will assist in securing equipment lease—average $21,000 to $35,000.
TRAINING: Thorough training program includes: all aspects of retail management, complete indoctrination in courses and teaching equipment, bookkeeping and

controls, promotion planning, merchandising, and purchasing procedures. Up to four weeks of training or until full proficiency is indicated.

MANAGERIAL ASSISTANCE: Full range of services include: new merchandise and course acquisition, advertising and publicity, sales forecasting, account management, store layout and design for special promotions, interstore relations program, and cooperative buying benefits.

*MARY MOPPET'S DAY CARE SCHOOLS, INC.
2404 West Huntington Drive
Tempe, AZ 85281
(602) 967–2063
Contact: M. E. Gillespie

BUSINESS: Day-care center for children.

FRANCHISES: 83 in 15 states.

FOUNDED: 1967.

REQUIRED CAPITAL: $30,000 minimum.

FINANCIAL ASSISTANCE: A total investment of $30,000 is required to open a center. $10,000 down payment, $10,000 when building is 50 percent completed, and $10,000 upon occupancy. The $10,000 down payment pays for expenses incurred in selection of sites, arranging leases, equipment, and so on. The company will carry back a portion of the franchising cost if the franchisee has good credit references. It is preferred that franchisees obtain their own financing.

TRAINING: An intensive-training program is held for one week at the company headquarters. Other training is done periodically during the year at the franchisee's operation.

MANAGERIAL ASSISTANCE: The company provides continued management counseling for the life of the franchise in the areas of bookkeeping, staff training, operational manuals, forms and directions for their use. Seminars are held during the year to answer questions and give qualified help in areas needing strength. The company also holds an annual convention in Phoenix, Arizona.

MIND POWER, INC.
P.O. Box 1464
Bethlehem, PA 18018
(215) 691–1300
Contact: Barkley Wyckoff

BUSINESS: Speed-reading and memory operation.

FRANCHISES: 175 in 18 states.

FOUNDED: 1969.

REQUIRED CAPITAL: $3,000.

FINANCIAL ASSISTANCE: The company provides assistance in obtaining financing.

TRAINING: Two-day initial training program; all training sessions are open for retraining. All employees are also trained at any subsequent session.

MANAGERIAL ASSISTANCE: Continual assistance is provided by the company both by telephone and personal contact.

MUSIC DYNAMICS
Fine Arts Building
410 South Michigan Avenue
Chicago, IL 60605
(312) 341–1274
Contact: Paul S. Renard

BUSINESS: Sight-reading teaching systems to music dealers.
FRANCHISES: 7 in Illinois.
FOUNDED: 1974.
REQUIRED CAPITAL: $15,000—the company takes 20 percent of teaching monies. Franchisees must supply their own studios and equipment.
FINANCIAL ASSISTANCE: None.
TRAINING: Fifteen hours of training required to teach the sight-reading system. Training is also provided to show franchisee how to operate a studio.
MANAGERIAL ASSISTANCE: Continuous operating assistance given to franchisee by staff of the company. An operations and procedures manual is available for all franchisees.

PATRICIA INTERNATIONAL, INC.
4401 Birch Street
Newport Beach, CA 92660
(714) 546–7360
Contact: J. Russell Calvert
P.O. Box 31818
Omaha, NB 68131
(402) 348–1515
Contact: Leonard Theise

BUSINESS: Educational residence schools that teach merchandising, public relations, and executive secretarial skills, and offer professional modeling and finishing courses.
FRANCHISES: 20 in the United States.
FOUNDED: 1950.
REQUIRED CAPITAL: $25,000 minimum.
FINANCIAL ASSISTANCE: No financial assistance is provided.
TRAINING: Three weeks intensive training is provided at the company educational headquarters, where seminars for teachers are held quarterly, both beginning and advanced. Also franchisees are taught to operate schools from an administration standpoint.
MANAGERIAL ASSISTANCE: Periodic training in school operations. Also, national and local advertising aids are provided together with visual aids.

PRE-SCHOOLS, INC.
351 Budlong
Cranston, RI 02910
(401) 944–4340
Contact: William B. Shields

BUSINESS: Day-care preschool education centers.
FRANCHISES: 4 in Rhode Island and Florida.
FOUNDED: 1969.
REQUIRED CAPITAL: $15,000.
FINANCIAL ASSISTANCE: Equipment finance—$10,000. The company provides mortgage finance assistance.
TRAINING: Thirty days' training; 15 days at company headquarters and 15 days at franchisee's location.
MANAGERIAL ASSISTANCE: Continual operation assistance throughout life of franchise.

UP-GRADE TUTORING SERVICE, INC.
2745 Carley Court
North Bellmore, NY 11710
(516) 221–1795
Contact: Victoria Levy

BUSINESS: Private and institutional tutoring and teaching.
FRANCHISES: 17 in metropolitan New York area, franchises limited.
FOUNDED: 1964.
REQUIRED CAPITAL: $10,000 and up according to size of geographic area.
FINANCIAL ASSISTANCE: Sixty percent on closing, balance to be paid within one year.
TRAINING: Training initially at company headquarters lasting approximately one week. Operational manual and unlimited training.
MANAGERIAL ASSISTANCE: Continuous assistance as necessary; no time limit. Each franchisee is required to attend at least one group meeting a year. Newsletters are sent out at least six times a year, suggesting new business ideas and programs experimented with that proved successful in an area.

A-1 PERSONNEL FRANCHISE SYSTEMS, INC.
219 Park Avenue
Scotch Plains, NJ 07076
(201) 322–6902
Contact: Joe Gerber

BUSINESS: Professional, clerical, and technical employment service.
FRANCHISES: 11 in New Jersey and Pennsylvania.
FOUNDED: 1962.

REQUIRED CAPITAL: $25,000.
FINANCIAL ASSISTANCE: None.
TRAINING: Approximately three weeks at company headquarters.
MANAGERIAL ASSISTANCE: Constant guidance at franchisee's office.

ACME PERSONNEL SERVICE
P.O. Box 14466
Opportunity, WA 99214
(509) 924–8000
Contact: D. Scott MacDonald

BUSINESS: Employment agency.
FRANCHISES: 76 in 17 states and Canada.
FOUNDED: 1946.
REQUIRED CAPITAL: Franchise fee is from $9,500 to $19,500 depending on the size of the market territory. The company recommends from 75–100 percent for support capital.
FINANCIAL ASSISTANCE: None directly. The company will recommend a prospective franchisee with good credit to suitable financing sources.
TRAINING: Before opening the office, franchisee receives a one-week training course. Franchisee is given and taught how to use the 400-page company *Guide*. Franchisee is also trained to use the system of personnel placement, as well as all internal procedures necessary to the successful running of the business. After opening, franchisee receives a personal visit from the franchise director and/or corporate district manager. Annual conventions also offer training sessions.
MANAGERIAL ASSISTANCE: Continual assistance is available from the franchise director, and/or corporate district managers in franchisee's area, in advertising, applicant recruitment, job-order promotion, internal staffing and training, bookkeeping and other internal operations, and so on. All new forms, procedures, ideas, and aids of any sort are sent to franchisee on a regular basis, usually weekly. Franchise receives free national advertising exposure, free job-order promotion materials and other assistance as requested.

*ADIA-PARTIME SERVICES
750 Valley Forge Plaza
Valley Forge, PA 19482
(215) 265–8700
Contact: Brian G. Dailey

BUSINESS: Employment agency specializing in temporary help.
FRANCHISES: 58 in 16 states and South America.
FOUNDED: 1957.
REQUIRED CAPITAL: $25,000 plus, depending on market size.
FINANCIAL ASSISTANCE: The company finances entire temporary help payroll.
TRAINING: One full week of formal, centralized manager and staff training with additional field training provided immediately after office opening. The company

* Asterisk denotes franchisor is a member of the International Franchise Association.

also provides complete operating manuals on Partime Temporary Help System.

MANAGERIAL ASSISTANCE: Continued company guidance is provided through weekly newsletter and bimonthly, monthly, and quarterly reports with constant field training, follow-up visits, and national and regional seminars. Also, advice and assistance is offered in such areas as advertising, marketing, insurance, financing, and sales.

BAILEY EMPLOYMENT SYSTEM, INC.
51 Shelton Road
Monroe, CT 06468
(203) 261–2908
Contact: Sheldon Leighton

BUSINESS: Employment agency.

FRANCHISES: 33 in nine states.

FOUNDED: 1960.

REQUIRED CAPITAL: $20,000.

FINANCIAL ASSISTANCE: Available to qualified persons.

TRAINING: Four hundred hours of classroom seminars augment four weeks of "on premises" direction. The training courses may be audited by the franchise operator and his or her staff at their convenience. Additional training in advanced techniques of professional placementship is offered weekly at convenient locations. All such additional training is free of charge to all franchise operators and personnel.

MANAGERIAL ASSISTANCE: Experts in site selection, advertising and public relations, business procedures and placementship techniques, accounting and bookkeeping, teaching and instructional services, as well as on-site field representatives are available for the benefit of the franchise operators.

BAKER & BAKER EMPLOYMENT SERVICE, INC.
114½ Washington Avenue
Athens, TN 37303
(615) 745–8805
Contact: Kathleen Baker

BUSINESS: Employment agency in small towns of 20,000.

FRANCHISES: 29 offices open in ten states.

FOUNDED: 1967.

REQUIRED CAPITAL: $5,000 to $8,000 dependent on location, plus $1,500 working capital.

FINANCIAL ASSISTANCE: Fifty percent of fee can be company financed.

TRAINING: Comprehensive training course before opening and additional periodical on-the-job training at the franchisee's location.

MANAGERIAL ASSISTANCE: Selection of suitable locations, a nationally aimed public relations program and instructions and materials for obtaining maximum publicity in local advertising media, all forms required for the first 12 months of operation, an established accounting system, national placement Tele-System operating between offices and assistance in interpreting state laws and complying with license regulations. Trained assistants on call at all hours on any agency problems.

*BUSINESS MEN'S CLEARING HOUSE, INC.
150 South Wacker Drive
Suite 3200
Chicago, IL 60606
(312) 368–8383
Contact: Herbert F. Imhoff

BUSINESS: Employment agency, specializing in the placement of salaried and professional employees.
FRANCHISES: 10 in six states.
FOUNDED: 1969.
REQUIRED CAPITAL: $35,000.
FINANCIAL ASSISTANCE: None.
TRAINING: A classroom-type training program, at least ten working days in length, for instruction in procedures, practices, and methods of operation. Also, an on-site training program of 10 working days to be provided as follows: first 5 days commencing with the actual opening date of the agency and the remaining 5 days to be scheduled within the next 90 days.
MANAGERIAL ASSISTANCE: Assists and/or advises the franchisee in the following: licenses application, site selection, lease negotiation, office design, furniture selection, establishment of files, telephone system setup, advertising and promotional programs, credit and collection procedures, and training of all office personnel during initial on-site training program. Continuing services include on-site audits, training seminars, advertising critiques, quarterly newsletters, monthly recognition announcements and other assistance programs through correspondence, telephone, and personal instruction of all matters relating to the operation.

BUSINESS & PROFESSIONAL CONSULTANTS, INC.
3807 Wilshire Boulevard
Los Angeles, CA 90010
(213) 380–8200
Contact: W. J. LaPerch

BUSINESS: Executive search in the fields of banking, insurance, engineering, sales, marketing, accounting, financial, and management.
FRANCHISES: 4 in California.
FOUNDED: 1961.
REQUIRED CAPITAL: $25,000 to cover franchise fee and three months' operational expenses.
FINANCIAL ASSISTANCE: Will finance franchise fee on a no-interest basis.
TRAINING: Initial in-house training of two weeks with field training on a continuing basis.
MANAGERIAL ASSISTANCE: Field visits and company headquarters training.

CAREER EMPLOYMENT SERVICES, INC.
1975 Hempstead Turnpike
East Meadow, NY 11554
(516) 794–4850
Contact: Edward Grant

BUSINESS: Employment agency for trainee up to middle management.
FRANCHISES: 3 in New York, Connecticut, and Massachusetts.
FOUNDED: 1959.
REQUIRED CAPITAL: Varies from $10,000 and up depending upon size and population of the market.
FINANCIAL ASSISTANCE: Franchise fee can be financed.
TRAINING: No prior agency experience is required. Owner or manager will spend one week of training at the company's headquarters. Training includes: placement instruction, counselor instruction, management controls, business operation, advertising techniques, and all pertinent forms.
MANAGERIAL ASSISTANCE: Assistance in the selection of site, negotiation of lease, office layout, selection of furniture and equipment, setting up of filing systems, telephone systems, and so on. Also interchange of job openings, and applicants, throughout the franchise and continuous telephone contact, site visits, and management assistance designed to support each franchise as needed.

DR. PERSONNEL, INC.
2045 Franklin Street
Denver, CO 80205
(303) 861–4977
Contact: M. Ray Fenster

BUSINESS: Employment agency providing paramedical and paradental personnel to physicians and dentists.
FRANCHISES: 38 in 17 states.
FOUNDED: 1975.
REQUIRED CAPITAL: $14,000 to $25,000.
FINANCIAL ASSISTANCE: None.
TRAINING.   Locate and assist in setting up each location. Provide approximately two weeks' training in franchisee's office by experienced medical personnel managers. A comprehensive operations manual is also provided.
MANAGERIAL ASSISTANCE: Franchisees are required to submit a weekly operations' report. Through continued analysis of these reports, management is generally able to define problem areas and recommend solutions in the early stages of development.

*DUNHILL PERSONNEL SYSTEM, INC.
One Old Country Road
Carle Place, NY 11514
(516) 741–5081
Contact: John F. Leddy

BUSINESS: Employment agency.
FRANCHISES: 215 in 43 states, District of Columbia, Canada, and Puerto Rico.

FOUNDED: 1952.

REQUIRED CAPITAL: Based on a franchise fee of $20,000: 50 percent of franchise fee ($10,000), setting-up expenses of $3,000 to $4,000 and three month's operating expenses of $9,000, total $22,000 to $25,000 plus personal and relocation expenses.

FINANCIAL ASSISTANCE: Franchisor will accept balance of franchise fee in promissory notes at current interest rates.

TRAINING: Two weeks' intensive training in Carle Place, New York, operations and training center, covering managing, marketing, marketing research, financial planning, applicant interviewing, selling, recruiting, advertising, and publicity. In addition, pretraining for setting-up and posttraining visits by experienced staff. Also, complete manuals and forms are provided together with current promotional materials.

MANAGERIAL ASSISTANCE: Continuous follow-ups and support. Field trips to franchisee's offices and constant telephone contact by field operations staff as well as all new systems and procedures inaugurated by the company, regional meetings, and one annual meeting of all offices.

ELLS PERSONNEL SYSTEMS, INC.
1129 Plymouth Building
Minneapolis, MN 55402
(612) 335–1131
Contact: Richard E. Peterson

BUSINESS: Employment agency.

FRANCHISES: 3 in Minnesota.

FOUNDED: 1912.

REQUIRED CAPITAL: About $10,000.

FINANCIAL ASSISTANCE: $3,000 down payment.

TRAINING: Formal training varies up to one month and continues during franchise agreement.

MANAGERIAL ASSISTANT: Continuous managerial assistance. Frequent exchange of job orders and applicants. Mutual advertising program.

EMPLOYERS OVERLOAD COMPANY
EO Building
8040 Cedar Avenue South
Minneapolis, MN 55420
(612) 859–5000
Contact: Max Fallek

BUSINESS: Employment agency specializing in temporary help.

FRANCHISES: 22 in ten states.

FOUNDED: 1947.

REQUIRED CAPITAL: Agency investment may vary from $10,000 to $25,000 depending on the size of the agency area.

FINANCIAL ASSISTANCE: The company will give consideration to making complete financial arrangements including, but not limited to, financing of accounts receivable, payroll, and payroll taxes.

TRAINING: One-week training at the company headquarters, plus a supply of all manuals. Also, one-week training at the franchisee's office.

MANAGERIAL ASSISTANCE: The company provides assistance in site selection, purchasing furniture and supplies, hiring personnel, advertising and public relations, yellow pages advertising, data processing and accounting, direct mail program, and analysis of franchisee's sales. In addition, field supervisor visits franchisee's office to help in development of promotional sales.

ENGINEERING CORPORATION OF AMERICA
2408 East Main Street
Ventura, CA 93003
(803) 643–9971
Contact: Vernon W. Haas

BUSINESS: Consulting engineering company specializing in placement of temporary engineering and technical personnel.

FRANCHISES: 6 in five states.

FOUNDED: 1951.

REQUIRED CAPITAL: $15,000.

FINANCIAL ASSISTANCE: The company provides financing for all payroll.

TRAINING: Thirty hours' training plus four manuals.

MANAGERIAL ASSISTANCE: Assistance upon request in all phases of the operation.

F-O-R-T-U-N-E FRANCHISE CORPORATION
505 Fifth Avenue
New York, NY 10017
(212) 697–4314
Contact: Roy S. Sanders

BUSINESS: Middle management and executive personnel employment agency.

FRANCHISES: 26 in 19 states.

FOUNDED: 1973.

REQUIRED CAPITAL: $15,000 to $30,000.

FINANCIAL ASSISTANCE: The $15,000 to $30,000 is cost of franchise, part of which the company may elect to finance. Additional funds are required to meet preopening expenses and working capital, which in aggregate should be $15,000 to $20,000. This amount may vary depending on the size of office and number of personnel employed.

TRAINING: Intensive, 20-day training program is required. Fifteen days of which are conducted at company headquarters on business fundamentals and management controls. Five days are spent on location by company executives training franchise owner and staff.

MANAGERIAL ASSISTANCE: The company provides ongoing management assistance in the areas of franchise controls, exchange programs for applicants and companies, and daily operational support. Communication is maintained by regular telephone contact, workshop, and periodic on-site visits. Special attention is paid and as much time as required given to the support of each newly opened office until it is well established.

*GILBERT LANE PERSONNEL SERVICE
750 Main Street
Hartford, CT 06103
(203) 278–7700
Contact: Howard Specter, President

BUSINESS: Employment agency.
FRANCHISES: 11 in six states.
FOUNDED: 1957.
REQUIRED CAPITAL: Franchise vary in cost from $7,000 to $12,000 depending on population in the particular marketing areas.
FINANCIAL ASSISTANCE: Total investment would include franchise fee and for preopening expenses to include rent deposit, utility deposit, advertising, legal fees, and so on. Additionally, a minimum of $10,000 recommended for use as operating capital. The company will give consideration to making financial arrangements.
TRAINING: The owner/manager is required to attend an intensive two-week training session at the company headquarters.
MANAGERIAL ASSISTANCE: The company provides continuous guidance and assistance in all areas of agency management. Also job openings and applicants are interchanged throughout the franchise.

*MANAGEMENT RECRUITERS INTERNATIONAL, INC.
1015 Euclid Avenue
Cleveland, OH 44115
(216) 696–1122
Contact: Alan R. Schonberg

BUSINESS: Search and recruiting firm—personnel placement.
FRANCHISES: 250 in 40 states.
FOUNDED: 1965.
REQUIRED CAPITAL: $20,000 to $50,000, depending on location.
FINANCIAL ASSISTANCE: None.
TRAINING: The company staff provides the franchisee with an intensive initial training program of approximately three weeks conducted at the company headquarters plus an initial on-the-job training program of approximately three weeks. In addition, the company staff will assist and advise the licensee in securing suitable office space and the negotiation of the lease, the design and layout of the office, the selection of office furniture and equipment, the negotiation of the purchase or lease agreement, and the establishment of a suitable telephone system.
MANAGERIAL ASSISTANCE: The licensee is provided with a detailed operations manual containing information, procedures and know-how for operating the business and the franchisor will furnish the licensee with continuing advice, guidance and assistance through national and regional meetings, seminars, correspondence, telephone and personal instruction with respect to the licensee's personnel placement service operations and procedures and their improvement and revision.

*MANPOWER, INC.
5301 North Ironwood Road
Milwaukee, WI 53201
(414) 961–1000
Contact: William J. Gallagher

BUSINESS: Temporary help service.
FRANCHISES: 412 worldwide.
FOUNDED: 1948.
REQUIRED CAPITAL: $50,000 minimum.
FINANCIAL ASSISTANCE: Financial advice and counsel is available upon request. The prospective franchisee is responsible for an investment to cover initial costs and operating capital.
TRAINING: A comprehensive one-week training program is offered. In addition, there are periodic meetings and seminars designed to maintain proficiency in operations.
MANAGERIAL ASSISTANCE: The company provides continuing advice, counsel, and assistance. Operating manuals, forms, and procedures are provided. The Franchise Center at company headquarters renders assistance through correspondence, telephone, and personal instruction. Management personnel make periodic visits and meetings and seminars are conducted to improve expertise and efficiency.

NATIONAL TEACHER PLACEMENT BUREAU, INC.
3428 Memphis Avenue
Cleveland, OH 44109
(216) 741–3771
Contact: Don F. Cermak

BUSINESS: Employment agency for educators to supplement their earnings.
FRANCHISES: 6 in Ohio and Illinois.
FOUNDED: 1969.
REQUIRED CAPITAL: $2,500 to $5,000.
FINANCIAL ASSISTANCE: None.
TRAINING: Two days intensive training conducted at company headquarters, or at prospective franchisee's home.
MANAGERIAL ASSISTANCE: The company conducts continuing training programs for all of its personnel in order to improve expertise, upgrade efficiency, and maintain morale.

NORRELL TEMPORARY SERVICES, INC.
3092 Piedmont Road, N.E.
Atlanta, GA 30305
(404) 262–2100
Contact: Robert J. Gibson

BUSINESS: Service providing skilled office, clerical, and data processing personnel to all types of businesses on a temporary basis.

FRANCHISES: 8 in six states.
FOUNDED: 1963.
REQUIRED CAPITAL: $15,000 operating capital and furnished office.
FINANCIAL ASSISTANCE: Payroll and accounts receivable financing.
TRAINING: Complete training program which includes comprehensive three-day basic office training, five days sales training, and periodic seminars.
MANAGERIAL ASSISTANCE: Continuous training and support from company headquarters which includes recruiting programs, weekly, and monthly reports of office activities, direct mail advertising-sales development, computer payrolling, customer billing, operations manuals, supplies and forms, and brochures.

*THE OLSTEN CORPORATION
1 Merrick Avenue
Westbury, Long Island, NY 11590
(516) 997–7200
Contact: Edward J. Wilsmann

BUSINESS: Temporary employment service.
FRANCHISES: 35 in 21 states.
FOUNDED: 1950.
REQUIRED CAPITAL: $15,000 minimum, plus working capital.
FINANCIAL ASSISTANCE: The company will provide accounts receivable financing to assist with working capital requirements.
TRAINING: One-week classroom training and two weeks' field training as well as periodic visits during the start-up period.
MANAGERIAL ASSISTANCE: The company supplies full operating manuals and in addition, provides continuous, ongoing assistance in all facets of the business including technical assistance, insurance, marketing, sales, advertising, and other areas of temporary help. The company also furnishes sales leads in franchisee's area whenever possible.

*PERSONNEL POOL OF AMERICA, INC.
521 South Andrews Avenue
Fort Lauderdale, FL 33301
(800) 327–1396
Contact: R. L. Myers, Vice President

BUSINESS: Medical, office and industrial temporary personnel service.
FRANCHISES: 170 in 35 states, District of Columbia, and Canada.
FOUNDED: 1946.
REQUIRED CAPITAL: $50,000 to $70,000 depending on market size.
FINANCIAL ASSISTANCE: Growth capital financing for franchises whose growth is greater than anticipated. Normally, loans of 12 months or less duration with monthly amortization at current interest rates.
TRAINING: Two weeks' training at company headquarters, plus two weeks on-the-job training at franchisee's office after opening.
MANAGERIAL ASSISTANCE: Advice, assistance, and preparation of advertising, marketing, recruiting and screening procedures, insurance coverages with some master policies available, training and selection of additional personnel, com-

parative sales and operating statistics, help with financial and accounting procedures, and review and analysis of operating problems and procedures.

PLACE MART FRANCHISING CORP.
20 Evergreen Place
East Orange, NJ 07018
(201) 678–8500
Contact: M. B. Kushma

BUSINESS: Employment agency.
FRANCHISES: 15 in New Jersey.
FOUNDED: 1962.
REQUIRED CAPITAL: $10,000 to $15,000.
FINANCIAL ASSISTANCE: The company will provide financing for qualified applicants.
TRAINING: Intensive three to six weeks' training at company headquarters with follow-up training at franchisee's location.
MANAGERIAL ASSISTANCE: Continuous training and supervision from field personnel, seminars, training sessions, and newsletters. Periodic franchise meetings to discuss policies and administrative problems.

POSITIONS, INC., INTERNATIONAL
20 William Street
Wellesley Office Park
Wellesley, MA 02181
(617) 235–8758
Contact: William F. Markey, Jr., CEC

BUSINESS: Employment agency.
FRANCHISES: 7 in Massachusetts and Connecticut.
FOUNDED: 1968.
REQUIRED: $30,000 to $40,000 depending on location.
FINANCIAL ASSISTANCE: None.
TRAINING: An intensive franchisee training program lasting approximately three weeks will be conducted at company headquarters. Also, the company will conduct an initial two-week training program for franchisee and staff in the franchisee's office. Periodic visits will be made to franchisee's location.
MANAGERIAL ASSISTANCE: The company provides continual assistance to franchisee in all aspects of operating franchised office. This includes training sessions, office critiques, advertising and promotional support, job order exchange programs, management techniques, profit planning, training bulletins, and so on.

*RETAIL RECRUITERS INTERNATIONAL, INC.
530 Industrial Bank Building
Providence, RI 02903
(401) 421–6742
Contact: Jacques J. Lapointe, President

BUSINESS: Employment agency.
FRANCHISES: 7 in six states and District of Columbia.

FOUNDED: 1969.

REQUIRED CAPITAL: $15,000 to $25,000 which includes working capital.

FINANCIAL ASSISTANCE: Up to 30 percent of franchise fee.

TRAINING: Complete training in all aspects of operation. Intensive 30-day training of new franchisee and new employees of initial franchise. Training can be conducted at company headquarters or new franchisee's first office. Continuous and follow-up training as needed. Assist in securing suitable office space, help negotiate lease, design layout of office, selection of proper office furniture and equipment, and proper telephone system.

MANAGERIAL ASSISTANCE: Company provides detailed training manual and tapes that contain information and know-how for operating personnel business. The company will provide advice, guidance, and assistance through meetings, seminars, correspondence, telephone, and personal instruction to improve expertise and efficiency. Also, visits are made on a continuous basis to ensure proper operation of business.

RICHARD P. RITA PERSONNEL SYSTEM, INC.
One Weybosset Hill
Providence, RI 02903
(401) 331–0010
Contact: Eugene W. Majewski

BUSINESS: Employment agency.

FRANCHISES: 20 in ten states.

FOUNDED: 1956.

REQUIRED CAPITAL: $20,000 to $40,000, depending on market area.

FINANCIAL ASSISTANCE: The company will aid in the securing of financing.

TRAINING: Three weeks of training and then continual assistance.

MANAGERIAL ASSISTANCE: Franchisor will support and assist franchisee in all phases of the operation.

S-H-S INTERNATIONAL
The Schneider-Hill-Spangler Network
121 South Broad Street
Philadelphia, PA 19107
(215) 732–4560
Contact: Arthur M. Schneider

BUSINESS: Employment agency.

FRANCHISES: 16 in five states.

FOUNDED: 1956.

REQUIRED CAPITAL: A minimum of $30,000.

FINANCIAL ASSISTANCE: The amount of the franchise fee varies according to area. Of this fee, a portion can be paid over a period of time, at no interest charge.

TRAINING: A comprehensive, mandatory, two-week program is held in Philadelphia. First week is account executive training, the second week is devoted to management. An additional week is spent training all staff upon opening. Further training and visitations are provided during the first six months of operation and thereafter on a regularly scheduled basis. A full set of training tapes, tests, and aids are also available. There are regional seminars conducted for all account executives.

MANAGERIAL ASSISTANCE: The company provides continual assistance in the form of visitations, seminars, national conventions, a management newsletter, an account executive newsletter, updated manager, account executive and receptionists' manuals, research, national surveys, financial, legal, and advertising assistance in addition to sales and advertising incentive programs.

SALES CONSULTANTS INTERNATIONAL
A Division of Management Recruiters International, Inc.
1016 Euclid Avenue
Cleveland, OH 44115
(216) 696–1122
Contact: Alan R. Schonberg

BUSINESS: Personnel placement agency specializing in sales and sales management talent, sales engineers, and marketing personnel.

FRANCHISES: 70 offices in 33 states.

FOUNDED: 1957.

REQUIRED CAPITAL: $20,000 to $40,000, depending on location.

FINANCIAL ASSISTANCE: None.

TRAINING: The company staff will provide the franchisee with an intensive initial training program of approximately three weeks conducted at the company headquarters plus an initial on-the-job training program of approximately three weeks conducted in the licensee's first office.

In addition to the above, the company staff will assist and advise the licensee in securing suitable office space and the negotiation of the lease for same, the design and layout of the office, the selection of office furniture and equipment and the negotiation of the purchase or lease agreement and the establishment of a suitable telephone system.

MANAGERIAL ASSISTANCE: The licensee is provided with a detailed operations manual containing information, procedures, and know-how for operating the business. The company will furnish the franchisee with continuing advice, guidance, and assistance through national and regional meetings, seminars, correspondence, telephone, and personal instruction with respect to the franchisee's personnel placement service operations and procedures and their improvement and revision.

SNELLING & SNELLING, INC.
International Headquarters
Snelling Plaza
4000 South Tamiami Trail
Sarasota, FL 33581
(813) 922–9616
Contact: William G. Allin, Group Vice President

BUSINESS: Employment service.

FRANCHISES: 600 in 47 states and South America.

FOUNDED: 1951.
REQUIRED CAPITAL: $20,000 to $60,000.
FINANCIAL ASSISTANCE: None.
TRAINING: Two weeks' training at company headquarters. Additional training in the field for franchisee and employees. The franchisee's employees may be sent at any time, free of charge, to training classes given at the company headquarters and throughout the country. Training includes the use of training manuals. The company is available for counseling and 17 regional directors travel throughout the United Sates providing assistance in office operations.
MANAGERIAL ASSISTANCE: Continued company guidance through communication systems and periodic field training visits and national and field seminars.

SPEER PERSONNEL CONSULTANTS
3384 Peachtree Road, N.E.
Atlanta, GA 30303
(404) 262–7804
Contact: Carol Speer

BUSINESS: Employment agency.
FRANCHISES: 3 in three states.
FOUNDED: 1969.
REQUIRED CAPITAL: $15,000 to $25,000 average.
FINANCIAL ASSISTANCE: None.
TRAINING: Franchisee receives three weeks' initial training. Two weeks at company headquarters, and one week in franchisee's office. The training includes all phases of agency operations and counselor functions. Sales motivation and sales techniques are emphasized. On a continuing basis, the company cross lists applicants and job orders on a national basis. Company staff makes visits quarterly.
MANAGERIAL ASSISTANCE: Franchisee is required to submit monthly report. Report is analyzed and recommendations are made as needed. In addition to the quarterly training visits by a qualified staff member, the franchisee is free to visit company headquarters at any time for additional consultation.

STAFF BUILDERS INTERNATIONAL, INC.
122 East 42nd Street
New York, NY 10017
(212) 867–2345
Contact: Walter E. Ritter

BUSINESS: Employment agency specializing in temporary help.
FRANCHISES: 19 in 12 states, District of Columbia, and Canada.
FOUNDED: 1961.
REQUIRED CAPITAL: $25,000.
FINANCIAL ASSISTANCE: The company may finance temporary payroll for franchisee up to 80 percent of weekly sales.
TRAINING: Two weeks at company headquarters for initial training. Manuals, procedures, and systems are all provided as part of the course.
MANAGERIAL ASSISTANCE: Continuous communication with franchisee via telephone, mail (bulletins, supplies, materials, and so on) and visits. Promotional

aids, sales programs, recruiting assistance, and financial advice are all part of the ongoing programs.

UNIFORCE TEMPORARIES
41 East 42nd Street
New York, NY 10017
(212) 687–4300
Contact: John Fanning

BUSINESS: Employment agency specializing in temporary help.
FRANCHISES: 45 in 15 states.
FOUNDED: 1970.
REQUIRED CAPITAL: $10,000 franchise fee and $15,000 operating capital.
FINANCIAL ASSISTANCE: The company finances entire accounts receivable.
TRAINING: Intensive three days' training at company headquarters and on-site. Continuous assistance in all phases of the business.
MANAGERIAL ASSISTANCE: The company provides complete operations manuals and supplies all necessary operational forms, direct mail, skilled tests, and monthly interoffice publication. The company also engages in unlimited phone consultation, plus periodic management visits and client sales calls.

APPARELMASTER, INC.
7609 Production Drive
Cincinnati, OH 45222
(513) 761–3130
Contact: James R. Wahl

BUSINESS: Uniform, career apparel, dust control, and miscellaneous rental system.
FRANCHISES: 207 in 48 states, District of Columbia, Canada, and England.
FOUNDED: 1971.
REQUIRED CAPITAL: $12,700 or $9,900 if paid in lump sum.
FINANCIAL ASSISTANCE: None.
TRAINING: Initial training augmented with periodic training in all facets of the business.
MANAGERIAL ASSISTANCE: Operation and other manuals provided. Managerial and technical assistance provided on every aspect of the industry for life of franchise.

*TAYLOR RENTAL CORPORATION
570 Cottage Street
Springfield, MA 01104
(413) 781–7730
Contact: Wilbert L. Bourque

BUSINESS: A general, all-purpose rental operation.
FRANCHISES: 436 in 43 states.

* Asterisk denotes franchisor is a member of the International Franchise Association.

FOUNDED: 1947.

REQUIRED CAPITAL: $20,000 to $30,000 (including down payment).

FINANCIAL ASSISTANCE: Down payments to franchisor range from $10,000 to $20,000 depending on recommended opening equipment, and supplies shipment of $40,000 to $65,000. The balance can be financed through bank participation loan (five year—60 payments). Financing for growth inventory is normally offered with no down payment requirement. Franchisee has option to arrange own outside financing. There is a one-time marketing and start-up fees of $4,000 payable at the time the franchise is awarded. Down payments are applied directly to equipment and supply purchases.

TRAINING: Comprehensive training at a company-owned training and operating center for ten days at no charge to franchisee. Advanced on-the-job training for a minimum of one week in another established center.

MANAGERIAL ASSISTANCE: Assistance is offered in locating proper site. The company provides either regional or headquarter dealer service representatives to assist both new and established dealers in all phases of operations. A computerized money status report to franchisees provides current income and inventory data on every piece of rental equipment on a percentage return against original cost basis. A computerized management analyses accounting system is available to all franchisees. The company provides all franchisees with a descriptive product book including a suggested rental rate guide which is updated continuously to reflect current equipment and rate changes. Budgets, cash flow and projection assistance are provided to increase current and long-range profitability. Complete operational, health and life insurances are included in the program.

TIME TOOL AND EQUIPMENT RENTALS, INC.
10795 North Irma Drive
Denver, CO 80233
(303) 452–3096
Contact: Vic Neumann

BUSINESS: Tools and equipment rental.

FRANCHISES: 38 in 17 states.

FOUNDED: 1969.

REQUIRED CAPITAL: $10,000 and working capital. No franchise fees, no royalty.

FINANCIAL ASSISTANCE: Company assistance to qualified applicants for local bank loans and lease purchase. Some 100 percent loans.

TRAINING: In-store at opening and continuous follow-up.

MANAGERIAL ASSISTANCE: Location feasibility studies made and assistance provided in securing proper location and lease negotiation.

*UNITED RENT-ALL, INC.
10131 National Boulevard
Los Angeles, CA 90034
(213) 836–4900
Contact: Licensing Manager

BUSINESS: General rental store.

FRANCHISES: Approximately 120 in 30 states.

FOUNDED: 1948.

REQUIRED CAPITAL: Approximately $35,000, plus working capital.

FINANCIAL ASSISTANCE: A portion of the franchise fee normally can be financed. At the election of the franchisee, equipment can be purchased through the company headquarters, which offers benefits of broad-based purchasing power and discounts. Land and custom-designed building may be leased for the term of the franchise. Blanket or group all-risk liability, casualty conversion, health, accident, and life insurance coverages are available.

.TRAINING: Normally, a two-week classroom and practical on-the-job training at the franchisee-owned store is provided, which includes discussion of rental concepts, equipment familiarization and maintenance, counter systems, cash and accounting methods, inventory control and management, advertising, promotion, customer relations, store security, employee management, telephone techniques, insurance, purchasing, cooperative and commission renting. Subsequent training is also given by regional directors on an ongoing basis.

MANAGERIAL ASSISTANCE: Company's complete staff available for consultation at the request of the franchisee. Operations manual updated periodically and periodic in-store consultations with field regional directors. Consultation in stores includes training on budgets, cash revenue, forecasts, inventory substitutions, sales, promotions, outside costs, personnel, and other aspects of operating the business. Purchasing, operations, advertising, legal and marketing departments maintained in the company headquarters.

COUNTRY STYLE DONUTS
8370 Woodbine Avenue
Buttonville, Ontario
LOH 1GO
Canada
(416) 495–1464
Contact: Licensing Manager

BUSINESS: Coffee and donut shop.

FRANCHISES: 60 stores in Canada and 5 stores in the United States.

FOUNDED: 1962.

REQUIRED CAPITAL: Total investment for a franchise is $80,000. This is broken down into $30,000 down payment, $5,000 working capital, and $45,000 to be financed, if required.

FINANCIAL ASSISTANCE: The company will arrange financing for the $45,000 loan on equipment.

TRAINING: A four-week training course is provided for each franchisee at the company training center. The course includes intensive training in the art of baking donuts, directions for store operation, employee management, bookkeeping, and so on.

MANAGERIAL ASSISTANCE: Each franchisee will have a field supervisor at the store for the first few days of opening. Continued assistance is available through the operations manager who makes visits to each store for the purpose of inspection and consultation. Also the company is continually testing and developing new formulas and products before introducing them on the store level. Promotional material is available to all franchisees from the head office. Bulletins are sent to all stores informing franchisees of all price changes and new products available.

DONUTLAND, INC.
P.O. Box 409
Marion, IA 52302
(319) 377–9416
Contact: Michael R. Nicholls

BUSINESS: Retail coffee and donuts.
FRANCHISES: 30 in Illinois, Iowa, Wisconsin, and Georgia.
FOUNDED: 1965.
REQUIRED CAPITAL: $15,000.
FINANCIAL ASSISTANCE: Company will assist in financing the balance of $20,000 needed for a franchise. Guarantee of lease.
TRAINING: Training in the making of the product and in the operation of franchisee's shop.
MANAGERIAL ASSISTANCE: Continual training and supervision. Constant inspection of physical plant for the life of franchise.

*DUNKIN' DONUTS OF AMERICA, INC.
P.O. Box 317
Randolph, MA 02368
(617) 461–4000
Contact: Thomas Schwarz

BUSINESS: Coffee and donut shop.
FRANCHISES: 851 in 40 states, Canada, Japan, and Puerto Rico.
FOUNDED: 1950.
REQUIRED CAPITAL: Franchise fee, $27,000 or $32,000 depending on geographical area. Working capital, approximately $12,000.
FINANCIAL ASSISTANCE: Equipment package may be financed for three years through the company. Signs may be financed directly through sign companies.
TRAINING: Five-week training course for franchisees at Dunkin' Donuts University in North Quincy, Massachusetts, consisting of production and shop management training. Initial training of donutmaker and managers for franchisees and retraining is carried out at Dunkin' Donuts University without additional charge.
MANAGERIAL ASSISTANCE: Continuous managerial assistance is available from the district sales manager assigned to the individual shop. The company maintains quality assurance, research and development, and new products programs. The franchisee-funded marketing department provides marketing programs for

* Asterisk denotes franchisor is a member of the International Franchise Association.

all shops. The marketing programs are administered by an area marketing manager who develops plans on a TV market basis.

*MISTER DONUT OF AMERICA, INC.
Subsidiary of International Multifoods Corporation
1200 Multifoods Building
Minneapolis, MN 55402
(612) 340–3300
Contact: Richard A. Niglio

BUSINESS: Coffee and donut shop.
FRANCHISES: 665 in 36 states, Canada, Japan, and Puerto Rico.
FOUNDED: 1955.
REQUIRED CAPITAL: Equipment package, $31,000; franchise fee, $6,000; and working capital, $5,000. Additional cash required $21,500 plus costs of real estate and building which is responsibility of franchisee but location is subject to Mister Donut's approval.
FINANCIAL ASSISTANCE: Equipment can be financed by company with 25 percent down payment. Financing over 60 months at current interest rates.
TRAINING: Continuous professional five weeks' training program consisting of practical as well as classroom training at company school in St. Paul, Minnesota.
MANAGERIAL ASSISTANCE: An area representative is permanently located at company expense in each area of the United States and Canada for managerial assistance to franchise operators. The company maintains a quality control service as well as a research and development department, marketing and advertising services to assist franchise owners. Location analysis, lease negotiation, and building design and construction is also provided by the company.

TASTEE DONUTS, INC.
P.O. Box 2708
Rocky Mount, NC 27801
(919) 443–6123
Contact: R. D. Gorham, Jr.

BUSINESS: Retail donut and pastry shops.
FRANCHISES: 40 in five states.
FOUNDED: 1962.
REQUIRED CAPITAL: $33,000 cash.
FINANCIAL ASSISTANCE: Advice and counsel on local bank financing.
TRAINING: Five weeks of classroom and on-the-job training at the training center in Rocky Mount, North Carolina.
MANAGERIAL ASSISTANCE: Operating manuals with continuous update and bulletins and visits by company personnel to assist with general operations and specific problems.

CHEESE SHOP INTERNATIONAL, INC.
25 Amogrone Crossway
Greenwich, CT 06830
(203) 661–1096
Contact: Cornelius Hearn III

BUSINESS: Retail sale of cheese, gourmet foods, related gift items, and wines where permissible.

FRANCHISES: 95 in 25 states.

FOUNDED: 1965.

REQUIRED CAPITAL: $35,000 to $65,000.

FINANCIAL ASSISTANCE: None.

TRAINING: Four weeks, five days per week working in an existing shop under the direction of a company expert.

MANAGERIAL ASSISTANCE: In addition to the training, the company provides an expert to help during the grand opening week. On a continuous basis, plans and advice on all purchases necessary to run the business. This service includes discussing the following: availability of product, freshness, specials, quality, next arrivals, trucking routes, air freight, costs, and so on. It also includes recommending where to place a given order for a certain product at a particular time. This service is optional and typically done on a weekly basis. Also, continuous supervision and advice in all phases of retail operations is provided.

THE CIRCLE K CORPORATION
Contract Operations
P.O. Box 20230
Phoenix, AZ 85036
(602) 268–1351
Contact: Robert Charles

BUSINESS: Convenience-type food stores.

FRANCHISES: 165 in six states.

FOUNDED: 1957.

REQUIRED CAPITAL: $6,000 ($1,600 security deposit, $4,400 inventory deposit).

FINANCIAL ASSISTANCE: The company provides the complete merchandise inventory (approximately $20,000, at cost). The inventory less the down payment is financed by the company at an interest rate not to exceed 10 percent per annum. The loan may be paid in full at any time.

TRAINING: Eight weeks of on-the-job training in all phases of the operation conducted in a store that is owned and operated by the company. The company will pay the franchisee $155 per week while in training.

MANAGERIAL ASSISTANCE: The company provides continual management service for the life of the franchise in all areas of operation such as accounting, advertising, merchandising, and inventory control. All forms and directions are provided. Zone, division, and area managers are available in all areas to work closely with the franchisee and make regular visits to stores to assist in solving operational problems.

*CONVENIENT FOOD MART, INC.
John Hancock Center
875 North Michigan Avenue, Suite 1401
Chicago, IL 60611
(312) 751–1500
Contact: William R. Sandberg, Executive Vice President

BUSINESS: Grocery Superette open from 7 A.M. to 12 midnight all year round. Available through licensed regional franchisors throughout the United States and Canada.
FRANCHISES: 800 throughout the United States.
FOUNDED: 1958.
REQUIRED CAPITAL: $22,000 to $30,000.
FINANCIAL ASSISTANCE: Financing of five to seven years up to $45,000 for fixtures, equipment, and signs, interest at available rates. Chicago area, short-term financing is available up to $15,000 for grocery inventory to qualified applicant. Practices vary from region to region.
TRAINING: Prestore opening training up to six weeks (four weeks minimum) given to franchisee in classroom and in operating store. Continuous training throughout life of business provided by up-to-date manuals, bulletins, and on-the-spot counseling usually once a week by qualified personnel to include, but not limited to, merchandising, advertising, promotion, inventory control, and store management.
MANAGERIAL ASSISTANCE: Continuous in-field counseling, quality control, and annual area educational meetings and seminars.

CONVENIENT INDUSTRIES OF AMERICA, INC.
P.O. Box 660
Louisville, KY 40201
(502) 584–1281
Contact: Charles W. Cooper, Jr.

BUSINESS: Grocery store open from 7 A.M. to 12 midnight seven days a week.
FRANCHISES: 285.
FOUNDED: 1960.
REQUIRED CAPITAL: $30,000.
FINANCIAL ASSISTANCE: Franchisee must provide original capital investment of $30,000.
TRAINING: One week of training school plus four weeks in-store training. Also coordinators are available for additional training and supervision. Periodic training sessions are held for franchisee when needed in specific areas.
MANAGERIAL ASSISTANCE: Stores are provided with management training, complete bookkeeping services, cash control, merchandising and advertising, suggested retail pricing, and approved suppliers.

* Asterisk denotes franchisor is a member of the International Franchise Association.

*HICKORY FARMS OF OHIO, INC.
1021 North Raynolds Road
Toledo, OH 43615
(419) 535–1491
Contact: Richard Bordeaux

BUSINESS: Retail store selling packages and bulk specialty food featuring the Hickory Farms summer sausage, a variety of imported and domestic cheeses, candies and other related food products.

FRANCHISES: 450 in 45 states and Canada.

FOUNDED: 1951.

REQUIRED CAPITAL: Approximately $80,000 plus leasehold improvements.

FINANCIAL ASSISTANCE: None, however, associate lease agreement may be available in some situations. Capital requirements may vary by location.

TRAINING: Two weeks at company headquarters in planning, purchasing, stocking and merchandising, advertising, and business management. Two weeks prior to opening, a training counselor and store organizer take charge of the new store operation.

MANAGERIAL ASSISTANCE: Continuous communication by bulletins, correspondence, direct phone, in-store visits by company personnel, and an annual national convention, interim regional meetings, and training sessions are conducted.

JITNEY-JINGLE, INC.
440 North Mill Street
P.O. Box 3409
Jackson, MS 39207
(601) 948–0361
Contact: Howard V. Blair

BUSINESS: Convenience food store, "Junior Food Marts."

FRANCHISES: 261 in 14 states.

FOUNDED: 1919.

REQUIRED CAPITAL: $14,500 to $19,500 to purchase inventory and supply working capital for store.

FINANCIAL ASSISTANCE: None needed. Company finds locations, secures leases, constructs buildings, and fixtures for the store.

TRAINING: District manager provides in-store training, assists in merchandising store, accounting procedures, store operation, store auditing, grand opening, vendor contacting, and seasonal merchandising.

MANAGERIAL ASSISTANCE: District manager makes regular visits to assist in the operation of the store.

LI'L SHOPPER, INC.
811 East State Street
Sharon, PA 16146
(412) 347–4505
Contact: Ronald V. Pacello

BUSINESS: Convenience grocery store.

FRANCHISES: 27 in Ohio and Pennsylvania.

FOUNDED: 1970.

REQUIRED CAPITAL: $15,000 to purchase inventory.

FINANCIAL ASSISTANCE: Company financing available to qualified applicant with minimum $4,000 cash down payment. Balance can be paid out of operation over an extended period.

TRAINING: Store operations manual and intensive in-store training initially, with continuing counseling by field representatives.

MANAGERIAL ASSISTANCE: Continuous assistance in all phases of accounting, operations, and merchandising is provided.

*MAJIK MARKET
Subsidiary of Munford, Inc.
68 Brookwood Drive, N.E.
Atlanta, GA 30309
(404) 873–6641
Contact: R. D. Blythe

BUSINESS: Convenience food store which operates seven days a week.

FRANCHISES: 1,400 in 16 states.

FOUNDED: 1948.

REQUIRED CAPITAL: Area franchisee fee varies and applicant must have substantial net worth.

FINANCIAL ASSISTANCE: None.

TRAINING: Four-week training provided at company headquarters covering all phases of the business including daily operating procedures, security, merchandising, advertising, and bookkeeping.

MANAGERIAL ASSISTANCE: Continuous operating assistance provided by skilled account representatives in all areas of operations. Constant monthly merchandising program offered. Financial statements and operating analysis submitted monthly. Also a manual of operating procedures and all accounting forms are made available to the franchisee.

*OPEN PANTRY FOOD MARTS, INC.
3055 East 63rd Street
Cleveland, OH 44127
(216) 277–2400
Contact: Jim Mamick

BUSINESS: Grocery store open from early morning to midnight every day of the year.

FRANCHISES: Over 300 in 25 states.

FOUNDED: 1962.

REQUIRED CAPITAL: $15,000 for individual store franchise.

FINANCIAL ASSISTANCE: The company arranges for financing of equipment fixtures and initial inventory.

TRAINING: Regional franchisors are provided complete headquarter training, plus continuous assistance throughout life of contract by expert field representatives. Store franchises receive three weeks in-store training, plus continued assistance from regional field experts.

MANAGERIAL ASSISTANCE: Continued management service is furnished throughout the life of the franchise. In case of store franchise, the services rendered include, but are not limited to, bookkeeping, merchandising, advertising, supervision, inventory, correct product mix, and fiscal control.

QUIK STOP MARKETS, INC.
P.O. Box 1745
Fremont, CA 94538
(415) 657–8500
Contact: Larry Kranich

BUSINESS: Convenience grocery store.

FRANCHISES: 100 in California.

FOUNDED: 1965.

REQUIRED CAPITAL: $5,000 to $7,000 which pays for franchise fee, security deposits, change fund, and training.

FINANCIAL ASSISTANCE: Financial assistance for the merchandise inventory of approximately $20,000 can be arranged. It is carried on an open account by the company and is paid off from profits of the business.

TRAINING: A complete manual of instruction is provided as well as in-store training under experienced supervision.

MANAGERIAL ASSISTANCE: The company provides continual management service including accounting, advertising, market and pricing information, and store performance analysis. Field representatives visit store regularly to offer assistance.

7–ELEVEN. See The Southland Corporation.

*THE SOUTHLAND CORPORATION
d.b.a. 7–Eleven
2828 North Haskell Avenue
P.O. Box 719
Dallas, TX 75221
(214) 828–7611
Contact: S. R. Dole

BUSINESS: Convenience grocery stores.

FRANCHISES: 2,234 in 22 states and District of Columbia.

FOUNDED: 1956.

REQUIRED CAPITAL: $22,000.

FINANCIAL ASSISTANCE: $10,000 cash down toward inventory and franchise fee. Balance paid out of operation over a reasonable time period.

TRAINING: One week of specialized classroom training, two weeks in an operational 7-Eleven store, plus ample in-store training.

MANAGERIAL ASSISTANCE: Continuous assistance is supplied by field representative.

*SWISS COLONY STORES, INC.
1112 Seventh Avenue
Monroe, WI 53566
(608) 328–8555
Contact: John Grey Davis

BUSINESS: Retail stores offering domestic and imported cheeses, sausages, European-style pastries, candy, specialty foods, and gifts.
FRANCHISES: 180 in 40 states.
FOUNDED: 1969.
REQUIRED CAPITAL: Approximately $85,000 plus leasehold improvements.
FINANCIAL ASSISTANCE: Equipment leasing available up to approximately $45,000.
TRAINING: Ten-day mandatory, thorough training at company headquarters, covering all phases of store operation. Additional training at company-owned stores, optional.
MANAGERIAL ASSISTANCE: Continuous supervision in store at intervals by company personnel. Constant high-volume monthly merchandise program offered.

TELECAKE INTERNATIONAL
2265 East 4800 South
Salt Lake City, UT 84117
(801) 278–0413
Contact: Clarence L. Jolley

BUSINESS: Cake by phone service. Franchise is a two-level retail bakery or regional sales center.
FRANCHISES: Over 2,600 locations in all states and Canada.
FOUNDED: 1971.
REQUIRED CAPITAL: (1) $210 for local bakery. (2) Minimum $10,000 for regional sales center.
FINANCIAL ASSISTANCE: None.
TRAINING: Training is given at regional sales center.
MANAGERIAL ASSISTANCE: Continual direction of the operation is provided.

*WHITE HEN PANTRY
Division of Jewel Companies, Inc.
666 Industrial Drive
Elmhurst, IL 60126
(312) 833–3100
Contact: Robert L. Swanson

BUSINESS: Convenience grocery store which is open from 7 A.M. to 12 P.M., seven days a week.
FRANCHISES: 213 in Illinois, Indiana, Wisconsin, and Massachusetts.
FOUNDED: 1965.

REQUIRED CAPITAL: $8,000.

FINANCIAL ASSISTANCE: Total investment averages $18,000 to $20,000. Investment includes minimum $15,600, merchandise, $1,600 security deposit, $200 cash register fund, $400 supplies, $100 to $200 for licenses and $1,000 processing fee. A minimum investment of $8,000 is required. Financial assistance is available.

TRAINING: Classroom and in-store training precede store opening. A special training facility is established for this purpose. Detailed operations manuals are provided. Store counselor visits are regular and frequent.

MANAGERIAL ASSISTANCE: Services provided include all merchandising, accounting, advertising, and group medical insurance (optional).

BARNHILL'S ICE CREAM PARLOR AND RESTAURANT
2855 West Market Street
Akron, OH 44313
(216) 864–3948
Contact: Robert W. Barnhill

BUSINESS: Gay 90s-style ice cream parlors and restaurants.

FRANCHISES: Primarily in Ohio.

FOUNDED: 1966.

REQUIRED CAPITAL: Approximately $100,000, plus leasehold improvements.

FINANCIAL ASSISTANCE: None.

TRAINING: Required 30-day minimum on-the-job training in the company operation in Akron, Ohio. The training covers fountain, kitchen, floor, candy and gift, and office procedures.

MANAGERIAL ASSISTANCE: The company provides all normal supervision for the life of the franchise operations; in addition, manuals, accounting systems, and so on.

BASKIN-ROBBINS, INC.
1201 South Victory Boulevard
Burbank, CA 91506
(213) 843–1060
Contact: Paul Fischer

BUSINESS: Ice cream store.

FRANCHISES: Over 2,000 throughout the United States, Canada, Japan, and Europe.

FOUNDED: 1945.

REQUIRED CAPITAL: Approximately $25,000 to $65,000 depending on location.

FINANCIAL ASSISTANCE: Financial assistance available.

TRAINING: A complete training program is provided. On-the-job training in operating store under the guidance of experienced supervisors.

MANAGERIAL ASSISTANCE: Continuous merchandising program, accounting procedures, counsel, and insurance program are provided.

*BRESLER'S 33 FLAVORS, INC.
4010 West Belden Avenue
Chicago, IL 60639
(312) 227–6700
Contact: C. D. Baxstresses

BUSINESS: Ice cream store.
FRANCHISES: 325 in 32 states and Canada.
FOUNDED: 1962.
REQUIRED CAPITAL: Approximately $30,000 plus working capital.
FINANCIAL ASSISTANCE: A present total investment of approximately $60,000 is required plus working capital of which approximately 50 percent is in cash. Franchisee may obtain own financing, or the company will attempt to obtain financing to the extent of 50 percent of the total required initial investment, repayable over a minimum five-year period.
TRAINING: A minimum of three weeks of classroom and in-store training.
MANAGERIAL ASSISTANCE: The company assists franchisee in all aspects of shop operation, record keeping, advertising and promotion, and selling techniques. Manuals of operations and counseling are provided. Company field personnel make regular visits to stores.

CALICO COTTAGE CANDIES, INC.
11 Crescent Street
Hewlett, NY 11557
(516) 374–4460
Contact: Lawrence J. Wurzel

BUSINESS: A fudge shop which may be added to an existing business.
FRANCHISES: 180 in 34 states.
FOUNDED: 1965.
REQUIRED CAPITAL: $5,000 which covers fudge-making equipment, utensils, and initial inventory.
FINANCIAL ASSISTANCE: None.
TRAINING: Two days' training covering all facets of the operation.
MANAGERIAL ASSISTANCE: Continuous guidance in technical, sales, and merchandising areas.

CARVEL CORPORATION
201 Sawmill River Road
Yonkers, NY 10701
(914) 969–7200
Contact: Raymond Urezzio

BUSINESS: Ice cream store.
FRANCHISES: Over 700 stores in 14 states.
FOUNDED: 1948.
REQUIRED CAPITAL: Approximately $95,000.
FINANCIAL ASSISTANCE: Contacts and counsel in arranging needed finance.

* Asterisk denotes franchisor is a member of the International Franchise Association.

TRAINING: Complete in-store, three-week training period covering actual store operation and a standard operating procedure manual.

MANAGERIAL ASSISTANCE: Continuous in-field counseling covering merchandising, quality control, advertising, and promotion are provided. In addition, the company holds annual area educational seminars.

COURTESY INTERSTATE CORPORATION
P.O. Box 2071
1411 West Palm Street
San Diego, CA 92101
(714) 297–0101
Contact: Duane C. Remsnyder

BUSINESS: In-the-room hotel/motel coffee service.

FRANCHISES: 35 throughout the United States.

FOUNDED: 1961.

REQUIRED CAPITAL: Depends on location. Reasonable working capital.

FINANCIAL ASSISTANCE: Open account credit based on analysis of franchisee's capacity.

TRAINING: One- to three-day training depending upon territory and franchisee involved.

MANAGERIAL ASSISTANCE: Continuous guidance in technical, sales, and merchandising problems. Sales leads resulting from trade show and trade journals are provided.

CRAIG'S, INC., CANDY & ICE CREAM SHOPS
Box 50233
Indianapolis, IN 46250
(317) 299–5799
Contact: Robert Craig Mogg

BUSINESS: Candy, ice cream and sandwich store.

FRANCHISES: 4 in Indiana.

FOUNDED: 1975.

REQUIRED CAPITAL: A total investment of $25,000 to $45,000 is required depending on store location and preparation.

FINANCIAL ASSISTANCE: None.

TRAINING: On-the-job training is provided in an operating store where franchisee can learn proper system firsthand.

MANAGERIAL ASSISTANCE: Complete and continued assistance provided.

DAIRY ISLE & 3 IN 1 RESTAURANTS
Division of Commissary Corporation
45224 Cass Avenue
Utica, MI 48087
(313) 739–1112
Contact: David K. Chapoton

BUSINESS: Soft ice cream store and fast-food operation.

FRANCHISES: 130 in eight states.

FOUNDED: 1949.

REQUIRED CAPITAL: $10,000 to $25,000.

FINANCIAL ASSISTANCE: Company assists qualified applicants in arranging financing.

TRAINING: Three days or more depending on individuals being trained plus follow-up calls during the operating season.

MANAGERIAL ASSISTANCE: Operation of unit follow up promotional ideas and equipment purchasing.

HAZLERT ENT., INC.
MAIN STREET ORIGINAL ICE CREAM PARLORS
P.O. Box 13396
St. Petersburg, FL 33711
(813) 823–1723
Contact: Dean L. Hazlert, President

BUSINESS: Old-fashioned ice cream parlors.

FRANCHISES: 14 in Florida and Hawaii.

FOUNDED: 1972.

REQUIRED CAPITAL: $95,000–$125,000.

FINANCIAL ASSISTANCE: The company assists qualified applicants in arranging financing.

TRAINING: Initial in-store training program, approximately two weeks, is provided to not less than three employees of the franchisee, including the franchisee and the operator/manager. Manufacturing training provided to designated in-store ice cream maker.

MANAGERIAL ASSISTANCE: Continuous assistance available in store operation, product manufacturing and control, advertising, promotional guidance, and Annual Systems Conclave.

INTERCONTINENTAL COFFEE SERVICE, INC.
5312 North Elston Avenue
Chicago, IL 60630
(312) 282–5555
Contact: D. O. Bielenberg

BUSINESS: Provide free restaurant quality coffee-making equipment to a place of business and supply coffee, cream, sugar, and so on.

FRANCHISES: 18 in 14 states.

FOUNDED: 1965.

REQUIRED CAPITAL: $5,000 and up.

FINANCIAL ASSISTANCE: Liberal monthly rental programs on all equipment are given. Initial $2,500 cash advance is paid and no franchise fees are paid except on the basis of monthly sales.

TRAINING: Both company headquarters training and in-the-field training of as much as two weeks are required and provided. Complete services and training in sales, accounting, purchasing, and mechanical service are covered.

MANAGERIAL ASSISTANCE: Continuous weekly and monthly technical and motivational assistance is part of the ongoing relationship between a franchisee and the company. Complete manuals of operations, sales, and company policies are provided. Company personnel continues to work closely with each franchisee for the duration of the life of the franchise. Yearly meetings are conducted at the company headquarters at company's expense.

*KARMELKORN SHOPPES, INC.
101 31st Avenue
Rock Island, IL 61201
(309) 778–8416
Contact: Robert J. Caparula

BUSINESS: Popcorn, popcorn confections, a variety of kitchen candies, and related snack food store.
FRANCHISES: 224 in 42 states.
FOUNDED: 1930.
REQUIRED CAPITAL: $30,000 to $40,000 when standard financing is available.
FINANCIAL ASSISTANCE: The total investment in the franchised shop varies according to construction costs, and most in 1978 ranged from $60,500 to $78,500. Franchisees arrange their own financing. Karmelkorn will assist franchisee in applying for his or her original financing upon request.
TRAINING: Preliminary information by mail followed by intensive training in franchisee's shop. Length of training period varies with experience and needs of individual franchise, but most complete the training within a week. All training is conducted by experienced company training supervisors.
MANAGERIAL ASSISTANCE: Franchisee receives and is instructed in the use of a specially designed bookkeeping system and a complete operations manual. Training program includes managerial instruction. Training supervisors visit shops periodically and on an "as needed" basis. Monthly publication provides updated operational information. Management and supervisory service are provided for the life of the franchise.

*MISTER SOFTEE, INC.
901 East Clements Bridge Road
Runnemede, NJ 08078
(609) 931–0200
Contact: James F. Conway

BUSINESS: Soft ice cream products from a mobile unit.
FRANCHISES: 1,243 in 31 states.
FOUNDED: 1956.
REQUIRED CAPITAL: $10,000 to $12,000.
FINANCIAL ASSISTANCE: Financing can be arranged for qualified individuals.
TRAINING: Franchisee is trained in the mobile unit, in the franchised area for one week, in merchandising, route planning, operation of the mobile unit, sanitation, and maintenance.

MANAGERIAL ASSISTANCE: Area representative visits franchise periodically and suggests improvements when needed. Standard operating procedure manual, service manual, accounting ledgers, and inventory control forms are provided to each franchisee.

THE SOBRIETY SARSAPARILLA AND SANDWICH SHOPPE FRANCHISE CORPORATION
P.O. Box 15577
Lakewood, CO 80215
(303) 237–6844
Contact: John Heckman

BUSINESS: Food shop, specializing in ice cream.
FRANCHISES: 1 in Colorado.
FOUNDED: 1971.
REQUIRED CAPITAL: $90,000.
FINANCIAL ASSISTANCE: Need 50 percent of franchise fee ($23,000) at time contract is signed. Will negotiate on remaining half.
TRAINING: Total operations training and manual provided. One month training before opening and one month after, and continual supervision.
MANAGERIAL ASSISTANCE: Continuous supervision in all phases of management.

SWENSEN'S ICE CREAM COMPANY
915 Front Street
San Francisco, 94111
(415) 989–8466
Contact: Charles A. Segalas

BUSINESS: Turn-of-the-century ice cream parlor.
FRANCHISES: 225 in 35 states, District of Columbia, Canada, Mexico, and Saudi Arabia.
FOUNDED: 1963.
REQUIRED CAPITAL: $80,000 minimum; equity capital requirements may vary depending on size of the store.
FINANCIAL ASSISTANCE: The company assists in arranging loans to franchisees by independent financial institutions.
TRAINING: Training consists of a one-month program in company training facility where franchisees learn ice cream-making techniques, preparation of fountain and other items, store operation, accounting, store maintenance, inventory control, and all other aspects of the operation.
MANAGERIAL ASSISTANCE: In addition to initial training, complete operations manuals and forms are provided. Franchisees are periodically provided with new flavor recipes and related promotional material. The company maintains full-time operations and product personnel who regularly visit stores to assist in managerial and product-related areas. These operations personnel are available at any time to assist franchisees upon request in addition to their regular visits.

Franchisees submit monthly operating statements to the company headquarters for analysis and comment.

SWIFT DAIRY & POULTRY COMPANY
115 West Jackson Boulevard
Chicago, IL 60604
(312) 431–2000
Contact: J. L. Anson

BUSINESS: Retail ice cream shop.
FRANCHISES: 225 in 15 states, Nassau, and Japan.
FOUNDED: 1963.
REQUIRED CAPITAL: Approximately $30,000.
FINANCIAL ASSISTANCE: Financial assistance is available from the company.
TRAINING: A complete program is provided which includes preopening training and on-the-job training.
MANAGERIAL ASSISTANCE: The shop owner is continuously assisted in all phases of merchandising and shop operations.

ZIP'Z
P.O. Box 5630
4470 Monroe Street
Toledo, OH 43617
(419) 475–8615
Contact: D. K. Combs

BUSINESS: Soft ice cream and yogurt shop.
FRANCHISES: 250 in 20 states and Canada.
FOUNDED: 1972.
REQUIRED CAPITAL: $9,500 minimum cash.
FINANCIAL ASSISTANCE: A total investment of $60,000 is necessary to open a franchise. This amount varies, plus or minus 10 percent depending on local code and amount of equipment. The company charges $9,500 for franchise licenses and will supply equipment to operator if requested. The company does not finance or lease equipment to operator. Franchisee must arrange own financing.
TRAINING: Seven-day minimum, 14-day maximum training school with complete bookkeeping, machine maintenance, operations, product, personnel training, and so on, at the company training school. Also provided is audiovisual training with an extensive operations manual. A supervisor opens every store and trains personnel in the store at opening.
MANAGERIAL ASSISTANCE: The company provides supervision of stores and outlets to purchase merchandise but does not sell food products directly to franchisees. The products must be bought from purveyors and must meet company standards. All printed materials must have the company logo and other

identification. Also, the company provides point of purchase materials for all stores and manual updates for new product developments.

GENERAL FRANCHISING CORPORATION
1350 Avenue of the Americas
Suite 2700
New York, NY 10019
(212) 586–2966
Contact: Jean Louis Poncet

BUSINESS: French restaurant specializing in crepes.

FRANCHISES: 30 in nine states.

FOUNDED: 1966.

REQUIRED CAPITAL: $85,000 which represents approximately one half of total investment.

FINANCIAL ASSISTANCE: Up to 50 percent of total investment through general contractors, provided potential franchisees shows financial stability. No outside assistance provided.

TRAINING: Five weeks of training in all phases and departments of the restaurant field.

MANAGERIAL ASSISTANCE: See "Training" above.

*INTERNATIONAL HOUSE OF PANCAKES
6837 Lankershim Boulevard
North Hollywood, CA 91605
(213) 982–2620
Contact: Joel R. Justice

BUSINESS: Fast-food, family-sytle restaurant featuring pancakes, steak and chicken dinners, and sandwiches.

FRANCHISES: Over 400 units in 38 states.

FOUNDED: 1958.

REQUIRED CAPITAL: $35,000 cash.

FINANCIAL ASSISTANCE: Total franchise fee is $65,000. Franchisee pays $35,000 cash down payment, balance payable at minimum interest rate, weekly. Franchisee also pays $10,000 cash for small equipment package.

TRAINING: Six weeks on-the-job training.

MANAGERIAL ASSISTANCE: The company provides complete turnkey operation, opening supervision, hiring of capable personnel plus weekly visits and assistance from field coordinators. Complete manual of operations specifies in detail precisely how each menu item is prepared and served and how the business is to be operated profitably.

* Asterisk denotes franchisor is a member of the International Franchise Association.

MARY BELLE RESTAURANTS
P.O. Box 531
1659 State Highway 88
Brick Town, NJ 08723
(201) 367–2333
Contact: Frank Georgalis

BUSINESS: Family-style restaurants.
FRANCHISES: 28 in New York, New Jersey, Connecticut, and Florida.
FOUNDED: 1974.
REQUIRED CAPITAL: $35,000 minimum.
FINANCIAL ASSISTANCE: Company will assist in locating financing. Rate of interest and term of financing dependent on franchisee's financial statement.
TRAINING: Up to 30-day training period provided in operating store with company in-store assistance.
MANAGERIAL ASSISTANCE: Management and technical assistance included in training period, with ongoing support from representatives. National and state-wide advertising programs will be developed by the company for implementation in franchisees area.

UNCLE JOHNS FAMILY RESTAURANTS
Division of Roxbury of America, Inc.
9808 Wilshire Boulevard, Suite 300
Los Angeles, CA 90212
(213) 878–3030
Contact: Stan Levy

BUSINESS: Family restaurant.
FRANCHISES: 14 in 13 states.
FOUNDED: 1958.
REQUIRED CAPITAL: Approximately $800,000.
FINANCIAL ASSISTANCE: None.
TRAINING: A minimum of four weeks on-the-job training for both the owner/operator or designee and an assistant manager.
MANAGERIAL ASSISTANCE: The company provides specifications and plans for the building, sign, and equipment. Also the company provides site selection approval, store opening supervision, an accounting system, advertising and marketing programs, purveyor orientation, product specifications, and guidance and counseling.

VAN'S BELGIAN WAFFLES, INC.
540 North Francisca Avenue
Redondo Beach, CA 90277
(213) 372–2620
Contact: Col. Douglas J. Horlander

BUSINESS: Belgian waffles and crepes.
FRANCHISES: 17 in five states.

FOUNDED: 1968.
REQUIRED CAPITAL: Approximately $45,000.
FINANCIAL ASSISTANCE: None.
TRAINING: Up to two weeks at franchisor's location in California.
MANAGERIAL ASSISTANCE: Ongoing assistance at no charge to the franchisee.

VILLAGE INN PANCAKE HOUSE, INC.
400 West 48th Avenue
Denver, CO 80216
(303) 892–5858
Contact: Scott Anderson

BUSINESS: Full-service restaurants specializing in pancakes.
FRANCHISES: 97 in 26 states.
FOUNDED: 1958.
REQUIRED CAPITAL: $75,000.
FINANCIAL ASSISTANCE: The company provides land and building, and sub-leases to franchisee. Also, the company provides assistance, when needed, in financing balance of equipment.
TRAINING: Ten weeks or more in Denver, Colorado, prior to opening, plus crew training after opening.
MANAGERIAL ASSISTANCE: Ongoing field supervisor; accounting service provided at no extra cost to franchisee.

*WAFFLE KING OF AMERICA, INC.
P.O. Box 2687
Huntington, WV 25726
(304) 525–7725
Contact: J. P. Andrews

BUSINESS: Coffee shop with sandwiches and full course dinners.
FRANCHISES: 3 in West Virginia, Virginia, and Kentucky.
FOUNDED: 1973.
REQUIRED CAPITAL: Approximately $25,000 exclusive of real estate.
FINANCIAL ASSISTANCE: No direct financial assistance; however, company will assist in preparing all loan applications and assist franchisee with the presentation of the application. Equipment leases have been arranged through private sources.
TRAINING: One-month training program for each franchisee prior to the opening of the store including classroom work and on-the-job training in an existing company store. Company personnel assist at each new location at time of opening.
MANAGERIAL ASSISTANCE: Managerial and technical assistance is provided throughout the term of the franchise. Regular visits by company personnel are designed to keep each franchisee up to date with the latest ideas regarding the business, and regular management meetings for both company and franchise managers are held.

*A & W INTERNATIONAL, INC.
922 Broadway
Santa Monica, CA 90406
(213) 395–3261
Contact: (Mrs.) Patricia A. Southall

BUSINESS: Drive-in, walk-in restaurants.
FRANCHISES: 1,700 in 44 states.
FOUNDED: 1919.
REQUIRED CAPITAL: Depends on market.
FINANCIAL ASSISTANCE: None.
TRAINING: Mandatory two-week training course.
MANAGERIAL ASSISTANCE: Continuous assistance from field personnel.

ACROSS THE STREET RESTAURANTS OF AMERICA, INC.
620 United Founders Tower
Oklahoma City, OK 73112
(405) 848–3501
Contact: Woody Farha

BUSINESS: Family charcoal hamburger restaurant specializing in one-quarter pound
hamburgers.
FRANCHISES: 14 in three states.
FOUNDED: 1964.
REQUIRED CAPITAL: $55,000 and up.
FINANCIAL ASSISTANCE: The company will counsel franchisee in obtaining a
loan.
TRAINING: The company provides 14 days of training for franchisee's management
at training center in Oklahoma City concerning all phases of operation: food
preparation, cooking, makeup, procedures, and so on. Company training personnel
sent to franchisee's restaurant to assist for ten days during restaurant opening.
MANAGERIAL ASSISTANCE: Company building plans and specifications provided
to franchisee. Also, the company provides site selection and operations manual
including policies, procedures, recipes, forms, and so on.

THE ALL AMERICAN BURGER, INC.
1888 Century Park East
Los Angeles, CA 90067
(213) 277–6161
Contact: Aaron M. Binder

BUSINESS: Fast-food restaurant.
FRANCHISES: 7 in California.
FOUNDED: 1968.
REQUIRED CAPITAL: $225,000 for freestanding store; $150,000 in-line store.
FINANCIAL ASSISTANCE: None.
TRAINING: Six weeks full store and office training.
MANAGERIAL ASSISTANCE: Continuous supervision and inspection teams. Fran-
chisor provides full supervision 30 days from opening of store.

   * Asterisk denotes franchisor is a member of the International Franchise Association.

AMFOOD INDUSTRY INC.
505 West Algonquin Road
Arlington Heights, IL 60004
(312) 593–2920
Contact: Anthony De Rosa

BUSINESS: Fast-food restaurant.

FRANCHISES: Approximately 29 in the United States.

FOUNDED: 1954.

REQUIRED CAPITAL: Franchisee's fee $5,000, must finance own property, building, and equipment.

FINANCIAL ASSISTANCE: None.

TRAINING: An intensive-training course is mandatory which provides the franchisee with managerial, promotional, operational, and skills. Also, actual drive-in operating conditions are part of the course.

MANAGERIAL ASSISTANCE: In addition to the operations manual which covers management, training, buying, accounting, and operational procedures, the company negotiates with purveyors to assure lowest wholesale chain store prices. Advertising, publicity and promotional programs are made available to the franchisee. Periodic visits are made by field consultants to each operator to discuss improvement of techniques, and so on.

ANGELINA'S PIZZA, INC.
596 Cleveland Street
Elyria, OH 44035
(216) 366–6151
Contact: John V. Naidenoff

BUSINESS: A pizza restaurant.

FRANCHISES: 3 in Ohio and Florida.

FOUNDED: 1956.

REQUIRED CAPITAL: $5,000—present franchise fee only.

FINANCIAL ASSISTANCE: Limited to the franchise fee.

TRAINING: Two weeks at a company store and one week at franchisee's store.

MANAGERIAL ASSISTANCE: The company furnishes operators manual, daily register sheets, assists in advertising and gives start-up assistance and continuous advice when needed.

ANGELO'S ITALIAN RESTAURANTS OF ILLINOIS, INC.
300 West North Street
Springfield, IL 62704
(217) 528–0449
Contact: Angelo Yannone

BUSINESS: Restaurant specializing in Italian food.

FRANCHISES: 20 in Illinois and Missouri.

FOUNDED: 1968.

REQUIRED CAPITAL: $45,000 excluding building and leasehold improvements. Cash investment about $12,000.

FINANCIAL ASSISTANCE: Assistance to franchisee in obtaining local financing.

TRAINING: Training is provided in a course of no less than 200 hours in an established operating restaurant. Training includes food preparation, merchandising, inventory control, cost and quality control, selection and training of personnel and money management.

MANAGERIAL ASSISTANCE: Periodic inspections and assistance are provided by company's management staff on a continual basis for the life of the franchise.

ARMAN'S SYSTEMS, INC.
6165 Central Avenue
Portage, IN 46368
(219) 762-6654
Contact: Arman Sarkisian

BUSINESS: Fast-food restaurant.
FRANCHISES: 12 in Indiana.
FOUNDED: 1967.
REQUIRED CAPITAL: $40,000 down; $85,000 total.
FINANCIAL ASSISTANCE: None. The company builds and leases to franchisee.
TRAINING: Training on the job at a company-owned store. Also two weeks after restaurant is open with company supervision.
MANAGERIAL ASSISTANCE: Periodic training in all phases of the business is provided franchisee.

*ARTHUR TREACHER'S FISH & CHIPS, INC.
1328 Dublin Road
Columbus, OH 43215
(614) 486-3636
Contact: Jim Jongeneel

BUSINESS: Fast-food restaurant.
FRANCHISES: 141 in 35 states, District of Columbia, and Canada.
FOUNDED: 1969.
REQUIRED CAPITAL: $50,000 to $300,000.
FINANCIAL ASSISTANCE: Terms for initial fee payment.
TRAINING: Ten-day training for franchisee or personnel at Arthur Treacher's institute, opening assistance, and continuous unit retraining.
MANAGERIAL ASSISTANCE: Periodic training in all phases of the business is provided franchisee.

BEEF-A-ROO, INC.
5419 North Second Street
Loves Park, IL 61111
(815) 877-6071
Contact: Dave L. DeBruler

BUSINESS: Fast-food restaurant.
FRANCHISES: Locations in Michigan, Iowa, Wisconsin, and Illinois.
FOUNDED: 1967.
REQUIRED CAPITAL: $15,000.

FINANCIAL ASSISTANCE: Assistance in arranging financing provided on individual basis.

TRAINING: Two weeks on-the-job training. Also two weeks at company training unit, opening assistance, retraining, and advisory services as necessary.

MANAGERIAL ASSISTANCE: Managerial and technical assistance on a regular bimonthly basis.

BIG DADDY'S RESTAURANTS
420 Lincoln Road Mall
Miami Beach, FL 33139
(305) 531–8881
Contact: Robert M. Napp, President
Larry Napp, Vice President

BUSINESS: Fast-food restaurant.

FRANCHISES: 5 in New York, Florida, and Canada.

FOUNDED: 1964.

REQUIRED CAPITAL: $75,000 to $100,000.

FINANCIAL ASSISTANCE: Total cost of turnkey investment is $100,000 to $200,000. Company will build unit and take back mortgage, which are required above $75,000 down payment.

TRAINING: Six to eight weeks, in Florida.

MANAGERIAL ASSISTANCE: Constant supervision and assistance provided.

BLACK ANGUS SYSTEMS, INC.
13001 North East 14th Avenue
North Miami, FL 33161
(305) 891–1120
Contact: Harry S. Langerman

BUSINESS: Restaurant and lounge.

FRANCHISES: 6 in Florida and Louisiana.

FOUNDED: 1958.

REQUIRED CAPITAL: $75,000 minimum.

FINANCIAL ASSISTANCE: None.

TRAINING: The franchisee and/or managerial staff are trained for a minimum of two weeks in an operating Black Angus restaurant. Additional supervision is given at the time of opening.

MANAGERIAL ASSISTANCE: The company will provide instruction in bookkeeping and auditing services.

BLIMPIE INTERNATIONAL, LTD.
370 Seventh Avenue
New York, NY 10001
(212) 795–1300
Contact: Peter De Carlo

BUSINESS: Sandwich shop.

FRANCHISES: 125 in 15 states and the District of Columbia.

FOUNDED: 1964.
REQUIRED CAPITAL: $20,000 to $25,000.
FINANCIAL ASSISTANCE: Total investment ranges from $50,000 to $60,000 with the balance financed over three years by the company.
TRAINING: Comprehensive two-week program. In addition training and coverage as needed during first few weeks of opening.
MANAGERIAL ASSISTANCE: Continual visits made by area consultant.

*BONANZA INTERNATIONAL, INC.
1000 Campbell Centre
8350 North Central Expressway
Dallas, TX 75206
(214) 363–1011
Contact: Edward Kosan

BUSINESS: Family restaurant.
FRANCHISES: Over 600 in 40 states and Canada.
FOUNDED: 1965.
REQUIRED CAPITAL: Amount depends on size of operation and franchising plan selected.
FINANCIAL ASSISTANCE: The company assists in securing financing.
TRAINING: One month of on-the-job training, plus one week of preopening training in company classrooms.
MANAGERIAL ASSISTANCE: Field sales consultants call upon franchisee at least twice per month.

BOY BLUE STORES, INC.
10919 West Janesville Road
Hales Corners, WI 53130
(414) 425–5160
Contact: Earl J. Phillips

BUSINESS: Restaurant.
FRANCHISES: 67 in 5 states and Canada.
FOUNDED: 1963.
REQUIRED CAPITAL: $15,000 to $20,000.
FINANCIAL ASSISTANCE: The company will assist the operator in finding sources of financing and will assist in the preparation of the necessary financial statements.
TRAINING: The franchisee is required to complete a ten-day training program at the National Headquarters training school and pass all the tests connected with the course.
MANAGERIAL ASSISTANCE: Semiannual advertising meetings and profit seminars for the franchisees.

BQF STEAKHOUSES
7850 Market Street
Youngstown, OH 44512
(216) 758–0997
Contact: Kenneth S. Moll

BUSINESS: Restaurant specializing in steaks.

FRANCHISES: 10 in five states.

FOUNDED: 1971.

REQUIRED CAPITAL: $25,000 to $40,000.

FINANCIAL ASSISTANCE: The company recommends sources it has experience and influence with, but no direct financing by company.

TRAINING: Intensive two-week on-the-job training for all new franchisees plus two weeks at franchisees outlet under the supervision of company staff members.

MANAGERIAL ASSISTANCE: The company provides continual management service for the life of the franchise in areas such as bookkeeping, advertising, inventory control, and complete manuals of operations. An area representative works with franchisees and visits stores regularly to assist in solutions to problems.

*BROWNS CHICKEN
800 Enterprise Drive
Oak Brook, IL 60521
(312) 654–0730
Contact: Phil Rohm

BUSINESS: Restaurant specializing in chicken.

FRANCHISES: 100 in five states.

FOUNDED: 1965.

REQUIRED CAPITAL: $100,000 to $150,000 plus, depending on franchisee's ability to obtain financing.

FINANCIAL ASSISTANCE: None.

TRAINING: Six weeks training school plus continual training on an inspection basis or request from franchisee.

MANAGERIAL ASSISTANCE: Formal training school, monthly field inspection, special assistance upon request, annual franchise seminar and spring and fall advertising meeting.

*BURGER CHEF SYSTEMS, INC.
P.O. Box 927
Indianapolis, IN 46206
(317) 299–8400
Contact: Richard S. Bollinger,
Public Relations Manager

BUSINESS: Fast-food restaurant.

FRANCHISES: Approximately 700 throughout the United States.

FOUNDED: 1954.

REQUIRED CAPITAL: $50,000 to $75,000 with a net worth of at least $150,000.

FINANCIAL ASSISTANCE: The company assists in locating and identifying financial sources.

TRAINING: Complete training program for manager (up to three) in all phases of restaurant operation and management.

MANAGERIAL ASSISTANCE: Managerial assistance on an ongoing basis through regular assigned area managers.

*BURGER KING CORPORATION
P.O. Box 520783
General Mail Facility
Miami, FL 33152
(305) 596–7011
Contact: Jeff Sieberger

BUSINESS: Fast-food restaurant.

FRANCHISES: Over 1,500 throughout the United States, Grand Bahama, Puerto Rico, Canada, and Spain.

FOUNDED: 1954.

REQUIRED CAPITAL: $90,000 with a net worth of at least $120,000.

FINANCIAL ASSISTANCE: Financing available in local banks and selected national finance companies.

TRAINING: Company-operated management training school providing extensive and detailed instruction in restaurant operation, equipment, administration for franchisees, management, or both.

MANAGERIAL ASSISTANCE: Operational assistance is provided every 30 to 45 days or as needed through regional and district offices.

*BURGER QUEEN ENTERPRISES, INC.
P.O. Box 6014
4000 Dupont Circle
Louisville, KY 40206
(502) 897–1766
Contact: George E. Clark

BUSINESS: Fast-food restaurant.

FRANCHISES: 116 in six states.

FOUNDED: 1962.

REQUIRED CAPITAL: $45,000.

FINANCIAL ASSISTANCE: Assistance in acquiring equipment loan.

TRAINING: Four-week development training program which includes combined unit and classroom work at special training unit. Also, follow-up visits at franchisee's unit by training director during next 25 weeks.

MANAGERIAL ASSISTANCE: Continued assistance in operations, accounting and taxes through coordinators and correspondence from the company headquarters.

BURGER TRAIN SYSTEMS, INC.
6508 South Barnes
Oklahoma City, OK 73159
(405) 685–5353
Contact: Edmond Hollie

BUSINESS: Fast-food restaurant.

FRANCHISES: 4 in Oklahoma and Texas.

FOUNDED: 1968.

REQUIRED CAPITAL: $20,000 and up, depending upon franchisee's ability to finance.

FINANCIAL ASSISTANCE: The company assists in locating financing. About $95,000 is the total investment required, which does not include building or land. Approximately $20,000 minimum for operating expenses required.

TRAINING: Four weeks mandatory training course for all new franchisees and operating personnel, alternating from office to store as needed.

MANAGERIAL ASSISTANCE: The company provides management service through the term of the franchise in all areas related to the operation, including, but not limited to, quality control, safety, public acceptance, advertising, innovation, counsel, and so on. The company also conducts product and marketing research.

CAPTAIN D'S
P.O. Box 1260
1724 Elm Hill Pike
Nashville, TN 37202
(615) 256–5201
Contact: Jim Hardy

BUSINESS: Fast-food restaurant.

FRANCHISES: 120 in 15 states.

FOUNDED: 1969.

REQUIRED CAPITAL: $35,000 and up depending on franchisee's ability to finance.

FINANCIAL ASSISTANCE: None.

TRAINING: Six weeks formal and in-store training plus continuing on-the-job supervision.

MANAGERIAL ASSISTANCE: All operation and technical services of the company are available to the franchisee.

CASEY JONES JUNCTION, INC.
6235 West Kellogg
Wichita, KS 67209
(316) 943–2363
Contact: M. Eugene Torline

BUSINESS: A family restaurant.

FRANCHISES: 8 in six states.

FOUNDED: 1968.

REQUIRED CAPITAL: From $10,000 to $40,000.

FINANCIAL ASSISTANCE: Financial assistance depends on the type of building, credit rating of the franchisee, judgment of franchisee's ability, the location of the restaurant, or furnish plans for a new building.

TRAINING: It is mandatory that the franchisee take at least two weeks' training at the company headquarters and participate in all functions of operating the restaurant as well as accounting and bookkeeping. In addition, the franchisee must be under the supervision of a company official for at least one week after the operation is opened.

MANAGERIAL ASSISTANCE: Technical assistance provided throughout term of franchise. Company will assist in any accounting problems at any time needed. Company will monitor all purchases and must approve of all purveyors as to quality of food, and so on, and will receive copies of invoices so that they may compare prices, quality, and so forth, with the entire system. Franchise operation inspected minimum of once every six months. Complete accounting statements must be provided to the franchisor each month. Should things appear to be wrong, immediate assistance is given the franchisee whether or not it is requested.

*CASSANO'S, INC.
1700 E. Stroop Road
Dayton, OH 45429
(513) 294–8400
Contact: Hank Ferrazza or Manager of Franchise Sales

BUSINESS: Restaurant specializing in pizza, seafood, sandwiches, and pastas.
FRANCHISES: 19 in six states.
FOUNDED: 1953.
REQUIRED CAPITAL: Total package (excluding building and leasehold improvements) amounts to approximately $170,000. Minimum cash investment, $100,000.
FINANCIAL ASSISTANCE: None.
TRAINING: Four weeks in-store and classroom instruction in company headquarters training stores.
MANAGERIAL ASSISTANCE: Marketing and advertising assistance, real estate assistance, accounting system both daily and monthly records, and engineering staff assistance. Field representatives make regularly scheduled visits.

CHICASEA, INC.
2004 Dabney Road
Richmond, VA 23230
(804) 353–7434
Contact: Martin E. Bandas

BUSINESS: Fast-food restaurant.
FRANCHISES: 20 in North Carolina and Virginia.
FOUNDED: 1967.
REQUIRED CAPITAL: $30,000.
FINANCIAL ASSISTANCE: $30,000 covers franchise fee, equipment, initial inventory, and beginning operating capital. Franchisees with good credit ratings are usually able to obtain financing for a portion of the initial capital needed.

TRAINING: The company provides training for the franchisee or a designee in the techniques and procedures of operating a franchise. Staff assistance is provided for the opening and is available as needed.

MANAGERIAL ASSISTANCE: The company staff is available for assistance in site location, planning and construction, equipment purchasing, and advertising. Trained personnel also advise on the use of the operations manual, which includes restaurant procedures, record keeping, forms and their use. The management staff is available at all times for counseling and guidance. Continuing inspections and supervisory training are provided throughout the term of the franchise agreement.

*CHICKEN DELIGHT
227 East Sunshine
Suite 119
Springfield, MO 65807
(417) 862–7875
Contact: Wendell E. Lejeune

BUSINESS: Fast-food restaurant.
FRANCHISES: 104 in ten states.
FOUNDED: 1952.
REQUIRED CAPITAL: $25,000 and ability to acquire equipment financing.
FINANCIAL ASSISTANCE: None.
TRAINING: On-the-job training which includes all phases of operation.
MANAGERIAL ASSISTANCE: Continual assistance in all phases of operation is offered.

CHICKEN UNLIMITED FAMILY RESTAURANTS
105 West Adams Street
Chicago, IL 60603
(312) 977–2345
Contact: Charles Wortman

BUSINESS: Fast-food restaurant.
FRANCHISES: 106 in eight states.
FOUNDED: 1964.
REQUIRED CAPITAL: Approximately $25,000.
FINANCIAL ASSISTANCE: After the down payment, which is included in the $25,000, the balance of the package will be financed for a seven-year term.
TRAINING: Owner/operator and/or manager and any staff people receive three weeks' training at company-owned and operated training units in Chicago, Miami, and Denver. During the first week of operation in franchisee's unit, an operations specialist is present to work with the operator and assist in the training of the new personnel.
MANAGERIAL ASSISTANCE: The company has a team of field operations specialists who visit each unit approximately once every two weeks for continuing management guidance, training, and assistance with promotions. Franchisee must follow computerized bookkeeping style.

COUNTRY KITCHEN INTERNATIONAL, INC.
7851 Metro Parkway
Suite 200
Bloomington, MN 55420
(612) 854–6333
Contact: Roy S. Lemaire, Director of Development

BUSINESS: Family restaurant.
FRANCHISES: 300 in 26 states.
FOUNDED: 1959.
REQUIRED CAPITAL: $57,000 not including land and building.
FINANCIAL ASSISTANCE: If necessary, guarantee lease and equipment financing is provided which includes a 10 percent signing fee.
TRAINING: On-the-job training and classroom up to 16 weeks plus assistance during opening.
MANAGERIAL ASSISTANCE: Supervision for the life of the contract, special menu service, meeting and advertising expertise, and consulting services. Construction supervision and site selection. Complete manuals and sound-on-slide training system.

COZZOLI CORPORATIONS
1027 6th Avenue
New York, NY 10001
(212) 221–2288
Contact: Michael P. Cozzoli

BUSINESS: Fast-food restaurant.
FRANCHISES: 39 in New York, New Jersey, and Florida.
FOUNDED: 1951.
REQUIRED CAPITAL: $30,000 to $40,000.
FINANCIAL ASSISTANCE: Complete financial assistance beyond the down payment.
TRAINING: Two weeks in existing store and at least one week in franchisee's store under supervision.
MANAGERIAL ASSISTANCE: Periodic training in all phases of the business is provided franchisee.

*CRAIG FOOD INDUSTRIES
P.O. Box 9255
Ogden, UT 84409
(801) 621–5464
Contact: E. D. Craig

BUSINESS: Fast-food restaurant specializing in Mexican food.
FRANCHISES: 102 in ten states.
FOUNDED: 1967.
REQUIRED CAPITAL: $30,000 to $40,000.
FINANCIAL ASSISTANCE: None.
TRAINING: The franchisee and any key personnel will be trained a maximum of four weeks in classrooms and on the job.

MANAGERIAL ASSISTANCE: Company representatives will be available on a continuous basis for consultation and advice on operations. Field representatives will call periodically on the franchisee's business operation, make suggestions, and generally assist the franchise operator.

DAIRY CHEER STORES
2914 Forgey Street
Ashland, KY 41101
(606) 324–5061
Contact: W. H. Culbertson

BUSINESS: Fast-food restaurant.
FRANCHISES: 12 in Kentucky, Tennessee, West Virginia, and Ohio.
FOUNDED: 1949.
REQUIRED CAPITAL: $5,000 franchise fee; building, $60,000; equipment, $50,000.
FINANCIAL ASSISTANCE: Equipment financed 100 percent.
TRAINING: On-the-job training before and after opening.
MANAGERIAL ASSISTANCE: Instructions in technical operations, inspections, advertising, formulas, and recipes.

DAIRY SWEET COMPANY
610 Des Moines Street
Ankeny, IA 50021
(515) 964–4226
Contact: C. O. Howell

BUSINESS: Fast-food restaurant.
FRANCHISES: 205 in ten states.
FOUNDED: 1952.
REQUIRED CAPITAL: $10,000.
FINANCIAL ASSISTANCE: 75 percent financing to qualified applicants.
TRAINING: On-the-job training at time of installation. Time depends on the individual and how much is necessary. Usually two days is sufficient.
MANAGERIAL ASSISTANCE: Continuous as long as franchisee wants assistance.

DER WIENERSCHNITZEL INTERNATIONAL, INC.
4440 Bon Karman Boulevard
Newport Beach, CA 92660
(714) 752–5800
Contact: Dan Ryan

BUSINESS: Fast-food restaurant specializing in hot dogs and hamburgers.
FRANCHISES: 300 in 22 states.
FOUNDED: 1961.
REQUIRED CAPITAL: $45,000 to $130,000.
FINANCIAL ASSISTANCE: None.
TRAINING: Six weeks of training provided.
MANAGERIAL ASSISTANCE: Periodic training in all phases of the business is provided franchisee.

DICKIES FISH & CHIPS
10133 East 30th Street
Tulsa, OK 74129
(918) 663-9363
Contact: F. L. Swanson

BUSINESS: Fast-food restaurant.
FRANCHISES: 5 in Oklahoma.
FOUNDED: 1970.
REQUIRED CAPITAL: $20,000.
FINANCIAL ASSISTANCE: Limited.
TRAINING: Three months in company-owned stores.
MANAGERIAL ASSISTANCE: Continued monitoring and assistance when and
where needed.

*DINO'S INC.
2085 Inkster Road
Garden City, MI 48135
(313) 261-9460
Contact: Harold C. Gant

BUSINESS: Pizzeria restaurant.
FRANCHISES: 140 in five states.
FOUNDED: 1961.
REQUIRED CAPITAL: $25,000.
FINANCIAL ASSISTANCE: Financial assistance arranged through local lending
institutions to $30,000 to $43,000.
TRAINING: A special training program is provided to familiarize the franchisee or
manager with the operation. The schooling includes on-the-job training. The
company also supplies an operating manual. A specialist will work in the unit
until the first week of operation or at the grand opening.
MANAGERIAL ASSISTANCE: Full-time quality controller visits all locations on a
regularly scheduled basis.

*DOG N SUDS RESTAURANTS
1420 Crestmont Avenue
Camden, NJ 08101
(609) 996-7500
Contact: Michael W. Fessler, Executive Vice President

BUSINESS: Fast-food restaurant.
FRANCHISES: 160 in 19 states and Canada.
FOUNDED: 1953.
REQUIRED CAPITAL: $18,000 to $25,000. Franchisee responsible for land and
building financing.
FINANCIAL ASSISTANCE: Direction for financial assistance is given.
TRAINING: Extensive training at Rover College plus opening assistance by field
service department.
MANAGERIAL ASSISTANCE: Continued assistance by regional managers.

142

*DOMINO'S PIZZA, INC.
2865 Broadwalk Drive
Ann Arbor, MI 48104
(313) 668–4000
Contact: Oscar Schreiber

BUSINESS: Restaurant specializing in pizza, carryout and delivery only.
FRANCHISES: 175 in 17 states.
FOUNDED: 1960.
REQUIRED CAPITAL: $18,500 minimum (some particular situations require more).
FINANCIAL ASSISTANCE: Suggestional consultation offered.
TRAINING: Training and supervision is provided on the job in company stores until ready, up to nine months.
MANAGERIAL ASSISTANCE: The company keeps close ties with its franchisees and provides on-call assistance for the franchise. Distributors, with jurisdiction over some large areas, keep communication lines open between the franchisees and the parent company through frequent correspondence, meetings, and a weekly newsletter. Domino's representatives visit the shops regularly. In addition, Domino's offers asistance to its franchisees in the form of recommendations concerning personnel, equipment, and production activities.

EL CHICO CORPORATION
1925 Valley View Lane
Dallas, TX 75234
(214) 247–9186
Contact: Bill Keith

BUSINESS: Mexican food restaurants.
FRANCHISES: 7 in Texas, Louisiana, and Arkansas.
FOUNDED: 1969.
REQUIRED CAPITAL: Approximately $100,000.
FINANCIAL ASSISTANCE: Lease guaranteed by franchisor on land and building.
TRAINING: Orientation with supervisor in overall operations of Mexican food specialty restaurant. Concentrated one-month training program of restaurant chefs, partially in company-owned facilities and partially in franchisee's restaurant.
MANAGERIAL ASSISTANCE: Continued supervision of food preparation and quality throughout life of franchise contract.

*FAMOUS RECIPE FRIED CHICKEN, INC.
11315 Reed Hartman Highway
Cincinnati, OH 45241
(513) 984–4000
Contact: Robert Acker

BUSINESS: Fast-food restaurant.
FRANCHISES: 175 in 20 states and Trinidad, W.I.

FOUNDED: 1965.

REQUIRED CAPITAL: $60,000.

FINANCIAL ASSISTANCE: The company does not provide financial assistance.

TRAINING: A two-week formal training and management course is required for all new franchisees or their managers and is conducted by qualified instructors at the company's training facilities in Cincinnati, Ohio, plus five days of supervision and training at franchisee's location during initial start-up period.

MANAGERIAL ASSISTANCE: The company provides standard building plans, advertising, operations, and equipment manuals. Assistance in lease negotiations is also available. Quarterly visits by regional supervisors to assist in any problem areas. Advertising division provides promotional and advertising materials and recommends programs for local markets. Annual national convention is conducted for exchange of new ideas, food preparation methods, and promotional programs.

FAST FOODS, INC.
Division of Jiffy Drive-Ins
136 St. Mathews Avenue
Louisville, KY 40207
(502) 896–1811
Contact: Ralph W. Pettit

BUSINESS: Fast-food restaurant.

FRANCHISES: 14 in Kentucky, Georgia, North Carolina, and Wyoming.

FOUNDED: 1953.

REQUIRED CAPITAL: $25,000.

FINANCIAL ASSISTANCE: Financing available in local banks and selected national finance companies.

TRAINING: Two-week on-the-job intensive training in company restaurants and company headquarters in all functions of operating the restaurant, inventory control, payroll procedure, and general accounting.

MANAGERIAL ASSISTANCE: The franchisee and/or manager must be under supervision of a company official throughout recruiting of restaurant employees, and 15 days after operation begins. Continued follow-up thereafter. Monthly SOP (standard operating procedures) inspections. Set up all food and paper suppliers. Negotiate and maintain price controls, also advertising and promotional guidance.

FROSTOP CORPORATION
12 First Street
Pelham, NY 10803
(914) 738–4333
Contact: J. J. Connolly

BUSINESS: Fast-food restaurant.

FRANCHISES: Over 400 in 30 states.

FOUNDED: 1926.

REQUIRED CAPITAL: Drive-ins, $10,000 and snack bars, $10,000 minimum.

FINANCIAL ASSISTANCE: Total investments vary according to land and building costs for drive-ins. Snack bars in discount stores range from $10,000 to $20,000. Balances after down payments are financed by franchisee's local banks.

TRAINING: Two weeks in-store training. Operational manuals are provided.

MANAGERIAL ASSISTANCE: The company provides continual management service for the life of the franchise in such areas as menu, advertising, and promotions. Complete manuals of operations, forms, and directions are also provided. In addition, the company sponsors meetings of franchisees and conducts marketing and product research to maintain high Frostop consumer acceptance.

GOLDEN CHICKEN FRANCHISES
3810 West National Avenue
Milwaukee, WI 53215
(414) 384–3160
Contact: Robert L. Bloom

BUSINESS: Fast-food restaurant.

FRANCHISES: 24 in Wisconsin and Minnesota.

FOUNDED: 1959.

REQUIRED CAPITAL: $3,500 for franchise fee plus net cost for equipment and setup.

FINANCIAL ASSISTANCE: A total investment of approximately $20,000 is needed. The company does no financing but will assist franchisee in securing sources. Primary source of financing has been leasing companies. Franchisee puts up $5,000 for franchise fee, lease and security deposits, and working capital. Balance usually financed over 60-month period.

TRAINING: Franchisee must spend seven days at a company store. A company representative spends 14 days with franchisee in the unit after opening.

MANAGERIAL ASSISTANCE: The company provides continual management service for the life of franchising agreement in such areas as bookkeeping, advertising, and promotions. The company visits stores a minimum of once a year, sponsors meetings of franchisees, and keeps franchisee informed of new products and promotions via newsletters.

*GOLDEN SKILLET COMPANIES
2819 Parham Road
Richmond, VA 23229
(804) 747–0650
Contact: Fran W. Brown

BUSINESS: Fast-food restaurant.

FRANCHISES: 200 in 16 states, Canada, Japan, and Puerto Rico.

FOUNDED: 1963.

REQUIRED CAPITAL: $30,000 with a $10,000 franchise fee included.

FINANCIAL ASSISTANCE: Equipment package including all signs and cash registers is $54,000. The company will assist in arrangement of leasing, if desired.

TRAINING: Franchisees receive 14 days of intensive mandatory training in all aspects of the operation. The first week's training is given at company headquarters.

MANAGERIAL ASSISTANCE: The company provides a full range of support services to its franchisees. These include plans and specifications for building, signs, equipment and supplies, advertising materials, bookkeeping and record-keeping systems, confidential operations manual, and the ongoing assistance by field personnel.

GREENTREE ENTERPRISES, INC.
d.b.a. Juice Factory
2247 North High Street
Columbus, OH 43201
(614) 291–5591
Contact: Barnett Greenbaum

BUSINESS: A restaurant specializing in meatless meals and a variety of fruit juices.

FRANCHISES: 3 in Ohio.

FOUNDED: 1975.

REQUIRED CAPITAL: $60,000 minimum.

FINANCIAL ASSISTANCE: Franchisee must have own source of financing.

TRAINING: Two weeks on-the-job training in existing units. One week at franchisee's outlet.

MANAGERIAL ASSISTANCE: Assistance in bookkeeping, advertisement, and inventory control. Also, the company publishes a newsletter discussing new products and visits by company personnel to outlets.

HAPPY JOE'S PIZZA & ICE CREAM PARLORS
1875 Middle Road
Bettendorf, IA 52722
(319) 359–7511
Contact: James K. Orr

BUSINESS: Fast-food restaurant.

FRANCHISES: 96 in 17 states.

FOUNDED: 1972.

REQUIRED CAPITAL: $80,000 minimum.

FINANCIAL ASSISTANCE: None.

TRAINING: Extensive on-the-job training including all facets of the operation lasting up to 30 days.

MANAGERIAL ASSISTANCE: Complete assistance and supervision in opening the business and an ongoing program of managerial and operational training and assistance from field supervisors. Additional assistance in advertising and promotion is also available.

THE HAPPY STEAK, INC.
1118 North Fulton Street
Fresno, CA 93728
(209) 485–8520
Contact: H. T. Brooks

BUSINESS: Family restaurant.
FRANCHISES: 35 in California.
FOUNDED: 1969.
REQUIRED CAPITAL: $35,000 franchise fee plus building construction, equipment and so on.
FINANCIAL ASSISTANCE: When required, company guarantees are provided. Personal notes are accepted by the company for franchise and equipment packages.
TRAINING: Approximately three weeks in-store training.
MANAGERIAL ASSISTANCE: Operations officer oversees the first two full weeks of operation.

*HARDEE'S FOOD SYSTEMS, INC.
P.O. Box 1619
1233 North Church Street
Rocky Mount, NC 27801
(919) 977–2000
Contact: Donald R. Mucci

BUSINESS: Fast-food restaurants.
FRANCHISES: 1,065 in 33 states, Central America, and Japan.
FOUNDED: 1962.
REQUIRED CAPITAL: $140,000 plus land and building.
FINANCIAL ASSISTANCE: No financial assistance available.
TRAINING: Five weeks' training in field and one at company headquarters. Recommended in-restaurant training prior to school attendance. Ten days' training and supervision at restaurant upon opening.
MANAGERIAL ASSISTANCE: Hardee's provides continued supervision on a scheduled basis and also provides bookkeeping methods, advertising direction, operating controls, complete operating manual, basic forms, and continued advice and counseling.

HEAVENLY FRIED CHICKEN, INC.
650 Americand
Annapolis, MD 21403
(301) 268–8187
Contact: Wayne Walter

BUSINESS: Fast-food restaurant.
FRANCHISES: 56 in 28 states.
FOUNDED: 1954.
REQUIRED CAPITAL: $2,000 to $3,800.

FINANCIAL ASSISTANCE: The company will finance $1,500.

TRAINING: Initially, two days of training with more available if necessary.

MANAGERIAL ASSISTANCE: The company provides process manuals, operating control systems, equipment layout and purchasing, labor and operating counseling.

*INTERNATIONAL DAIRY QUEEN, INC.
Box 35286
5701 Green Valley Drive
Minneapolis, MN 55435
(612) 836–0327
Contact: Bruce Bloom

BUSINESS: Fast-food restaurant.

FRANCHISES: 4,790 in the United States and 8 foreign countries.

FOUNDED: 1962.

REQUIRED CAPITAL: The franchise fee is $20,000. All prospective franchisees must meet certain financial requirements, one of which is $60,000 cash liquidity.

FINANCIAL ASSISTANCE: The company offers franchisees an opportunity to lease equipment for a period of five to seven years with a security deposit. Qualified franchisees may also purchase equipment on a conditional sales contract over a five-year payment period with the required down payment.

TRAINING: The company offers an intensive two-week training course to all new and existing franchisees. The course covers sanitation, sales promotion, inventory control, and basic functions of management. The company also offers new franchisees the services of a special opening team that assists operators at openings.

MANAGERIAL ASSISTANCE: The company maintains an operations specialty division in addition to regional and district managers, who provide continuing assistance involving store operation, product quality, customer convenience, product development, advertising, financial control, training, communication, and incentives. A research and development department is engaged in developing new products, cooking methods and procedures. Sales promotion programs are conducted through newspapers, radio, television, and billboards.

*JERRY'S RESTAURANTS
Jerrico, Inc.
P.O. Box 11988
Lexington, KY 40579
(606) 268–5343
Contact: Don Hippensteel

BUSINESS: Family restaurant.

FRANCHISES: 36 in Kentucky, Tennessee, Ohio, Indiana, and Florida.

FOUNDED: 1929.

REQUIRED CAPITAL: $100,000.

FINANCIAL ASSISTANCE: Assistance to qualified applicants.

TRAINING: Complete training course for management. Opening assistance in the form of traveling supervisory crew.

MANAGERIAL ASSISTANCE: Continued supervision program through field consultants.

JRECK ENTERPRISES, INC.
671 Mill Street
Watertown, NY 13601
(315) 782-0760
Contact: Ellis R. Martin

BUSINESS: Submarine sandwiches restaurant.
FRANCHISES: 28 in New York, Ohio, and Florida.
FOUNDED: 1967.
REQUIRED CAPITAL: $5,000 to $15,000.
FINANCIAL ASSISTANCE: Assistance in securing outside financing.
TRAINING: Three weeks of intensive in-store training, which includes bookkeeping, inventory control, and personnel expertise.
MANAGERIAL ASSISTANCE: Marketing, advertising assistance, lease negotiation, and legal assistance.

JUICE FACTORY. See Greentree Enterprises, Inc.

*KFC CORPORATION
P.O. Box 32070
Louisville, KY 40213
(502) 459-8600
Contact: John Cox

BUSINESS: Fast-food restaurant.
FRANCHISES: 690 in all states except Montana, Utah, and Florida.
FOUNDED: 1964.
REQUIRED CAPITAL: $30,000 cash plus ability to finance land, building, and equipment.
FINANCIAL ASSISTANCE: Finance up to 80 percent of equipment package with average equipment package amounting to $45,000 to $62,000.
TRAINING: Required of all new franchisees and recommended for key employees: One-week training seminar covering proper store operation including management, accounting, sales, advertising, catering, and purchasing. Ongoing training provided in areas of customer service, general restaurant management, and quality control. Also available are sales hostess instruction, seminars for instruction of specific company programs, and equipment such as the Automatic Cooker. Franchisees are also provided with confidential operating manuals.
MANAGERIAL ASSISTANCE: Engineering assistance regarding best suited building, blueprints, recommended floor plan layout, and placement of selected equipment. Also, the company provides field services assistance including store opening, periodic visits to assist in matters dealing with daily store operation, quality control standard. In addition, the company offers regional and local seminars and workshops.

LIL' DUFFER OF AMERICA, INC.
2208 Hancock Street
Bellevue, NB 68005
(402) 291–2040
Contact: J. W. Beardmore

BUSINESS: Fast-food restaurant.

FRANCHISES: 18 in Iowa, Nebraska, South Dakota, Kansas, and Missouri.

FOUNDED: 1966.

REQUIRED CAPITAL: At least $25,000 and substantial net worth.

FINANCIAL ASSISTANCE: The company assists franchisee in arranging needed financial assistance.

TRAINING: Franchisees are trained at their own expense for a minimum of two weeks in an existing store prior to opening. Company supervisors assist in training franchise personnel prior to and during the opening. Field supervisors give continuing assistance as long as agreement is in effect.

MANAGERIAL ASSISTANCE: Regular visits by field supervisors. Advertising program, accounting system, and management training provided by the company. Advice and consultation available on request.

LITTLE CAESAR ENTERPRISES, INC.
38700 Grand River Avenue
Farmington Hills, MI 48018
(313) 478–6200
Contact: Michael Ilitch

BUSINESS: Fast-food restaurants and carryout stores.

FRANCHISES: 102 in Michigan, Ohio, Pennsylvania, Florida, and Canada.

FOUNDED: 1962.

REQUIRED CAPITAL: Carryout store: $50,000–$60,000 including $17,000 franchise fee; restaurants: $350,000–$450,000 including franchise fee.

FINANCIAL ASSISTANCE: None.

TRAINING: Two weeks on-the-job training.

MANAGERIAL ASSISTANCE: Operations, real estate/construction, and accounting.

LONDON FISH 'N CHIPS, LTD.
306 South Maple Avenue
South San Francisco, CA 94080
(415) 873–1300
Contact: Fred Hoffman

BUSINESS: Fast-food restaurant.

FRANCHISES: 16 in California.

FOUNDED: 1967.

REQUIRED CAPITAL: $35,000 plus real estate modification.

FINANCIAL ASSISTANCE: The company will finance all equipment on a security agreement and personal note.

TRAINING: On-the-job training in company and franchisee's shop. Also, supervision in franchisee's shop as needed.

MANAGERIAL ASSISTANCE: Help with bookkeeping. Advice on new methods and products and selling procedures for duration of franchise. Provide periodic inspection and instruction as needed.

*LONG JOHN SILVER'S INC.
Subsidiary of Jerrico, Inc.
P.O. Box 11988
Lexington, KY 40511
(606) 269–8811
Contact: Eugene O. Getchell

BUSINESS: Fast-food restaurant.

FRANCHISES: 290 in the United States.

FOUNDED: 1929.

REQUIRED CAPITAL: $30,000 with lease, $300,000 and up with purchase of land and equipment. Company looks for multiunit franchisees.

FINANCIAL ASSISTANCE: None.

TRAINING: Two weeks of formal training course for management.

MANAGERIAL ASSISTANCE: Continued supervision program in all phases of management through field supervisors and company personnel.

LOSURDO FOODS, INC.
20 Owens Road
Hackensack, NJ 07601
(201) 343–6680
Contact: Michael Losurdo

BUSINESS: Italian restaurant which specializes in pizza.

FRANCHISES: 10 in New York, New Jersey, Pennsylvania, and North Carolina.

FOUNDED: 1968.

REQUIRED CAPITAL: $25,000.

FINANCIAL ASSISTANCE: None.

TRAINING: Two-week training period plus regular monthly training session.

MANAGERIAL ASSISTANCE: Continual assistance in product preparation and advertising.

*LOVE'S ENTERPRISES, INC.
6837 Lankershim Boulevard
North Hollywood, CA 91605
(213) 982–2620
Contact: Ronald C. Mesker

BUSINESS: Family restaurant and cocktail lounge.

FRANCHISES: 53 in six states.

FOUNDED: 1948.

REQUIRED CAPITAL: $75,000 plus $25,000 preopening inventory and liquor license. Also franchisee is responsible for acquiring lease and land.

FINANCIAL ASSISTANCE: The company provides assistance to applicants with proper credit standing.

TRAINING: Six weeks on-the-job training and classroom instruction.

MANAGERIAL ASSISTANCE: The company provides complete turnkey operation, opening supervision, hiring of capable personnel plus frequent visits, and assistance from field coordinators. Complete manual of operations specifies in detail precisely how each menu item is prepared and served and how the business is to be operated effectively.

*LUM'S RESTAURANT CORPORATION
8410 NW 53rd Terrace
Suite 200
Miami, FL 33166
(502) 426-6515
Contact: Donald L. Perlyn

BUSINESS: Fast-food restaurant.

FRANCHISES: 284 in 30 states.

FOUNDED: 1965.

REQUIRED CAPITAL: $70,000.

FINANCIAL ASSISTANCE: None.

TRAINING: Three weeks of classroom and practical training at company headquarters in Miami, Florida. Training covers all aspects of the business—operational procedures, bookkeeping, employee training, and management techniques. During the first two weeks of operation in the franchisee's restaurant, a team of operations consultants is present to supervise the opening and assist in the training of all new personnel.

MANAGERIAL ASSISTANCE: Company field consultants visit unit periodically for inspection and assistance. Company personnel available to render assistance as required. Franchisee is issued a complete standard operating procedure manual which is constantly updated The company sponsors seminars of franchisees and conducts marketing and product research. Bimonthly newsletter sent to franchisee.

MAID RITE PRODUCTS, INC.
100 East Second Street
Muscatine, IA 52761
(319) 263-5331
Contact: William F. Angell

BUSINESS: Fast-food restaurant.

FRANCHISES: 150 in most states.

FOUNDED: 1928.

REQUIRED CAPITAL: $3,000 average franchise fee.

FINANCIAL ASSISTANCE: None.

TRAINING: Complete on-the-job and classroom training.

MANAGERIAL ASSISTANCE: Company personnel available at all times to offer advice and counsel on any and all aspects of the operation. Franchisee is provided with complete operating manuals and procedures.

*McDONALD'S SYSTEM, INC.
Subsidiary of McDonald's Corporation
1 McDonald's Plaza
Oak Brook, IL 60521
(312) 887–3200
Contact: Licensing Manager

BUSINESS: Fast-food restaurant.

FRANCHISES: 4,207 in all 50 states and international.

FOUNDED: 1955.

REQUIRED CAPITAL: $100,000 and ability to acquire $140,000 minimum financing.

FINANCIAL ASSISTANCE: None.

TRAINING: Minimum of 100 hours pre-registration and 300 hours plus post-registration; formal training of two weeks in general area of franchisee plus 11 days of managerial training at Hamburger University in Elk Grove, Illinois.

MANAGERIAL ASSISTANCE: Operations, training, maintenance, and equipment manuals provided. Company makes available promotional advertising material plus field representative consultation and assistance.

MINUTE MAN OF AMERICA, INC.
P.O. Box 828
701 Collins
Little Rock, AR 72205
(501) 376–8271
Contact: Vernon L. Rodgers

BUSINESS: Fast-food restaurant.

FRANCHISES: 23 in two states.

FOUNDED: 1965.

REQUIRED CAPITAL: $65,000 turnkey plus lease on ground and building.

FINANCIAL ASSISTANCE: Advice and counsel only.

TRAINING: Six-week training required at company headquarters at the expense of franchisee. Trainee will receive $200 weekly while training.

MANAGERIAL ASSISTANCE: Real estate selection based on computer test volume. Help in lease negotiation and equipment purchasing. Manager manual and on-the-job help in hiring and training first crew. Complete advertising programs through National Advertising Committee. Continuous visitation and invitational meetings.

MISTER S'GETTI RESTAURANT
2015 South Calhoun Street
Fort Wayne, IN 46804
(219) 456–3596
Contact: Charles H. Sanderson

BUSINESS: Fast-food restaurant specializing in spaghetti.

FRANCHISES: 3 in Florida.

FOUNDED: 1968.

REQUIRED CAPITAL: $7,500.

FINANCIAL ASSISTANCE: A total investment of $20,000 to $50,000 is needed, depending on size of restaurant. The company will finance or secure financing for the franchisee with good credit references.

TRAINING: The franchisee is sent to the pilot restaurant for two weeks prior to the opening to obtain intensive training in every phase of the operation. A representative helps to open and works with the franchisee for two weeks and then checks and monitors the operation on a monthly basis.

MANAGERIAL ASSISTANCE: The franchisee has available a 24-hour, seven days a week open phone line to answer any questions pertaining to the operation. Monthly inspections are made to assure sanitary measures are being used, and quality control of the food and service are at top levels. Records are kept and figured in percentages to gross sales to eliminate unneeded expenses and to discourage pilferage. Percentages are computed monthly and if any one item is out of line, it is drawn to the attention of the franchisee immediately.

MOM'S PIZZA, INC.
4457 Main Street
Philadelphia, PA 19127
(215) 482–1644
Contact: Nicholos Castellucci

BUSINESS: Fast-food restaurant.

FRANCHISES: 18 in Pennsylvania, Maryland, and New Jersey.

FOUNDED: 1961.

REQUIRED CAPITAL: $90,000.

FINANCIAL ASSISTANCE: Bank financing assistance if applicant has good credit standing.

TRAINING: Two weeks.

MANAGERIAL ASSISTANCE: Continued help from company headquarters.

MR. DUNDERBAK, INC.
P.O. Box 912
Rocky Mount, NC 27801
(919) 443–3326
Contact: R. D. Gorham

BUSINESS: A specialty food shop featuring cheese, sausages, gourmet foods, deli-type sandwiches and German sausages.

FRANCHISES: 28 in 14 states.

FOUNDED: 1962.

REQUIRED CAPITAL: $50,000.

FINANCIAL ASSISTANCE: Advice and counsel on local bank financing.

TRAINING: Five weeks in company-operated store. Two weeks on-site at opening with company staff assistance.

MANAGERIAL ASSISTANCE: Operating manuals with continuous update and bulletins and visits by company personnel to assist with general operations and specific problems.

*MR. STEAK, INC.
International Headquarters
5100 Race Court
Denver, CO 80217
(303) 292–3070
Contact: Licensing Manager

BUSINESS: Family-style restaurant.
FRANCHISES: 275 in 36 states and Canada.
FOUNDED: 1962.
REQUIRED CAPITAL: $50,400.
FINANCIAL ASSISTANCE: The total cash investment required is approximately $50,000 if franchisees can secure their own financing. Cost varies with lease deposits for local area. A purchase agreement for the franchise in the amount of $5,000 secures the area with the balance of $15,500 due when land and building lease is secured on site location purchased. Franchisee is responsible for securing land and building lease and equipment financing.
TRAINING: Comprehensive seven weeks mandatory training is provided with the franchise fee for the restaurant manager. Salary, travel, food, and lodging are the responsibility of the trainee while in training.
MANAGERIAL ASSISTANCE: Opening and continuing assistance is provided by the company. Kinds and amount of assistance provided by the company is limited.

*NATHAN'S FAMOUS, INC.
1515 Broadway
New York, NY 10036
(212) 869–0600
Contact: Harold Norbitz

BUSINESS: Fast-food restaurant.
FRANCHISES: 12 in New York, Florida, and California.
FOUNDED: 1916.
REQUIRED CAPITAL: Varies depending upon size and location of restaurant.
FINANCIAL ASSISTANCE: None.
TRAINING: Intensive, mandatory training for key personnel. Training could be four weeks at company's location. Training is formalized and under direction of the company.
MANAGERIAL ASSISTANCE: Continual management supervision. The company provides assistance in operations, food preparation, food specification, accounting, and advertising. Complete manual of operation is provided and field supervision is conducted by the company to assist franchisee. In addition, the company continually engages in research and development.

*NICKERSON FARMS FRANCHISING COMPANY
4135 South 89th Street
Omaha, NB 68127
(402) 331–0404
Contact: Robert L. Francis

BUSINESS: A combination restaurant, gift shop, and gasoline retailer on interstate locations.
FRANCHISES: 3 in Indiana and Tennessee.
FOUNDED: 1966.
REQUIRED CAPITAL: $50,000 plus building and land.
FINANCIAL ASSISTANCE: None.
TRAINING: Ten weeks formal training including on-the-job training in a company-operated unit.
MANAGERIAL ASSISTANCE: Periodic field inspections and special assistance upon unit openings.

*NOBLE ROMAN'S INC.
2909 Buick Cadillac Boulevard
Bloomington, IN 47401
(812) 339–3533
Contact: Gary Clarke, Vice President, Unit Development

BUSINESS: Family restaurant specializing in pizza and Italian foods.
FRANCHISES: 48 in the Midwest.
FOUNDED: 1972.
REQUIRED CAPITAL: $7,500 to $12,500.
FINANCIAL ASSISTANCE: None.
TRAINING: Complete training is provided at a company-operated unit. The standard training period is approximately six weeks.
MANAGERIAL ASSISTANCE: Managerial and technical assistance is provided.

*ORANGE JULIUS OF AMERICA
3219 Wilshire Boulevard
Santa Monica, CA 90403
(213) 829–7611
Contact: Robert M. Singer

BUSINESS: Fast-food restaurant.
FRANCHISES: 333 in 42 states, Canada, Europe, Australia, and the Philippines.
FOUNDED: 1926.
REQUIRED CAPITAL: Approximately $30,000 to $50,000.
FINANCIAL ASSISTANCE: A total investment of approximately $75,000 to $120,000 is required. This amount is dependent upon the size of the store, menu selection, and the type of equipment required. The franchisees are required to arrange their own financing. Traditionally, franchisees have been able to contribute one-half in equity and finance one half of the total investment, through their own financial sources. Franchises are sold on the basis of individual units. The franchisee pays for the cost of construction. The company develops site location.

TRAINING: On-site training, approximately ten days, including preopening training and training subsequent to the initial opening of the franchise.

MANAGERIAL ASSISTANCE: Managerial and technical assistance is provided for site selection, construction, equipment purchase, training of personnel and management. Ongoing supervision is provided.

PACIFIC TASTEE FREEZ, INC.
1101 South Cypress Street
La Habra, CA 90631
(213) 694–1061
Contact: N. W. Axene

BUSINESS: Fast-food restaurant.

FRANCHISES: 74 in California and Oregon.

FOUNDED: 1955.

REQUIRED CAPITAL: Approximately $20,000 to $30,000, including operating capital.

FINANCIAL ASSISTANCE: Equipment financing and/or leasing assistance available.

TRAINING: Five weeks in-store training.

MANAGERIAL ASSISTANCE: Assistance through field representatives for duration of franchise agreement.

PAIL-O-CHICKEN, INC.
1996 North E. Street
San Bernardino, CA 92405
(714) 886–5512
Contact: William J. Schaeffer

BUSINESS: Carryout operation.

FRANCHISES: 3 in California.

FOUNDED: 1967.

REQUIRED CAPITAL: $70,000 minimum.

FINANCIAL ASSISTANCE: None.

TRAINING: In-store training and supervision.

MANAGERIAL ASSISTANCE: Periodic training in all phases of the business is provided franchisee.

PAPPY'S ENTERPRISES, INC.
300 East Joppa Road
Towson, MD 21204
(301) 296–1200
Contact: Robert B. Geller or Freeman Bixler

BUSINESS: Family-style restaurant.

FRANCHISES: 50 in six states.

FOUNDED: 1968.

REQUIRED CAPITAL: $7,500 franchise fee plus 25 percent deposit on building, land and equipment package of $450,000 and ability to finance balance.

FINANCIAL ASSISTANCE: None.

TRAINING: Three-week intensive training conducted at training store. Two-week training in franchisee's store by representative of the company.

MANAGERIAL ASSISTANCE: The company provides continuing advertising and promotions to franchisee. In addition, operations supervisor visits each store every four to six weeks. The company also provides an operations manual, forms, and bookkeeping systems.

*PASQUALE FOOD COMPANY, INC.
19 West Oxmoor Road
Birmingham, AL 35209
(205) 942–3371
Contact: Duane Watson

BUSINESS: Italian restaurant specializing in pizza.

FRANCHISES: 222 in 19 states.

FOUNDED: 1952.

REQUIRED CAPITAL: Approximately $60,000 plus real estate.

FINANCIAL ASSISTANCE: None.

TRAINING: Initial two weeks' training and periodically thereafter.

MANAGERIAL ASSISTANCE: Managerial and technical assistance provided.

THE PEDDLER, INC.
P.O. Box 1361
Southern Pines, NC 28387
(919) 692–8199
Contact: J. P. Morgan, Jr.

BUSINESS: Family-style restaurant specializing in steaks.

FRANCHISES: 42 in seven states.

FOUNDED: 1965.

REQUIRED CAPITAL: $60,000 to $90,000.

FINANCIAL ASSISTANCE: None.

TRAINING: Two weeks of training in an operating restaurant is provided for the manager. Two days of assistance given during the opening.

MANAGERIAL ASSISTANCE: Managerial and technical assistance is provided for site selection, layout, equipment purchase, training of personnel, and selection of suppliers. Assistance is continued through periodic inspection of operational procedure.

PEDRO'S FOOD SYSTEMS, INC.
P.O. Box 622
Columbus, MS 39701
(601) 327–8921
Contact: Louis May

BUSINESS: Fast-service restaurant specializing in Mexican food.

FRANCHISES: 217 in 16 states.

FOUNDED: 1974.

REQUIRED CAPITAL: $27,500.

FINANCIAL ASSISTANCE: A total investment of $70,000 plus real estate is necessary to open a restaurant. The required capital of $27,500 pays for franchise fee ($9,500), opening inventory, security deposits, permits and licenses, and down payment on equipment package.

TRAINING: The company provides an intensive ten-day training program encompassing every phase of running a successful Mexican restaurant. A complete operations manual is provided and additional training is conducted during and after restaurant is open.

MANAGERIAL ASSISTANCE: The company staff works closely with all franchisees to provide assistance and direction in all phases of marketing and operation of the restaurant.

THE PEWTER MUG
207 Frankfort Avenue
Cleveland, OH 44113
(216) 241–7298
Contact: Robert Wertheim

BUSINESS: English pub and restaurant.

FRANCHISES: 8 in Ohio.

FOUNDED: 1962.

REQUIRED CAPITAL: Total cost approximately $300,000.

FINANCIAL ASSISTANCE: None.

TRAINING: Training of all personnel in company restaurant in Cleveland and in store by training staff after opening.

MANAGERIAL ASSISTANCE: Assistance given in lease negotiations, general contracting, hiring of employees, and coordination of kitchen and bar operation. The company provides a supervisor in franchisee's restaurant one week prior to and following opening.

PEWTER POT MANAGEMENT CORPORATION
211 Middlesex Turnpike
Burlington, MA 01803
(617) 272–6360
Contact: Kevin Hartigan

BUSINESS: Family-style restaurant.

FRANCHISES: 9 in Massachusetts.

FOUNDED: 1965.

REQUIRED CAPITAL: $50,000 initial investment.

FINANCIAL ASSISTANCE: Independent sources.

TRAINING: Minimum four-week on-the-job in company-operated training unit. Franchisees supplied with confidential training manual.

MANAGERIAL ASSISTANCE: Engineering assistance regarding building and equipment plans. Field service assistance for opening and continuing quality control guidance.

*PIONEER TAKE OUT CORPORATION
3663 West 6th Street
Los Angeles, CA 90020
(213) 487–4820
Contact: Paul Wilmoth

BUSINESS: Fast-food restaurant specializing in chicken, fish, and shrimp.
FRANCHISES: 170 in California, Hawaii, Arizona, and Alaska.
FOUNDED: 1961.
REQUIRED CAPITAL: $50,000.
FINANCIAL ASSISTANCE: Company will carry back up to $7,500 of franchise fee for qualified individuals, with simple interest on balance. A total investment of $50,000 is needed which includes franchise fees, sign/lease, equipment down payment, and working capital.
TRAINING: Six weeks intensive and complete training program; four weeks' theory; two weeks on-the-job training under supervision of the training department.
MANAGERIAL ASSISTANCE: The company provides continuous management services for the life of the franchise in such areas as bookkeeping, advertising, quality control, service, and food preparation. Complete manuals of operations and food preparation are provided. Field coordinators work closely with franchisee and visit stores regularly to assist solving problems. The company regularly conducts franchise seminars and continuously performs market and product research to maintain high-volume, profitable locations.

THE PIZZA INN, INC.
2930 Stemmons Freeway
P.O. Box 22247
Dallas, TX 75222
(214) 638–7550
Contact: W. J. Sodeman

BUSINESS: Restaurant specializing in pizza and related Italian menu.
FRANCHISES: 378 throughout the United States, Japan, and South Africa.
FOUNDED: 1959.
REQUIRED CAPITAL: $50,000 to $75,000 plus net worth for lease, land and building.
FINANCIAL ASSISTANCE: Lease situation on equipment plus referral to developers who will build for qualified franchisees.
TRAINING: Two weeks' training in training school plus up to one-week opening assistance with reoccurring training available at all times and periodic follow-up inspections.
MANAGERIAL ASSISTANCE: Complete operations manual furnished upon request and franchise operations representatives available at all times; complete package of training, marketing and promotion programs furnished.

PIZZA-Q ENTERPRISES, INC.
526 Monroe Street
P.O. Box 744
Magnolia, AR 71753
(501) 234–1959
Contact: Licensing manager

BUSINESS: Restaurant specializing in pizza.
FRANCHISES: 3 in Arkansas.
FOUNDED: 1967.
REQUIRED CAPITAL: $12,500.
FINANCIAL ASSISTANCE: Company assists in arranging financing for applicants with good credit standing.
TRAINING: Two months' training.
MANAGERIAL ASSISTANCE: Consultation, training, and bookkeeping services for lifetime of franchise.

POLOCK JOHNNY'S, INC.
111 West Lexington Street
Baltimore, MD 21201
(301) 727–1900
Contact: Ken Bader

BUSINESS: Fast-food restaurant specializing in sausages.
FRANCHISES: 21 in Maryland.
FOUNDED: 1944.
REQUIRED CAPITAL: $30,000.
FINANCIAL ASSISTANCE: Assistance in acquiring equipment loan.
TRAINING: Two weeks on-the-job training at one of the company-operated stores. The company also provides two weeks of training for the supervisor at opening.
MANAGERIAL ASSISTANCE: Continuous assistance in areas such as advertising, inventory, and quality control.

PONDEROSA SYSTEM, INC.
P.O. Box 578
Dayton, OH 45401
(513) 890–6400
Contact: Director-Licensee Department

BUSINESS: Cafeteria-style, fast-food restaurant specializing in steaks.
FRANCHISES: 600 in 25 states and Canada.
FOUNDED: 1965.
REQUIRED CAPITAL: Approximately $100,000.
FINANCIAL ASSISTANCE: No direct financial assistance is provided. However, the company may negotiate lease for the franchisee unit at option of franchisee.
TRAINING: Four weeks of formal training in classroom and in restaurant with

training instructor. Follow-up training in restaurant as required to develop necessary skills.

MANAGERIAL ASSISTANCE: Complete operations manual detailing methods for scheduling labor, maintenance of equipment, training of employees, hiring practices, ordering supplies, and recording and controlling expenses. Field consultants provided on regular basis to help resolve operational problems. Seminars held to give advertising, promotional, and other managerial support to franchisee.

REABAN'S, INC.
10726 Manchester Road
Kirkwood, MO 63122
(314) 966–8330
Contact: John E. Reaban, Jr.

BUSINESS: Fast-food restaurant.

FRANCHISES: 36 in Illinois, Missouri, Montana, and Utah.

FOUNDED: 1958.

REQUIRED CAPITAL: $10,000.

FINANCIAL ASSISTANCE: A total investment of $25,000 is required for equipment, initial franchise fee, and working capital. Normally $10,000 will cover down payment of equipment, franchisee fee, and working capital with the company assisting in obtaining financing on the balance.

TRAINING: A minimum of two weeks on-site training at an existing restaurant.

MANAGERIAL ASSISTANCE: The company provides continuing assistance to the franchisee. Advertising programs are available on an optional basis. Regular visits are made to each operation.

THE RED BARN SYSTEM, INC.
Division of Servomation Corporation
6845 Elm Street
McLean, VA 22101
(703) 893–2111
Contact: Mrs. Pat Kuhlman

BUSINESS: Fast-food restaurant.

FRANCHISES: 50 in 25 states and Canada.

FOUNDED: 1961.

REQUIRED CAPITAL: Approximately $42,500, not including cost of building and land. Land acquisition is franchisee's responsibility.

FINANCIAL ASSISTANCE: None.

TRAINING: Two-week course consisting of practical training in company stores and instruction covering the theory of small business operation as it pertains to their franchise.

MANAGERIAL ASSISTANCE: Field supervisors act as troubleshooters and visit operations periodically.

RED DEVIL
Division of Messina Meat Products, Inc.
614-B East Edna Place
Covina, CA 91723
(213) 966–7585
Contact: Rey Ochoa

BUSINESS: Pizza restaurant.
FRANCHISES: 29 in California.
FOUNDED: 1974.
REQUIRED CAPITAL: $25,000.
FINANCIAL ASSISTANCE: The company will lease the real estate and equipment and sublease to franchisee upon franchisee's qualifications for credit.
TRAINING: Intensive 30-day training.
MANAGERIAL ASSISTANCE: Periodic consultation during life of franchise.

*THE ROUND TABLE FRANCHISE CORPORATION
1101 Embarcadero Road
Palo Alto, CA 94303
(415) 321–4760
Contact: Steve Linsley

BUSINESS: Family-style restaurant specializing in pizza.
FRANCHISES: 150 in western United States.
FOUNDED: 1962.
REQUIRED CAPITAL: Estimated cash requirement (including initial franchise fee) $75,000. Total cost, $135,000 to $150,000.
FINANCIAL ASSISTANCE: Franchisee is required to provide sufficient funds to establish and open restaurant.
TRAINING: The company offers mandatory on-site training course for new franchisees. Assistance and supervision in various other areas prior to opening restaurant is also provided.
MANAGERIAL ASSISTANCE: The company offers a variety of continuing managerial and technical advice including, but not limited to, advertising, store operations, and bookkeeping techniques.

*SHAKEY'S INCORPORATED
5565 First International Building
Dallas, TX 75202
(214) 741–5801
Contact: Sara Eigenmann

BUSINESS: Family-style restaurant specializing in pizza.
FRANCHISES: 514 in 45 states, Canada, Mexico, Japan, Philippines, and Guam.
FOUNDED: 1954.
REQUIRED CAPITAL: $40,000 to $50,000 with real estate.
FINANCIAL ASSISTANCE: Up to 80 percent equipment financing available from independent sources.

TRAINING: Complete training consisting of classroom and in-store curriculum provided. Twenty-one-day course conducted at University of Northern Colorado, only accredited fast-food course in the United States.

MANAGERIAL ASSISTANCE: The company provides continual service in such areas as advertising, quality control, and lease negotiations. Complete operating manuals are provided. Regional managers and dealer services consultants work closely with franchisees and visit restaurants to assist in any problem areas. Franchisees meet generally two to three times a year to exchange views and opinions with company advisory staff.

SIR BEEF LIMITED
4300 Morgan Avenue
Evansville, IN 47715
(812) 477–8931
Contact: Victor Guagenti

BUSINESS: Fast-food restaurant specializing in roast beef sandwiches.

FRANCHISES: 4 in Indiana, Illinois, and Kentucky.

FOUNDED: 1967.

REQUIRED CAPITAL: $50,000.

FINANCIAL ASSISTANCE: None.

TRAINING: Training provided at company unit.

MANAGERIAL ASSISTANCE: Periodic training in all phases of the business is provided franchisee.

SIZZLER FAMILY STEAK HOUSES
12731 West Jefferson Boulevard
Los Angeles, CA 90066
(213) 396–6241
Contact: William Kutzing

BUSINESS: Family-style restaurant specializing in steaks.

FRANCHISES: 350 in 34 states.

FOUNDED: 1959.

REQUIRED CAPITAL: Franchisee must be able to obtain financing for land and building in addition to minimum cash requirement of approximately $100,000.

FINANCIAL ASSISTANCE: None.

TRAINING: Eight weeks on-the-job and classroom training at regional training stores (Los Angeles, California) .

MANAGERIAL ASSISTANCE: The company provides continued field and management services for life of the franchise in areas of marketing, advertising, selection and training of key personnel, accounting, purchasing, restaurant management, and scheduled training schools and seminars. The company management guide, a confidential plan for successful management, is provided each new licensee. Field representatives contact franchisees periodically to review progress and to help institute new policies and procedures for improving service, sales, and profits.

STEWART'S DRIVE-INS
Division of Frostie Enterprises
1420 Crestmont Avenue
Camden, NJ 08103
(609) 966–7500
Contact: Michael W. Fessler

BUSINESS: Fast-food restaurant.
FRANCHISES: 110 in five states.
FOUNDED: 1924.
REQUIRED CAPITAL: $18,000 to $25,000.
FINANCIAL ASSISTANCE: Franchisor will assist in securing adequate financing.
TRAINING: Complete on-the-job training program provided. Training covers all aspects of the business-operational procedures, bookkeeping, employee training, advertising and promotion, and management techniques and menu selection.
MANAGERIAL ASSISTANCE: Regional managers continue to counsel franchisee in advertising, merchandising, and quality control for the life of the franchise; also, the company assists with local advertising and promotion.

*STUCKEY'S, INC.
P.O. Box 370
Eastman, GA 31023
(912) 374–4381
Contact: J. W. Spradley

BUSINESS: Interstates and main U.S. highway restaurant.
FRANCHISES: 160 in 40 states.
FOUNDED: 1931.
REQUIRED CAPITAL: Amount varies depending upon location.
FINANCIAL ASSISTANCE: None.
TRAINING: Two weeks of intensive classroom and practical training at company headquarters. This includes business operation procedures, bookkeeping procedures, management techniques, and on-the-job experience. Also, periodic regional meetings are held for continuous updating on procedures and operations.
MANAGERIAL ASSISTANCE: Managerial and technical assistance is provided in site location, site preparation, and building construction. Company representatives also visit units periodically for inspection and assistance in all phases of the business. Supervisors are always available to assist the franchisee in all areas of the business. A complete accounting and retail auditing service is available at a nominal monthly fee. A newsletter is also sent to all franchisees.

*SUBWAY
25 High Street
Milford, CT 06460
(203) 877–4281
Contact: Frederick A. DeLuca

BUSINESS: Fast-food restaurant specializing in submarine sandwiches.
FRANCHISES: 140 in 17 states.

FOUNDED: 1965.

REQUIRED CAPITAL: Approximately $22,500 to $47,500.

FINANCIAL ASSISTANCE: No financing or financial assistance is provided.

TRAINING: Approximately 80 hours consisting of five eight-hour day shifts and five eight-hour night shifts training franchisee in preparation of sandwiches, working with company quality and inventory control system, accounting procedures, stock ordering, labor management, and all facets of operating one unit.

MANAGERIAL ASSISTANCE: Monthly inspections by company field representative. Weekly computerized analysis of the operation and preparation of weekly operating statement. Ongoing assistance in advertising and all phases of business. Between monthly visits, or guidance as needed. Assistance continues through life of franchise.

TACO HUT, INC.
3621 South 73rd East Avenue
Tulsa, OK 74145
(918) 587–0413
Contact: Murray Schroyer

BUSINESS: Fast-food restaurant specializing in Mexican food.

FRANCHISES: 65 in ten states including Alaska and Hawaii.

FOUNDED: 1965.

REQUIRED CAPITAL: $35,000 to $45,000. This does not include building or real estate.

FINANCIAL ASSISTANCE: None.

TRAINING: Two weeks intensive management training in Tulsa, Oklahoma, or on site.

MANAGERIAL ASSISTANCE: Continuous.

TACO JOHN'S. See Woodson-Holmes Enterprises, Inc.

*TACO TIME INTERNATIONAL, INC.
3880 West 11th Street
Eugene, OR 97401
(503) 687–8222
Contact: Donald Payne

BUSINESS: Restaurants specializing in Mexican food.

FRANCHISES: 175 in 13 states and Canada.

FOUNDED: 1960.

REQUIRED CAPITAL: $35,000.

FINANCIAL ASSISTANCE: $250,000 for five-unit area franchise.

TRAINING: In store and classroom—four weeks.

MANAGERIAL ASSISTANCE: Inspections, bulletins research, and development improvements are provided periodically.

TASTEE FREEZ BIG T FAMILY RESTAURANT SYSTEMS
Division of Tastee Freez International, Inc.
1515 South Mount Prospect Road
Des Plaines, IL 60018
(312) 694–3900
Contact: Glen Mathews or Nancy Kemph

BUSINESS: Fast-food restaurant.

FRANCHISES: Over 2,000 in 50 states.

FOUNDED: 1950.

REQUIRED CAPITAL: A minimum cash down payment of $30,000 to $100,000 depending on size of market area. Total investments for equipment and license run from $70,000 to $100,000, depending on size of the restaurant, not including sales tax or operating capital and food inventory.

FINANCIAL ASSISTANCE: Guidance in arranging financing.

TRAINING: Intensive training for new franchisees and their personnel is conducted at company training center and franchisee's store. Course covers managerial, accounting, promotional, food preparation, and operational phases under actual operating conditions.

MANAGERIAL ASSISTANCE: State supervisors provide assistance in cost controls, new operational methods, advertising, merchandising, and quality control. The company assists with national TV and local advertising and promotion, and conducts a yearly national convention for licensees to exchange ideas on merchandising, advertising, salesmanship, and new food preparation methods.

TIPPY'S TACO HOUSE, INC.
2853 West Illinois
Dallas, TX 75233
(214) 339–4211
Contact: W. L. Locklier

BUSINESS: Fast-food restaurant specializing in Mexican food.

FRANCHISES: 25 in 12 states.

FOUNDED: 1967.

REQUIRED CAPITAL: $35,000 to $40,000, cash and credit combined.

FINANCIAL ASSISTANCE: None.

TRAINING: Preopening and opening week training at restaurant.

MANAGERIAL ASSISTANCE: Continuing assistance by representative visitations, letters, bulletins, and telephone.

WALT'S ROAST BEEF, INC.
1635 Cranston Street
Cranston, RI 02920
(401) 945–5736
Contact: Louis W. Spirite

BUSINESS: Restaurant specializing in roast beef sandwiches.

FRANCHISES: 14 in the New England states.

FOUNDED: 1967.

REQUIRED CAPITAL: $15,000 to $20,000.

FINANCIAL ASSISTANCE: Investment of $70,000, minimum of $15,000 down payment pays for equipment, franchise fee, and refurnishing of existing building. Company will help franchisee obtain financing.

TRAINING: A training period of four weeks is required.

MANAGERIAL ASSISTANCE: Company provides continual management service.

*WENDY'S OLD FASHIONED HAMBURGERS
% Wendy's International, Inc.
P.O. Box 256
Dublin, OH 43017
(614) 889–0900
Contact: Franchise Sales Department

BUSINESS: Fast-food restaurant.

FRANCHISES: 1,067 in 48 states.

FOUNDED: 1969.

REQUIRED CAPITAL: $100,000.

FINANCIAL ASSISTANCE: Total investment $350,000 plus. Company provides no financial assistance.

TRAINING: One two-week course for franchisee in classroom and on-the-job at Wendy's Management Institute in Columbus, Ohio.

MANAGERIAL ASSISTANCE: Company provides manuals and services to cover cost controls, personnel management, quality control, field consultation, operational efficiency, and purchasing.

*WIENER KING CORPORATION
1610 East Morehead Street
Charlotte, NC 28207
(704) 377–9333
Contact: Stephen M. Booker

BUSINESS: Fast-food restaurant specializing in hot dogs and chili.

FRANCHISES: 85 in 35 states.

FOUNDED: 1970.

REQUIRED CAPITAL: $25,000 minimum.

FINANCIAL ASSISTANCE: Company will assist in obtaining financing for applicants with good credit ratings.

TRAINING: Two weeks of training at company headquarters, both in operation of a unit and classroom lectures covering personnel, promotions, reporting, and so on. Annual franchisee meeting is held to discuss accomplishments and goals.

MANAGERIAL ASSISTANCE: Company provides continuous assistance throughout the term of franchise agreement. Each unit is visited monthly by a company representative to assist in maximizing profits and by the company quality control department.

WIFE SAVER FRANCHISES AND SUPPLY
2706 Milledgeville Road
Augusta, GA 30904
(404) 736–3924
Contact: George B. Cunningham

BUSINESS: Fast-food restaurant specializing in fried chicken and seafood.
FRANCHISES: 8 in Georgia and South Carolina.
FOUNDED: 1965.
REQUIRED CAPITAL: $16,500 minimum. Total investment approximately $205,000.
FINANCIAL ASSISTANCE: Company arranges leases for building and equipment and helps make banking contacts.
TRAINING: Minimum four weeks.
MANAGERIAL ASSISTANCE: Technical assistance provided throughout term of franchise.

WINKYS DRIVE-IN RESTAURANTS, INC.
Route 286
Saltsburg, PA 15186
(412) 568–9075
Contact: Licensing manager

BUSINESS: Fast-food restaurant.
FRANCHISES: 11 in Pennsylvania, West Virginia, and Ohio.
FOUNDED: 1962.
REQUIRED CAPITAL: $50,000.
FINANCIAL ASSISTANCE: Up to 75 percent financing available from independent financing sources.
TRAINING: Minimum six weeks.
MANAGERIAL ASSISTANCE: Continuous home office assistance, field supervision, and counsel.

WOODSON-HOLMES ENTERPRISES, INC.
d.b.a. Taco John's
P.O. Box 1589
Cheyenne, WY 82001
(307) 035–0101
Contact: Harold Holmes

BUSINESS: Fast-food restaurant specializing in Mexican food.
FRANCHISES: 245 in 27 states.
FOUNDED: 1969.
REQUIRED CAPITAL: $25,000 minimum.
FINANCIAL ASSISTANCE: A total investment of $70,000 to $80,000 is necessary to open a restaurant. The company will provide franchisee with background information and references to help him obtain financing at a local bank or the

Small Business Administration. If the franchisee desires to lease the building and equipment, the company has sources available to contact.

TRAINING: An intensive 12-day mandatory training course combining classroom work and production at an operating unit is scheduled in Cheyenne, Wyoming.

MANAGERIAL ASSISTANCE: The company provides continuous technical and managerial assistance. At opening, the company provides personnel for approximately one week. Periodic calls by company field personnel, complete manuals of operation, forms, and directions, advertising materials, a monthly newsletter are provided, and regional and national meetings are held throughout the year.

WOODY'S LITTLE ITALY RESTAURANTS
5300 Walnut Street
McKeesport, PA 15132
(412) 751–3225
Contact: Gurino Antonelli

BUSINESS: Restaurant specializing in Italian food.
FRANCHISES: 3 in Pennsylvania.
FOUNDED: 1968.
REQUIRED CAPITAL: $35,000.
FINANCIAL ASSISTANCE: Assistance in obtaining financing.
TRAINING: Two weeks at company location.
MANAGERIAL ASSISTANCE: Company trains all personnel, manages promotional programs, and assists franchise opening with company employees and managers.

BEN FRANKLIN
Division of City Products Corporation
1700 South Wolf Road
Des Plaines, IL 60018
(312) 298–8800
Contact: Lee Dombif

BUSINESS: A general merchandise store.
FRANCHISES: 2,100 in 50 states.
FOUNDED: 1977.
REQUIRED CAPITAL: $35,000.
FINANCIAL ASSISTANCE: Several financing plans are available to qualified persons, ranging from loans through commercial institutions to a direct participation in the equity of the business by the company. Financial plans are available for investors and retail managers interested in operating a store on a buy-out basis.
TRAINING: Training provided for franchisee and employees in store by company representative. Duration of training is flexible, depending upon background, qualifications, and needs of the franchisee.

MANAGERIAL ASSISTANCE: Assistance is available in finding locations, sales promotion and all phases of operation by periodic visits of company personnel.

COAST TO COAST STORES
Division of Central Organization Inc.
P.O. Box 80
Minneapolis, MN 55440
(612) 935–1711
Contact: Joe Karels

BUSINESS: Retail "total hardware" store.

FRANCHISES: Approximately 1,175 in 26 states.

FOUNDED: 1928.

REQUIRED CAPITAL: $50,000 to $200,000, depending on store size. There are no franchise or development fees.

FINANCIAL ASSISTANCE: Franchisee provides half the initial capital. The company helps negotiate additional financing through local community sources.

TRAINING: Three-day training school (with sessions, lodging, and meals at company expense) that covers all phases of store operations. Company representatives help franchisee with layout, display, setup, and grand opening; thereafter district manager makes continuing visits.

MANAGERIAL ASSISTANCE: Company provides complete bookkeeping and tax accounting; layout and display ideas; inventory control; prepriced tickets; optional electronic order entry system; group insurance programs, sales circulars, and merchandising helps; two merchandising meetings a year; training clinics; and continuing advice and assistance from company personnel.

GAMBLE–SKOGMO, INC.
Division of Gamble Stores
5100 Gamble Drive
Minneapolis, MN 55416
(612) 374–6123
Contact: Development Manager

BUSINESS: Complete retail store operation.

FRANCHISES: 1,013.

FOUNDED: 1933.

REQUIRED CAPITAL: $30,000 minimum.

FINANCIAL ASSISTANCE: A total investment of $100,000 is recommended. Franchisees may borrow capital from financial sources selected by them. Retailers Growth Fund, Inc. (a company of Gamble–Skogmo, Inc.), or Gamble–Skogmo, Inc.

TRAINING: A training program is provided at company office.

MANAGERIAL ASSISTANCE: The company provides a merchandising program, distribution centers, operational program with manuals and bookkeeping service. Company representatives visit store regularly.

RASCO STORES
Division of Gamble–Skogmo, Inc.
2777 North Ontario Street
Burbank, CA 91504
(213) 843–3773
Contact: E. E. Hackett, Director of Franchising

BUSINESS: Three types of franchises: Rasco Variety (a family store), Toy World (toy specialty stores), and Rasco Temp (mass-merchandise store).

FRANCHISES: 139 in eight states.

FOUNDED: 1934.

REQUIRED CAPITAL: Minimum down payment: Rasco Variety $5,000. Rasco Tempo $15,000, and Toy World $7,000.

FINANCIAL ASSISTANCE: Company provides financing to qualified people at reasonable rates.

TRAINING: Two to three days in Burbank, California, office with the balance of training in the franchisee's store.

MANAGERIAL ASSISTANCE: Company provides merchandising ideas, complete accounting services, store layout and opening assistance, advertising program, fixture rental plan, and operating assistance.

HEALTH AIDS/SERVICES

DIET CONTROL CENTERS, INC.
1021 Stuyvesant Avenue
Union, NJ 07083
(201) 686–0007
Contact: Ruth Landesberg

BUSINESS: Group weight control.

FRANCHISES: 39 in 11 states.

FOUNDED: 1968.

REQUIRED CAPITAL: Mini-franchise $3,500.

FINANCIAL ASSISTANCE: Financial assistance available.

TRAINING: Training on-the-job at executive center.

MANAGERIAL ASSISTANCE: Training is provided on a continuing basis for unlimited duration. Nutritional and home economic department guidance. Periodic meetings and weekly telephone contact. All group and bookkeeping supplies are included.

*THE DIET WORKSHOP
111 Washington Street
Brookline, MA 02146
(617) 739–2222
Contact: Lois Lindauer

BUSINESS: Group weight control.

FRANCHISES: 65 franchises in 30 states, Canada, and Bermuda.

* Asterisk denotes franchisor is a member of the International Franchise Association.

FOUNDED: 1965.

REQUIRED CAPITAL: Franchise cost $5,000. Recommended opening capital, $10,000.

FINANCIAL ASSISTANCE: None.

TRAINING: Five days' training in classroom and on the job, plus trips to franchisee's area. Four operating manuals, including all bookkeeping and group supplies for 300 people.

MANAGERIAL ASSISTANCE: Local and national seminars.

GLORIA STEVENS FIGURE SALONS
182 Forbes Road
Braintree, MA 02184
(617) 848–7380
Contact: Howard E. Alpert

BUSINESS: Group weight control for women.

FRANCHISES: 105 mostly in the New England states.

FOUNDED: 1969.

REQUIRED CAPITAL: Approximately $25,000.

FINANCIAL ASSISTANCE: Average $39,500 total price. After a 50 percent down payment the balance may be financed. Master franchises (larger territorial areas with subfranchising opportunities) are available to qualified persons.

TRAINING: Training course consisting of classroom and on-the-job training.

MANAGERIAL ASSISTANCE: Regular training meetings, seminars, and conventions open for owners and staff members. Company representative on call.

MacLEVY PRODUCTS CORPORATION
92–21 Corona Avenue
Elmhurst, NY 11373
(212) 592–6550
Contact: Monty MacLevy

BUSINESS: Weight control and health club.

FRANCHISES: 25.

FOUNDED: 1968.

REQUIRED CAPITAL: $10,000 to $25,000.

FINANCIAL ASSISTANCE: No financial assistance provided by company. Financing available through commercial credit organizations. Company terms of purchase are 30 percent deposit with order, balance C.O.D.

TRAINING: One- to seven-day training period at operating health clubs in different locations. Franchisor provides operation manuals as well as instructional material and business systems, architectural advice, plans and layouts, and suggested list of equipment. Personalized on-the-job training available at additional charge. Details and costs upon request.

MANAGERIAL ASSISTANCE: Managerial and technical assistance by telephone or through correspondence at no charge.

MEDIPOWER
P.O. Box 613
Bellaire, TX 77401
(713) 777–5787
Contact: Floyd MacKenzie

BUSINESS: Sale, rent, or lease of patient's aid, hospital beds, wheelchairs, walkers, crutches, and so on.
FRANCHISES: 3 in Texas.
FOUNDED: 1969.
REQUIRED CAPITAL: No franchise fee; investment limited to inventory; no minimum required.
FINANCIAL ASSISTANCE: None—on approved credit, 30-day open accounts.
TRAINING: Continuous sales training and on-location aid for first two weeks.
MANAGERIAL ASSISTANCE: Continuous assistance.

*QUALITY CARE INC.
65 Roosevelt Avenue
Valley Stream, NY 11580
(516) 791–8366
Contact: Herman M. Schuster

BUSINESS: Provides nursing, health care, and paramedical personnel to the patient in the home or institutions. Also provides all levels of health care personnel to the institution on an ongoing basis.
FRANCHISES: 39 in 29 states.
FOUNDED: 1972.
REQUIRED CAPITAL: $30,000 plus ability to establish line of credit to finance payrolls against receivables.
FINANCIAL ASSISTANCE: None.
TRAINING: Three to four weeks' training both on site of franchise and at company headquarters.
MANAGERIAL ASSISTANCE: The company provides continuous, ongoing management service for the life of the franchise in the areas of personnel recruitment, advertising, bookkeeping, business getting, quality control, and so on.

STAFF BUILDERS MEDICAL SERVICES
122 East 42nd Street
New York, NY 10017
(212) 867–2345
Contact: Walter E. Ritter

BUSINESS: Supplies medical services personnel to hospitals, nursing homes, institutions, doctors offices, and for home care. Provides temporary help services for office, industrial, data processing, marketing, and technical businesses.
FRANCHISES: 18 in 12 states.
FOUNDED: 1961.

REQUIRED CAPITAL: $25,000.

FINANCIAL ASSISTANCE: Partial financing of franchise investment or financing of temporary payroll.

TRAINING: Two weeks' training at New York headquarters, all expenses paid. Training includes manuals, procedures, and systems.

MANAGERIAL ASSISTANCE: Promotional aids, sales programs, recruiting assistance and financial advice are part of continuous communications with franchisee via telephone, mail, and visits.

HEARING AIDS

RCI, INC.
4915 West 35th Street
Minneapolis, MN 55416
(612) 926–7611
Contact: Ralph Campagna

BUSINESS: Hearing aids in Montgomery Ward retail stores.

FRANCHISES: 29 in eight states.

FOUNDED: 1961.

REQUIRED CAPITAL: $5,000 to $10,000.

FINANCIAL ASSISTANCE: None.

TRAINING: Two to four weeks initial training with additional training every month for three months. Enrollment in National Hearing Aid Service home study course.

MANAGERIAL ASSISTANCE: Company provides sales meetings, publications, industry workshops, and personal visits.

HOME FURNISHINGS/FURNITURE—RETAIL/REPAIR/SERVICES

ABBEY CARPET COMPANY
6643 Franklin Boulevard
Sacramento, CA 95823
(916) 422–8230
Contact: Phil Gutierre

BUSINESS: Retail carpet stores.

FRANCHISES: 56 in 13 states.

FOUNDED: 1967.

REQUIRED CAPITAL: Approximately $5,000 for existing carpet store.

FINANCIAL ASSISTANCE: None.

TRAINING: Company mail-order course plus three weeks in-store training.

MANAGERIAL ASSISTANCE: Company provides continuous management service program.

AMITY INC.
410 Atlas Avenue
Madison, WI 53716
(608) 221–3585
Contact: Jerry R. Cook, President

BUSINESS: Furniture stripping and products.
FRANCHISES: Over 400 in the United States and Canada.
FOUNDED: 1970.
REQUIRED CAPITAL: $3,995 to $5,000.
FINANCIAL ASSISTANCE: None.
TRAINING: Training provided at home office for the length of time required by franchisee. On-site training provided upon installation.
MANAGERIAL ASSISTANCE: The company provides managerial and technical assistance through monthly newsletter, telephone calls, home office visits, visits by company representative to shops, and annual national conventions. Advertising and promotional ideas and assistance offered. No marketing areas or restrictions. A total free enterprise.

CARPETERIA, INC.
1122 North Vine Street
Hollywood, CA 90038
(213) 462–6232
Contact: Andrew Reid

BUSINESS: Retail carpet.
FRANCHISES: 21 in California and Nevada.
FOUNDED: 1973.
REQUIRED CAPITAL: $50,000 to $75,000.
FINANCIAL ASSISTANCE: None.
TRAINING: Three months' training.
MANAGERIAL ASSISTANCE: Managerial and technical assistance is provided as needed.

CASTRO CONVERTIBLES
1990 Jericho Turnpike
New Hyde Park, NY 11040
(516) 488–3000
Contact: Robert J. Perdrizet

BUSINESS: Convertible sleep sofas and allied products.
FRANCHISES: 85 in United States.
FOUNDED: 1931.
REQUIRED CAPITAL: $70,000 to $150,000, depending on size of store and area.
FINANCIAL ASSISTANCE: The company provides assistance to qualified applicants.
TRAINING: Company will set up showroom and train all personnel on-the-job in all phases of the operation followed up with continuing assistance and supervision as needed.

MANAGERIAL ASSISTANCE: Daily telephone contact by company representative plus periodic visits.

CHEM-CLEAN FURNITURE RESTORATION CENTER
Division of Union Chemical Company, Inc.
Union, ME 04862
(207) 785–2625
Contact: Dr. R. G. Esposito

BUSINESS: Patented systems for furniture stripping and refinishing.
FRANCHISES: 70 in 16 states and Canada.
FOUNDED: 1967.
REQUIRED CAPITAL. $3,890 to $15,000 plus initial operating funds.
FINANCIAL ASSISTANCE: Lease purchase plans available. No royalties, franchisee owns all equipment outright.
TRAINING: Up to one week of instruction in a company-owned center.
MANAGERIAL ASSISTANCE: Company trains in operating procedures, including technical and managerial techniques. Annual meetings of franchisees.

CROSSLAND FURNITURE RESTORATION STUDIOS
5747 North Main Street
Sylvania, OH 43560
(419) 885–4000
Contact: Hugh J. Crossland

BUSINESS: Furniture stripping, refinishing and restoration; also refinishing products.
FRANCHISES: 89 in the United States and Canada.
FOUNDED: 1969.
REQUIRED CAPITAL: $45,000.
FINANCIAL ASSISTANCE: Company will finance 50 percent of initial investment for qualified applicants.
TRAINING: Complete training is provided.
MANAGERIAL ASSISTANCE: Company provides marketing assistance, business management aids, and technical help.

*DECORATING DEN
Division of American Drapery Consultants, Inc.
P.O. Box 68165
5753 West 85th Street
Indianapolis, IN 46278
(317) 293–9400
Contact: James C. Long

BUSINESS: Decorating products and services.
FRANCHISES: 160 in 30 states.
FOUNDED: 1970.

* Asterisk denotes franchisor is a member of the International Franchise Association.

REQUIRED CAPITAL: $5,525 to $13,000.
FINANCIAL ASSISTANCE: $2,000 down payment, balance financed over 12-month period at 21.57 annual percentage.
TRAINING: Minimum of two weeks of classroom training, one-week on-the-job training, plus local and regional training. Training is continuously available.
MANAGERIAL ASSISTANCE: Opening preparation and attendance. Planning and sales projection meeting. Periodic progress checks.

DELHI CHEMICALS, INC.
22 South Street
Stamford, NY 12167
(607) 652–7527
Contact: Andrew Pilato

BUSINESS: Furniture stripping and finish removal.
FRANCHISES: 382 in 43 states, Canada, and Italy.
FOUNDED: 1966.
REQUIRED CAPITAL: $15,500.
FINANCIAL ASSISTANCE: $5,000.
TRAINING: Three and one-half days of classroom and shop training at the company's headquarters in Stamford, or at 1 of 18 National Training Centers located throughout the United States.
MANAGERIAL ASSISTANCE: Continuing technical assistance upon request, usually by letter or telegram. Additional training is available at all times and all programs are without charge to franchisees.

G. FRIED CARPETLAND, INCORPORATED
800 Old Country Road
Westbury, NY 11590
(516) 333–3900
Contact: Al Fried

BUSINESS: Retail floor covering stores.
FRANCHISES: 26 in New York, New Jersey, Connecticut, Florida, and Ohio.
FOUNDED: 1969.
REQUIRED CAPITAL: Minimum $5,000 each with suggested two partners.
FINANCIAL ASSISTANCE: Company can arrange loan, equal to amounts of cash put up by franchisee.
TRAINING: Established professionals only will be considered.
MANAGERIAL ASSISTANCE: Constant company supervision.

GUARANTEE CARPET CLEANING & DYE COMPANY
2953 Powers Avenue
Jacksonville, FL 32207
(904) 733–6454
Contact: Frank Woodruff

BUSINESS: Carpet and upholstery cleaning and dying.
FRANCHISES: 200 in 42 states, Canada, and Puerto Rico.
FOUNDED: 1969.

REQUIRED CAPITAL: $6,000 minimum excluding van-type truck.

FINANCIAL ASSISTANCE: Franchise fees are $3,000 per 100,000 population with minimum franchise of $6,000 for 200,000 or less. Company requires one quarter down and balance payable weekly on a noninterest bearing note. Payments begin 45 days after franchise starts operating. Franchise fee may be paid in full at any time without penalty. Complete equipment and initial expendable materials $3,500.

TRAINING: Two weeks classroom and on-the-job training including management, marketing, and technical in Jacksonville.

MANAGERIAL ASSISTANCE: Company provides marketing and technical manuals and training for the duration of the franchise via nationwide toll free WATS line, two regional meetings each year in all areas, and annual national meeting and convention. Field assistance provided at no charge.

JACK THE STRIPPER
P.O. Box 16353
Memphis, TN 38116
(901) 948–2614
Contact: Mrs. Jack Aday, Jr.

BUSINESS: Furniture stripping.

FRANCHISES: 8 in Tennessee, Alabama, and Mississippi.

FOUNDED: 1965.

REQUIRED CAPITAL: About $10,000.

FINANCIAL ASSISTANCE: Franchisee buys the franchise and the equipment furnished with the initial purchase.

TRAINING: One-day training at franchisee's location. Additional training at franchisee's expense at company, if desired.

MANAGERIAL ASSISTANCE: None.

LEE'S BARS 'N STOOLS 'N DINETTES. See Lee's Purchasing, Inc.

LEE'S PURCHASING, INC.
d.b.a. Lee's Bars 'N Stools 'N Dinettes
19562 Ventura Boulevard
Tarzana, CA 91356
(213) 996–0403
Contact: Leon J. Shapiro

BUSINESS: Retail stores specializing in bars, barstools, dinettes, and game sets.

FRANCHISES: 8 in California.

FOUNDED: 1973.

REQUIRED CAPITAL: $60,000.

FINANCIAL ASSISTANCE: None.

TRAINING: As necessary.

MANAGERIAL ASSISTANCE: Company provides managerial and technical assistance in purchasing, advertising, sales aids, floor setup, floor display, criterias, and maintaining sales books.

RUG CRAFTERS
3321 South Fairview Street
Santa Ana, CA 92704
(714) 751–4260
Contact: Al Hoff

BUSINESS: Yarn craft stores which specialize in "speed-tufting."

FRANCHISES: 60 in 20 states.

FOUNDED: 1970.

REQUIRED CAPITAL: $30,000.

FINANCIAL ASSISTANCE: Total investment is about $60,000 and company will assist franchisee in obtaining local bank financing of about $32,000.

TRAINING: Company provides a training program including product knowledge, store operation, selling techniques, inventory control, and finance control. Program includes classroom and in-store training for 15 days.

MANAGERIAL ASSISTANCE: Company assists franchisee in store operations including the introduction of new products, record keeping, selling methods, advertising, and promotion. Company provides an operations manual and the services of a field coordinator, in addition to the assistance available through the headquarters staff.

SIESTA SLEEP SHOP, INC.
386 Lindelof Avenue
Stoughton, MA 02072
(617) 344–9877
Contact: Manuel Glickman

BUSINESS: Retail mattresses, beds, and platform beds.

FRANCHISES: 5 in Massachusetts.

FOUNDED: 1953.

REQUIRED CAPITAL: $15,000 to $30,000.

FINANCIAL ASSISTANCE: To qualified applicants.

TRAINING: Six to eight weeks intensive training plus three months extra supervision, as needed.

MANAGERIAL ASSISTANCE: Company provides assistance from stockroom to management to sales and advertising. Ongoing cooperation between franchisor and franchisee.

SPRING CREST COMPANY
505 West Lambert Road
Brea, CA 92621
(714) 529–9993
Contact: Thomas M. Icing

BUSINESS: Retail draperies, drapery hardware, and accessories.

FRANCHISES: 200 in 34 states, Canada, Japan, and Australia.

FOUNDED: 1968..

REQUIRED CAPITAL: $15,000 to $25,000.

FINANCIAL ASSISTANCE: Minimal.

TRAINING: One or two weeks' training at either company school or at franchise location, prior to opening. Additional training as needed, after opening.

MANAGERIAL ASSISTANCE: Procedural manual. Monthly newsletter, national magazine advertising, prepared television commercials, news releases, and newspaper ads. Two area meetings per year. One national convention per 18 months. Company consultation available by phone or letter.

STEAMATIC INCORPORATED
1601 109th Street
Grand Prairie, TX 75050
(214) 647–1244
Contact: Lindy Berry

BUSINESS: Carpet, upholstery, and drapery cleaning.

FRANCHISES: Over 185 in 37 states, Germany, Canada, Japan, Mexico, Ecuador, Lebanon, Nigeria, and Kuwait.

FOUNDED: 1967.

REQUIRED CAPITAL: $8,500 to $35,000.

FINANCIAL ASSISTANCE: If franchisee qualifies, one third of franchise fee can be financed through Fort Worth bank.

TRAINING: Two weeks at headquarters in Grand Prairie, two weeks at franchisee's location.

MANAGERIAL ASSISTANCE: Continuous assistance in sales, equipment service, advertising materials, research and development, computer management system.

A CLEANER WORLD
P.O. Box 5328
High Point, NC 27260
(919) 885–5218
Contact: S. S. McKarem

BUSINESS: Laundry and dry cleaning service.

FRANCHISES: 48 in North Carolina, South Carolina, Tennessee, Virginia, and Georgia.

FOUNDED: 1969.

REQUIRED CAPITAL: $25,000.

FINANCIAL ASSISTANCE: A total investment of $55,000. Initial $10,000 is for operating capital, advertising, licenses, permits, and supplies. Company will finance the balance for qualified persons (eight years). Franchisee may arrange own financing.

TRAINING: One week of classroom instruction and 11 weeks of in-plant training. Regular training seminars are conducted for the life of the franchise.

MANAGERIAL ASSISTANCE: A district manager is assigned to every 15 stores. Complete manual of operations, forms, and directions are provided with continual assistance in bookkeeping, advertising, and inventory control.

BIG B FRANCHISE INC.
P.O. Box 1000
Richmond, KY 40475
(606) 623–2550
Contact: Roland Barnett

BUSINESS: Fast-service laundry and dry cleaning stores.
FRANCHISES: 7 in Kentucky and Mississippi.
FOUNDED: 1971.
REQUIRED CAPITAL: Total cost approximately $40,000 to $50,000.
FINANCIAL ASSISTANCE: None.
TRAINING: Complete training at franchisee's expense.
MANAGERIAL ASSISTANCE: Company assistance and supervision in bookkeeping, equipment, and supplies.

COIT DRAPERY & CARPET CLEANERS, INC.
897 Hinckley Road
Burlingame, CA 94010
(415) 342–6023
Contact: Ernie Pressman

BUSINESS: Supply and maintenance of draperies.
FRANCHISES: 60 in 35 states, Canada, and Europe.
FOUNDED: 1963.
REQUIRED CAPITAL: Minimum $5,000.
FINANCIAL ASSISTANCE: Some credit to qualified individuals.
TRAINING: Initial training at company plant in California or regional plant with additional training at franchisee's plant.
MANAGERIAL ASSISTANCE: Training at regional meetings, manual of operating instructions, continuous managerial and technical assistance, quality control, and research and development programs. Bulletins, company magazine, and revisions to the manual are provided.

COOK MACHINERY COMPANY
Division of Ald, Inc.
4301 South Fitzhugh Avenue
Dallas, TX 75226
(214) 421–2135
Contact: Licensing Manager

BUSINESS: Laundry and dry cleaning stores.
FRANCHISES: 200 in all 50 states.
FOUNDED: 1970.
REQUIRED CAPITAL: $25,000 to $40,000.
FINANCIAL ASSISTANCE: Financing and leasing available for qualified applicants.
TRAINING: On-the-job training and monthly service schools at the factory.
MANAGERIAL ASSISTANCE: Managerial and technical assistance provided by local distributors.

DUTCH GIRL CONTINENTAL CLEANERS
175 Express Street
Plainview, NY 11803
(516) 822–5300
Contact: Michael U. Voelkel

BUSINESS: Dry cleaning store.
FRANCHISES: 150 in 20 states.
FOUNDED: 1964.
REQUIRED CAPITAL: $15,000 to $20,000.
FINANCIAL ASSISTANCE: Financing up to 90 percent of equipment costs.
TRAINING: Three weeks' training with initial training in operating school, followed by on-the-job training at franchisee's store.
MANAGERIAL ASSISTANCE: Assistance available in management, promotion, accounting, and technical problems.

*GIGANTIC CLEANERS & LAUNDRY, INC.
411 East 17th Avenue
Denver, CO 80203
(303) 861–8230
Contact: James Orlin

BUSINESS: Fast-service laundry and dry cleaning plants.
FRANCHISES: 17 in Colorado.
FOUNDED: 1960.
REQUIRED CAPITAL: $65,000.
FINANCIAL ASSISTANCE: None.
TRAINING: Two weeks in company plants and four to six weeks' on-the-job training in franchisee's plant.
MANAGERIAL ASSISTANCE: Assistance in site location, equipment, and installation. Company provides start-up supplies. Constant managerial and technical assistance, and monthly profit and loss statement provided.

*MARTIN SALES (MARTINIZING)
Division of American Laundry Machinery
McGraw-Edison Company
5050 Section Avenue
Cincinnati, OH 45212
(513) 731–5500
Contact: Charles Caldwell

BUSINESS: Fast-service dry cleaning stores.
FRANCHISES: 1,956 in 49 states.
FOUNDED: 1950.
REQUIRED CAPITAL: $5,000 franchise free.
FINANCIAL ASSISTANCE: None.

* Asterisk denotes franchisor is a member of the International Franchise Association.

AINING: On-the-job training provided by local independent dealer in an established store.

MANAGERIAL ASSISTANCE: Operational manual provided covering accounting, personnel, advertising, and so on. Periodic store inspection by company inspectors plus continuous assistance as required.

LAWN AND GARDEN SUPPLIES/SERVICES

LAWN-A-MAT CHEMICAL AND EQUIPMENT CORPORATION
153 Jefferson Avenue
Mineola, NY 11501
(516) 248–0122
Contact: Dan Dorfman

BUSINESS: Sales of lawn products and services.
FRANCHISES: 200 in 33 states and Canada.
FOUNDED: 1961.
REQUIRED CAPITAL: $6,500.
FINANCIAL ASSISTANCE: For qualified applicants.
TRAINING: Training at company training centers with continuous training on the job.
MANAGERIAL ASSISTANCE: Agronomical, managerial, technical, and sales training provided on a continuing basis at regular seminars and in the field. Company representative available for special problems.

*LAWN DOCTOR INCORPORATED
P.O. Box 186, Conover Road
Wickatunk, NJ 07765
(201) 946–9700
Contact: Anthony Giordano

BUSINESS: Automated lawn service.
FRANCHISES: 173 in 22 states.
FOUNDED: 1967.
REQUIRED CAPITAL: Minimum of $7,500.
FINANCIAL ASSISTANCE: None.
TRAINING: Two-week managerial, sales and technical training at the company office. One-week technical training for each employee at the company office. Weekly workshops and management seminars.
MANAGERIAL ASSISTANCE: All initial bookkeeping, advertising, and sales promotional materials supplied. Company representatives available for both telephone and in the field assistance as required. Cassette tapes of weekly workshops sent to the franchisees who cannot attend meetings.

* Asterisk denotes franchisor is a member of the International Franchise Association.

LAWN KING, INC.
14 Spielman Road
Fairfield, NJ 07006
(201) 227–3700
Contact: Joseph J. Sandler

BUSINESS: Automated lawn service.
FRANCHISES: 130 in 11 states.
FOUNDED: 1970.
REQUIRED CAPITAL: From $15,000 plus $5,000 operating capital.
FINANCIAL ASSISTANCE: Limited financing for qualified parties.
TRAINING: Two weeks' training covering managerial, technical, sales, advertising, and mechanical aspects, with continuous additional training for one year.
MANAGERIAL ASSISTANCE: Company provides bookkeeping, accounting service, contract forms, billing procedures, newspaper advertising layouts, direct mail program, television commercials, forms, and tools for estimates and lawn analyses.

LAWN MEDIC INC.
1024 Sibley Tower Building
Rochester, NY 14604
(716) 342–1870
Contact: Donald W. Burton

BUSINESS: Automated lawn service.
FRANCHISES: 163 in 27 states.
FOUNDED: 1968.
REQUIRED CAPITAL: $9,850.
FINANCIAL ASSISTANCE: Company finances qualified applicants.
TRAINING: Four-day classroom session plus two days on the job. Regular seminars and training meetings after franchise is established.
MANAGERIAL ASSISTANCE: Assistance in bookkeeping, advertising, inventory control, and tax advice. Continuous research in marketing, products, and service provided.

SUBURBAN LAWN SERVICES
28 West Hills Road
Huntington, NY 11746
(516) 549–0640
Contact: Louis Sax

BUSINESS: Garden center service.
FRANCHISES: 39 in nine states.
FOUNDED: 1962.
REQUIRED CAPITAL: $16,500.
FINANCIAL ASSISTANCE: Co-op chemical purchasing.
TRAINING: Two-week training on sales products and customer service.
MANAGERIAL ASSISTANCE. Weekly control sheets and perpetual profit and loss statements. Continuing management assistance.

TURF-O-MATIC, INC.
9 Monmouth Park Place
Oceanport, NJ 07757
(201) 542–5527
Contact: Charles Cortelyou

BUSINESS: Automated lawn service.
FRANCHISES: 3 in New Jersey.
FOUNDED: 1970.
REQUIRED CAPITAL: $14,500.
FINANCIAL ASSISTANCE: Financing available to qualified applicants.
TRAINING: Initial training at company office. Regular seminars and training meetings after franchisee is established.
MANAGERIAL ASSISTANCE: Advertising program. Lawn combine reconditioned annually at company factory.

MAINTENANCE/CLEANING/SANITATION—SERVICES/SUPPLIES

ABC MAINTENANCE DEVELOPMENT CORPORATION
18850 Ventura Boulevard
Suite 214
Tarzana, CA 91356
(213) 996–1554
Contact: Phillip A. Syphers

BUSINESS: Commercial building maintenance service. Area subfranchising rights available in selected areas.
FRANCHISES: 90 in California and Arizona.
FOUNDED: 1971.
REQUIRED CAPITAL: $500 to $25,000.
FINANCIAL ASSISTANCE: Partial financing available.
TRAINING: Classroom and on-the-job training from three days to two weeks for the service franchisee and one month for area subfranchisors.
MANAGERIAL ASSISTANCE: Company provides managerial services including computerized bookkeeping systems, billing, collecting, employee referrals, technical advice, sales assistance, company supervision, and continuous management counseling.

AMERICLEAN NATIONAL SERVICE CORPORATION
Hemlock Road
Boxford, MA 01921
(617) 887–8011
Contact: Carl F. Whitaker

BUSINESS: Residential and commercial cleaning service.
FRANCHISES: 6 in Massachusetts.

FOUNDED: 1968.

REQUIRED CAPITAL: $3,400 to $4,800 guaranteed repurchase agreement.

FINANCIAL ASSISTANCE: Company assists franchisee in locating financing through local or corporate sources.

TRAINING: Training by established local franchisees when available. Local business and training seminars held annually.

MANAGERIAL ASSISTANCE: Assistance in advertising development, sales promotion, training, bookkeeping, manuals, laboratory assistance, and legal and financial help. Company offers benefits including life, medical, and disability insurance, and a retirement savings plan.

ARMSTRONG BUILDING MAINTENANCE COMPANY
Franchise Division
P.O. Box 8306
Albuquerque, NM 87108
(505) 265–7963
Contact: Licensing Manager

BUSINESS: Janitorial and pest control services.

FRANCHISES: 8 in six states.

FOUNDED: 1954.

REQUIRED CAPITAL: $10,800.

FINANCIAL ASSISTANCE: Partial financial assistance available.

TRAINING: Two weeks' training at company office and two weeks' training on the job.

MANAGERIAL ASSISTANCE: Continuous management assistance and periodic staff visits. Pest control service is a separate franchise and operates as Armstrong Pest Control. Same required capital.

CHEM-MARK INTERNATIONAL, INC.
200 South Cypress Street
Orange, CA 92666
(714) 633–8560
Contact: Darol W. Carlson

BUSINESS: Sales and rental of commercial low-temperature dishwashing machines, detergents, cleaning supplies, sanitation products, and restaurant and bar equipment.

FRANCHISES: 89 in 46 states.

FOUNDED: 1959.

REQUIRED CAPITAL: $18,000.

FINANCIAL ASSISTANCE: None.

TRAINING: One week in home office, plus two weeks' on the job in franchisee's territory.

MANAGERIAL ASSISTANCE: Continued managerial and technical assistance.

*DOMESTICARE, INC.
190 Godwin Avenue
Midland Park, NJ 07432
(201) 447–3737
Contact: R. C. Figurell

BUSINESS: Residential cleaning services.
FRANCHISES: 200 in 18 states.
FOUNDED: 1964.
REQUIRED CAPITAL: $3,000 down payment plus working capital.
FINANCIAL ASSISTANCE: Company will assist in financing the remaining $3,500 over two and a half years. Package includes territory, training, equipment, initial supplies, business system, accounts receivable financing, and computerized central billing system.
TRAINING: Eighteen days at company's headquarters.
MANAGERIAL ASSISTANCE: District managers offer assistance, furnish manuals, reporting forms, regular seminars, and periodic field visits.

*DURACLEAN INTERNATIONAL
Duraclean Building
Deerfield, IL 60015
(312) 945–2000
Contact: James Ball

BUSINESS: Carpet and upholstery cleaning.
FRANCHISES: 1,068 in all 50 states and Canada.
FOUNDED: 1930.
REQUIRED CAPITAL: $1,985 down payment with cash payment of $5,200.
FINANCIAL ASSISTANCE: Franchisor will finance balance of franchise cost after down payment.
TRAINING: Five-day resident training school. One-day training with experienced franchisee.
MANAGERIAL ASSISTANCE: Advertising, sales promotion, bookkeeping, and laboratory services on cleaning and technical spotting. Regional meetings and international conventions biannually.

GENERAL SEWER SERVICE, INC.
P.O. Box 83
Iselin, NJ 08830
(201) 636–2265
Contact: Frank Shingle

BUSINESS: Residential and commercial electric sewer cleaning.
FRANCHISES: 15 in New Jersey, New York, Pennsylvania, and Connecticut.
FOUNDED: 1967.
REQUIRED CAPITAL: $25,000 average.
FINANCIAL ASSISTANCE: None.
TRAINING: Minimum 13 days.
MANAGERIAL ASSISTANCE: Continual availability of company personnel. On-

* Asterisk denotes franchisor is a member of the International Franchise Association.

location assistance as required. Dispatch and operational manual. Periodic seminars planned.

*LIEN CHEMICAL COMPANY
9229 West Grand Avenue
Franklin Park, IL 60131
(312) 455–5000
Contact: Richard Crane

BUSINESS: Commercial sanitation services.
FRANCHISES: 46 in 25 states.
FOUNDED: 1929.
REQUIRED CAPITAL: $15,000 minimum.
FINANCIAL ASSISTANCE: None.
TRAINING: Training includes administration, sales, and service at company headquarters.
MANAGERIAL ASSISTANCE: Supervised start-up of the operation and ongoing individual consultations by company representatives. Periodic seminars and a yearly national conference, technical bulletins, newsletters, and performance analysis are continuously provided.

MR. ROOTER CORPORATION
4220 N.W. 23rd Street
Oklahoma City, OK 73107
(405) 946–3000
Contact: Lee Russell

BUSINESS: Sewer and drain cleaning.
FRANCHISES: 48 in 17 states.
FOUNDED: 1970.
REQUIRED CAPITAL: Maximum of $7,500.
FINANCIAL ASSISTANCE: None.
TRAINING: Training including bookkeeping as well as on-the-job training.
MANAGERIAL ASSISTANCE: Company maintains a continuous advisory service, including guidance in both managerial and technical aspects, for the lifetime of the agreement. Dealers may take refresher training at any time.

NATIONAL SURFACE CLEANING CORPORATION
4959 Commerce Parkway
Cleveland, OH 44128
(216) 292–4777
Contact: David A. Sheridan

BUSINESS: Cleaning exteriors of masonry or metal buildings.
FRANCHISES: 231 in 38 states.
FOUNDED: 1971.
REQUIRED CAPITAL: $8,950.
FINANCIAL ASSISTANCE: Limited financing available.
TRAINING: Company office training for one week. Training in franchisee's area

for three days. Additional on-the-job training available at no charge upon reasonable request.

MANAGERIAL ASSISTANCE: Company provides continual management service in advertising, operations, and sales with manuals of operations, forms, and directories. Field managers are available to work closely with franchisees and visit regularly to assist in solving problems. The company sponsors meetings and conducts marketing and product research.

PORT-O-LET COMPANY, INC.
Subsidiary of Thetford Corporation
2300 Larsen Road
Jacksonville, FL 32207
(904) 396–2031
Contact: James P. Smith

BUSINESS: Temporary toilet facilities.
FRANCHISES: 60 in 21 states and Puerto Rico.
FOUNDED: 1954.
REQUIRED CAPITAL: $5,000 to $25,000.
FINANCIAL ASSISTANCE: Rental units are furnished.
TRAINING: One week at company headquarters plus additional training on the job.
MANAGERIAL ASSISTANCE: Company furnishes equipment, does all invoicing, record keeping, accounts receivable, collections, and so on.

*ROTO-ROOTER CORPORATION
300 Ashworth Road
West Des Moines, IA 50265
(515) 223–1343
Contact: William F. Dau

BUSINESS: Sewer and drain cleaning service.
FRANCHISES: 725 in the United States.
FOUNDED: 1935.
REQUIRED CAPITAL: $5,000.
FINANCIAL ASSISTANCE: None.
TRAINING: Training available at home office, but most new franchisees prefer training at an operating franchise near their location.
MANAGERIAL ASSISTANCE: Continued assistance through field staff, manuals, bulletins, and so on.

SERMAC
Division of Servicemaster Industries, Inc.
2300 Warrenville Road
Downers Grove, IL 60515
(312) 964–1300
Contact: Delbert D. Stoner

BUSINESS: Industrial cleaning and restoration services.
FRANCHISES: 35 in 19 states.

FOUNDED: 1975.

REQUIRED CAPITAL: $7,500 minimum.

FINANCIAL ASSISTANCE: Choice of two franchise offers. SR3000 mobile power cleaning unit $39,500. SR1500 mobile power cleaning unit $14,990. Financing is available to qualified prospects or franchisee has option to arrange outside financing. One-third down payment on SR3000, with balance payable in 35 monthly installments plus final installment payment. One-half down payment on SR1500, with balance payable in 48 monthly installments. A minimum of $10,000 in additional operating capital also required.

TRAINING: Two-week on-the-job training provided at company headquarters, followed by two-day training in franchisee location. Management, marketing, and technical manuals are provided.

MANAGERIAL ASSISTANCE: Company provides continual technical, management and marketing services to franchisee through personal visits, telephone contacts, and regional and national workshops.

*SERVICEMASTER INDUSTRIES, INC.
2300 Warrenville Road
Downers Grove, IL 60515
(312) 964–1300
Contact: R. Thomas Gibson

BUSINESS: Residential and commercial cleaning.

FRANCHISES: 1,718 in 50 states.

FOUNDED: 1947.

REQUIRED CAPITAL: $6,500.

FINANCIAL ASSISTANCE: Company will finance qualified applicants.

TRAINING: Home study course, two weeks on-the-job with established franchisee, one day in the field with counselor, one-week resident training school. Continuous program provided for all franchisees.

MANAGERIAL ASSISTANCE: Managerial assistance is available on a continuous basis, from the company and from the master franchise coordinator of franchisees in the field. The company makes available advertising, sales promotion, formal training, laboratory services, and regional and international meetings.

*SERVPRO INDUSTRIES, INC.
4545 Orange Grove Avenue
Sacramento, CA 95841
(916) 483–6076
Contact: Tal Denney

BUSINESS: Cleaning service.

FRANCHISES: Over 275 in 32 states.

FOUNDED: 1967.

REQUIRED CAPITAL: $13,500.

FINANCIAL ASSISTANCE: A total investment of $27,000. Company will finance 50 percent. Franchisee has option to arrange own financing.

TRAINING: On-the-job training, setup training, classroom training, and continuous training through national convention and regional seminars.

MANAGEMENT ASSISTANCE: Company provides continual training, including bookkeeping, advertising, and inventory control.

SPARKLE WASH, INC.
177 East Washington Street
Chagrin Falls, OH 44022
(216) 247–7611
Contact: Otto V. Jackson

BUSINESS: Cleaning service for vehicles, airplanes, boats, commercial buildings, and mobile homes.

FRANCHISES: 135 in 41 states and Canada.

FOUNDED: 1965.

REQUIRED CAPITAL: Plan A—$13,000 and Plan B—$26,950.

FINANCIAL ASSISTANCE: Plan A requires $13,000 initial capital outlay for qualified individuals; to include license fee and initial lease payment for the mobile power cleaning unit, 30–60 day chemical supply, marketing, and business package. Plan B requires $26,950 obtained through local financing by the prospective licensee. Company provides support information necessary. Company also provides complete accounting system.

TRAINING: Initial training in equipment operation, maintenance, chemicals, and marketing provided at company headquarters. In the field training utilizes the licensee's unit and operators.

MANAGERIAL ASSISTANCE: Company provides publication containing up-to-date marketing and technical information. Company also provides computer printouts of truck fleet operators, market survey, advertising materials, and marketing packages for specific markets. Company personnel available on a regular basis.

U.S. ROOTER CORPORATION
18 Remount Road
North Little Rock, AR 72118
(501) 663–6363
Contact: Troy L. Ratliff

BUSINESS: Sewer and drain cleaning service.

FRANCHISES: 10 in California, Louisiana, and Arkansas.

FOUNDED: 1968.

REQUIRED CAPITAL: $3,000 minimum rents one set of machines and accessories.

FINANCIAL ASSISTANCE: Available to qualified applicants.

TRAINING: Two weeks' training, or more if desired at company headquarters or the nearest franchised area.

MANAGERIAL ASSISTANCE: Company advises by mail or telephone on advertising. Also provides a manual of operation.

VON SCHRADER MANUFACTURING COMPANY
1600 Junction Avenue
Racine, WI 53404
(414) 634–1956
Contact: F. U. von Schrader

BUSINESS: Cleaning service.
FRANCHISES: Over 25,000 in the United States.
FOUNDED: 1935.
REQUIRED CAPITAL: $400 to $2,200.
FINANCIAL ASSISTANCE: Twelve-month partial financing.
TRAINING: Business manuals and instruction books, personal factory, and in-the-field instructions, together with available company consulting staff for individual specific problems.
MANAGERIAL ASSISTANCE: Technical and managerial assistance available. Services are available at the company and in the field at no cost.

AMERICAN TRAVEL INNS
4th South and Main Streets
Salt Lake City, UT 84101
(801) 322–5395
Contact: Wesley Sine

BUSINESS: Full-service lodging chain.
FRANCHISES: 12 in the United States.
FOUNDED: 1953.
REQUIRED CAPITAL: $60,000 to $120,000.
FINANCIAL ASSISTANCE: None.
TRAINING: Continuous consulting privileges, scheduled meetings, and training seminars.
MANAGERIAL ASSISTANCE: Guidance as requested.

DOWNTOWNER/ROWNTOWNER MOTOR INNS
Division of Passport Inns of America, Inc.
5350 Poplar Avenue
Memphis, TN 38117
(901) 761–3280
Contact: Don T. Baker, Executive Vice President

BUSINESS: Motels and restaurants.
FRANCHISES: 60 in 22 states.
FOUNDED: 1960.
REQUIRED CAPITAL: Depending on financial strength and record of individual or company involved.
FINANCIAL ASSISTANCE: Guidance and counseling.
TRAINING: Orientation program for owner and manager, plus on-the-job training.

MANAGERIAL ASSISTANCE: Guidance on company policies, procedures, forms, and methods, plus manuals and job description for all departments.

*ECONO-TRAVEL MOTOR HOTEL CORP.
3 Koger Executive Center
P.O. Box 12188
Norfolk, VA 23502
(804) 461–6111
Contact: Lloyd T. Tarbutton

BUSINESS: Motor hotels.
FRANCHISES: Over 100 in 17 states.
FOUNDED: 1967.
REQUIRED CAPITAL: Dependent upon location.
FINANCIAL ASSISTANCE: None. Indirectly company helps locate mortgage lenders.
TRAINING: Training for all motel managers.
MANAGERIAL ASSISTANCE: General assistance in areas of bookkeeping system, site selection, analysis, economics of housekeeping and maintenance, motel inspection periodically by company representatives. Seminars conducted several times yearly; advertising expertise.

FAMILY INNS OF AMERICA, INC.
1111 Northshore Drive
P.O. Box 2191
Knoxville, TN 37901
(615) 588–2974
Contact: Kenneth M. Seaton

BUSINESS: Motor hotels with food and beverage facilities.
FRANCHISES: 25 in 10 states.
FOUNDED: 1971.
REQUIRED CAPITAL: Between $100,000 and $250,000 depending upon size.
FINANCIAL ASSISTANCE: Feasibility studies, plans, guidance, and counseling with financial institutions, national contracts for lower construction cost.
TRAINING: Training in all phases of motel business, room renting, restaurant and lounge setup and planning as long as needed.
MANAGERIAL ASSISTANCE: Guidance and counseling on company policies, complete audit and accounting forms. Complete inspections by company, annual meetings, and help available at any time.

HAPPY INNS OF AMERICA, INC.
8849 Richmond Highway
Alexandria, VA 22309
(703) 780–0003
Contact: Clark Morris

BUSINESS: Motor inns.
FRANCHISES: 17 in seven states.

* Asterisk denotes franchisor is a member of the International Franchise Association.

FOUNDED: 1970.

REQUIRED CAPITAL: Approximately 20 percent of construction cost.

FINANCIAL ASSISTANCE: Will assist franchisee in obtaining local financing.

TRAINING: Thirty days on-the-job training for managers. Operations manual, continually updated.

MANAGERIAL ASSISTANCE: Continual management assistance as needed for life of franchise.

*HOLIDAY INNS, INC.
3796 Lamar Avenue
Memphis, TN 38118
(901) 362–4248
Contact: Gary D. Parker

BUSINESS: Motor hotels and restaurants.

FRANCHISES: 1,514 worldwide.

FOUNDED: 1954.

REQUIRED CAPITAL: $400,000 cash—$2,000,000 net worth.

FINANCIAL ASSISTANCE: None.

TRAINING: Three-week course at company.

MANAGERIAL ASSISTANCE: Continuing guidance as needed.

MASTER HOSTS INNS
Division of Red Carpet Inns of America, Inc.
444 Seabreeze Boulevard
P.O. Box 2510
Daytona Beach, FL 32015
(904) 255–1492
Contact: William A. Harwood

BUSINESS: Motor hotels.

FRANCHISES: 145 in 30 states.

FOUNDED: 1969.

REQUIRED CAPITAL: 30 percent of total cost.

FINANCIAL ASSISTANCE: Assistance in preparation of mortgage package and introduction to financial institutions.

TRAINING: On-the-job training given at company-owned operations during planning stages.

MANAGERIAL ASSISTANCE: Management company for the purpose of managing franchised motels.

MORRISON, INC.
P.O. Box 2608
Mobile, AL 36625
(205) 432–9711
Contact: E. F. Congdon

BUSINESS: Motor hotels.

FRANCHISES: 8 in six states.

FOUNDED: 1946.
REQUIRED CAPITAL: $200,000 to $300,000.
FINANCIAL ASSISTANCE: Assistance in locating sources of financing, along with overall construction, selection of furnishing fixtures and equipment.
TRAINING: Assistance in training personnel throughout entire term of franchise.
MANAGERIAL ASSISTANCE: Assistance at all levels of management, as well as in accounting, legal, wage and salary, and so forth.

QUALITY INNS INTERNATIONAL, INC.
10750 Columbia Pike
Silver Spring, MD 20901
(301) 593-5600
Contact: James H. Rempe, Executive Vice President

BUSINESS: Motor inns with food and beverage facilities.
FRANCHISES: 300 in the United States, Canada, and Europe.
FOUNDED: 1941.
REQUIRED CAPITAL: $275,000 to $325,000 plus land and financing.
FINANCIAL ASSISTANCE: Assistance in preparing and presenting mortgage application; furnishings may be financed through company's wholly owned subsidiary.
TRAINING: Orientation program for franchisee or managers prior to motel opening. Continuing seminar programs. Complete operations manual available.
MANAGERIAL ASSISTANCE: Guidance on company policies, procedures, accounting forms, and methods included in training course.

*RAMADA INNS, INC.
3838 East Van Buren Street
Phoenix, AZ 85008
(602) 273-4040
Contact: Francis R. Loetterk

BUSINESS: Motor hotels.
FRANCHISES: 807 in the United States.
FOUNDED: 1959.
REQUIRED CAPITAL: A minimum of 20 percent of total gross investment.
FINANCIAL ASSISTANCE: Market surveys, contracts, guidance, and counseling.
TRAINING: Continuous training sessions at the Management Development Center.
MANAGERIAL ASSISTANCE: Continual consulting privileges with company executives. Regional and annual meetings. Four annual inspections are made. Complete management services available.

RED CARPET INNS OF AMERICA, INC. See Master Hosts Inns.

REGAL 8 INNS
P.O. Box 1268
Mt. Vernon, IL 62864
(618) 242–7240
Contact: Mrs. Dee Smith

BUSINESS: Motels.
FRANCHISES: 17 in 12 states.
FOUNDED: 1970.
REQUIRED CAPITAL: $5,000.
FINANCIAL ASSISTANCE: None.
TRAINING: Three weeks manager training at an existing motel plus quarterly visits and assistance as requested.
MANAGERIAL ASSISTANCE: As above on straight franchise. Complete management on management contract.

RODEWAY INNS OF AMERICA
2525 Stemmons Freeway
Suite 800
Dallas, TX 75207
(214) 630–9300
Contact: James Wellbeloved

BUSINESS: Motor hotels.
FRANCHISES: 143 in 30 states and Mexico.
FOUNDED: 1962.
REQUIRED CAPITAL: Approximately 20 percent of total cost.
FINANCIAL ASSISTANCE: Company assists franchisee in obtaining financing and feasibility study.
TRAINING: Seminars and on-the-job training at company project.
MANAGERIAL ASSISTANCE: Managerial and technical assistance provided in design, decor, plans, financing, site location, feasibility studies and in management.

*SHERATON INNS, INC.
60 State Street
Boston, MA 02109
(617) 367–3600
Contact: Irving Zeldman

BUSINESS: Hotels and inns.
FRANCHISES: 375 in 43 states.
FOUNDED: 1962.
REQUIRED CAPITAL: Approximately 20 percent of total cost.
FINANCIAL ASSISTANCE: Company assists in obtaining financing.
TRAINING: Seminars for franchisees and general managers prior to opening. Sales and company seminars four times per year.

MANAGERIAL ASSISTANCE: Continual management assistance, including operating manuals, sales, and advertising guidance, marketing assistance, and quarterly visits from regional director, and regional and national meetings.

SUPER 8 MOTELS, INC.
224 Sixth Avenue, S.E.
Aberdeen, SD 57401
(605) 255–2272
Contact: Dennis E. Bale

BUSINESS: Motels.
FRANCHISES: 55 in 11 states.
FOUNDED: 1972.
REQUIRED CAPITAL: Up to $200,000 depending upon size.
FINANCIAL ASSISTANCE: Company assists in obtaining financing.
TRAINING: Training program is provided, including on-the-job training, films, classroom study, and examinations.
MANAGERIAL ASSISTANCE: Managerial, advertising and accounting services provided.

TRAVELODGE INTERNATIONAL, INC.
Travelodge Drive
El Cajon, CA 92090
(714) 442–0511
Contact: Jere M. Hooper

BUSINESS: Motels.
FRANCHISES: 193 in 45 states, District of Columbia, and worldwide.
FOUNDED: 1947.
REQUIRED CAPITAL: $100,000 to $400,000.
FINANCIAL ASSISTANCE: Company assists in obtaining financing.
TRAINING: One-week training at company office.
MANAGERIAL ASSISTANCE: Area meetings and seminars are held periodically. Quarterly inspections are standard procedure.

TREADWAY INNS CORPORATION
140 Market Street
Paterson, NJ 07505
(201) 881–7900
Contact: James F. Horrigan

BUSINESS: Motor inns.
FRANCHISES: 23 in seven states.
FOUNDED: 1912.
REQUIRED CAPITAL: For existing facilities, $50 per room. For building a new inn, $18,000 to $20,000 per room plus land cost.

FINANCIAL ASSISTANCE: Franchisee obtains own financing.

TRAINING: Company assists franchisee in selection of manager and department heads, who may attend on-the-job training for up to six weeks at one or more existing motels.

MANAGERIAL ASSISTANCE: Company provides operational manuals and consultation.

DAVIS PAINT COMPANY
1311 Iron Street
North Kansas City, MO 64116
(816) 471–4447
Contact: Jess Bagby

BUSINESS: Paint and wallpaper and decorating stores.

FRANCHISES: 90 in 8 states.

FOUNDED: 1944.

REQUIRED CAPITAL: $25,000 to $30,000.

FINANCIAL ASSISTANCE: Partial financing available to qualified individuals.

TRAINING: Training at company plant. Field training by company personnel and regional sales meetings.

MANAGERIAL ASSISTANCE: Complete assistance in site location, lease arrangements, store layout, advertising, sales promotion, bookkeeping, insurance, and management techniques. Franchisor personnel and field representatives make regular calls.

MARY CARTER INDUSTRIES, INC.
1191 South Wheeling
Wheeling, IL 60090
(312) 541–9000
Contact: Dick Schen

BUSINESS: Paint, wallpaper, and flooring store.

FRANCHISES: Over 800 in 45 states.

FOUNDED: 1948.

REQUIRED CAPITAL: $30,000.

FINANCIAL ASSISTANCE: For opening additional units after the original, financing available.

TRAINING: One-week training in an established store and an additional week in franchisee's newly opened store. Periodic training programs by company personnel.

MANAGERIAL ASSISTANCE: Guidance offered in establishing location, designing the floor planning and signs, sales promotions, grand opening and follow-up advertising, and periodic visits by field and management personnel. National sales meetings once a year.

DOCKTOR PET CENTERS, INC.
Dundee Park
Andover, MA 01810
(617) 475–8166
Contact: Leslie Charm, President

BUSINESS: Pets, supplies and accessories, and grooming services.
FRANCHISES: 111 in 28 states.
FOUNDED: 1966.
REQUIRED CAPITAL: Approximately $60,000.
FINANCIAL ASSISTANCE: None.
TRAINING: Four weeks at company headquarters. Training covers store operation, care of pets, accounting, management, inventory, maintenance, and personnel selection.
MANAGERIAL ASSISTANCE: Advice on stocking, fixture arrangement, receipt of livestock, and maintenance procedures. On-the-site company representative guides franchisee during first week of operations. Advertising materials and standardized accounting and report forms furnished. Company representatives visit stores to assist franchisees, train sales personnel, maintain retail concepts and advise on profitability.

PEDIGREE PET CENTERS
Division of Pedigree Industries, Inc.
11 Goldthwait Road
Marblehead, MA 01945
(617) 631–8210
Contact: Milton Docktor

BUSINESS: Pets, supplies, accessories, and grooming services.
FRANCHISES: 4 in Maine, Massachusetts, Florida, and New Jersey.
FOUNDED: 1975.
REQUIRED CAPITAL: Approximately $40,000.
FINANCIAL ASSISTANCE: Company may assist in obtaining financing.
TRAINING: Four weeks at company headquarters. Covers store operation, care of pets, accounting, management, inventory, maintenance, and personnel selection.
MANAGERIAL ASSISTANCE: Advice on stocking, fixture arrangement, receipt of livestock, and maintenance procedures. On-the-site company representative guides franchisee during first week of operations. Advertising materials and standardized accounting and report forms furnished. Company representatives visit stores to assist franchisees.

WESTERN METRO GUARD DOGS, INC.
23442 30th Avenue S.
Kent, WA 98034
(206) 824–7200
Contact: Dick McNeely

BUSINESS: Sales, training, and rental of guard dogs.
FRANCHISES: 8 in Alaska, Washington, Idaho, and Alabama.

FOUNDED: 1958.

REQUIRED CAPITAL: $1,495.

FINANCIAL ASSISTANCE: Partial.

TRAINING: One hundred and ten hours of prestudy at home and 80–100 hours of resident training at the company office.

MANAGERIAL ASSISTANCE: Constant: monthly bulletins, setup bookkeeping, and assistance in advertising. Quarterly retraining seminars at company office.

*BIG RED Q QUICKPRINT CENTERS
3131 Douglas Road
Toledo, OH 43614
(419) 473–1551
Contact: A. C. Hazlewood

BUSINESS: Instant printing and copying service.

FRANCHISES: 202 in 27 states.

FOUNDED: 1967.

REQUIRED CAPITAL: $15,000 plus $10,000 working capital.

FINANCIAL ASSISTANCE: Equipment package can be provided on a five-year lease, five-year bank loan or cash.

TRAINING: Two weeks at national training school on equipment, sales, and bookkeeping. Two weeks at opening of franchisee's new store by company field representative.

MANAGERIAL ASSISTANCE: Operations manual kept up to date, bookkeeping system, regular visits by company representative, bulletins, advertising materials, accounting assistance, sales ideas, and personnel provided for illness or vacations.

*INSTY-PRINTS, INC.
417 North Fifth Street
Minneapolis, MN 55401
(612) 774–6837
Contact: John O. Prater

BUSINESS: Instant printing service.

FRANCHISES: 168 in 26 states, plus Washington, D.C., Puerto Rico, South Africa, Israel, and Thailand.

FOUNDED: 1965.

REQUIRED CAPITAL: $19,000 minimum cash requirement.

FINANCIAL ASSISTANCE: Up to $20,000 of total $39,000 investment may be financed through company by qualified applicants. $19,000 minimum cash requirement covers (a) equipment down payment, (b) opening paper and supplies inventory, and (c) $5,000 business working capital retained by franchisee.

TRAINING: Four weeks at Minneapolis headquarters, covering use of equipment,

* Asterisk denotes franchisor is a member of the International Franchise Association.

advertising, estimating, paper, freight, bookkeeping, counter procedures, inventory and cost control, and general unit management. Fifth week in franchisee's own unit, under company supervision. Additional personnel training in Minneapolis headquarters at no additional charge throughout term of agreement.

MANAGERIAL ASSISTANCE: Annual regional workshops, continuing management and technical advice, instant WATS telephone communication, continuing advertising and promotion programs, complete operations and sales manuals, and periodic bulletins. National advertising fund.

KOPY KAT, INC.
National Franchise Division
Executive Plaza
Fort Washington, PA 19034
(800) 523–8950, (215) 643–5598 (Pennsylvania only)
Contact: Charles J. Ascenzi

BUSINESS: Instant printing and copying service.

FRANCHISES: 100 in 35 states.

FOUNDED: 1968.

REQUIRED CAPITAL: $10,900 down payment on $33,009 total cost. Balance payable monthly from proceeds of business over a five-year period.

FINANCIAL ASSISTANCE: Company will help arrange financing for qualified applicants after down payment.

TRAINING: Two weeks initial training program at company office. Courses provided in technical skills, advertising agency skills, bookkeeping method, marketing, and sales promotion. Additional training is provided at opening.

MANAGERIAL ASSISTANCE: Advertising and publicity program, newsletters, assistance in site selection, lease negotiation, bookkeeping, management, and printing merchandising.

*KWIK-KOPY CORPORATION
5225 Hollister
Houston, TX 77040
(713) 939–1010
Contact: Henry S. Eason

BUSINESS: Instant printing and copying service.

FRANCHISES: Over 250 in 28 states.

FOUNDED: 1967.

REQUIRED CAPITAL: $51,250.

FINANCIAL ASSISTANCE: A total investment of $51,250 required. The $23,918 equipment package can be financed on a 60-month leaseback.

TRAINING: Two weeks at training school at Breham, Texas and two weeks on-the-job. Training includes equipment operation, advertising, and sales and business methods.

MANAGERIAL ASSISTANCE: The company provides continued support services to its franchisees for the full life of the franchise agreement, including management and legal counsel, advertising, training of new employees, and retraining through periodic meetings and seminars, research of new methods and equipment, and visits by field representatives. Management is available for assistance and counseling by telephone at all times.

*POSTAL INSTANT PRESS (PIP)
8201 Beverly Boulevard
Los Angeles, CA 90048
(213) 653–8750
Contact: Larry G. Cummings, National Sales Director

BUSINESS: Instant printing and copying service.
FRANCHISES: 425 in 39 states, District of Columbia, and Canada.
FOUNDED: 1965.
REQUIRED CAPITAL: $15,000 ($12,000 operating capital) . Total of $47,000.
FINANCIAL ASSISTANCE: Up to $32,500 to qualified individuals.
TRAINING: Two weeks at company headquarters, covering technical instructions on machines used, as well as advertising and promotional ideas. Company representative at franchisee's location during first week. Continued field assistance thereafter.
MANAGERIAL ASSISTANCE: Regular visits from company coordinators. Collect phone calls to company for immediate problems. Bulletins, manuals and promotional aids, accounting guidance, local and national seminars.

THE PRINTING PLACE, INC.
P.O. Box 1040
Easton, PA 18042
(215) 258–3437
Contact: Arthur Alan Leaver

BUSINESS: Instant printing and copying service.
FRANCHISES: 3 in Pennsylvania and West Virginia.
FOUNDED: 1973.
REQUIRED CAPITAL: $12,000 to $18,000 down payment plus $5,000 to $6,000 working capital.
FINANCIAL ASSISTANCE: Total price is $30,000 to $46,000 not including working capital. Financing can be secured from various sources for qualified applicant. Company may assume some financing.
TRAINING: Two or three weeks' training in franchisee's shop or regional company training center. Instructions in sales, merchandising, and general business practices are also given at franchise location.
MANAGERIAL ASSISTANCE: Company provides continuing training on equipment, supplies, techniques and marketing practices, specialized advertising and promotion campaigns, and business operational requirements. Periodic visits by company representatives.

QUIK PRINT, INC.
250 North Rock Road, Suite 100
Wichita, KS 67206
(316) 686–3321
Contact: Wayne Jenkins

BUSINESS: Instant printing and copying service.
FRANCHISES: 83 in 17 states.
FOUNDED: 1967.
REQUIRED CAPITAL: $42,500.
FINANCIAL ASSISTANCE: Company assists in securing financing.
TRAINING: Four to six weeks at company headquarters, plus two weeks' on the job at franchisee's new location.
MANAGERIAL ASSISTANCE: Management services in the area of bookkeeping, advertising, equipment, and production techniques.

SIR SPEEDY INSTANT PRINTING CENTERS
P.O. Box 1790
892 West 16th Street
Newport Beach, CA 92663
(714) 642–9476
Contact: George F. Rombach, Vice President, Administration and Finance

BUSINESS: Instant printing and copying service.
FRANCHISES: 233 in 27 states.
FOUNDED: 1968.
REQUIRED CAPITAL: $48,000 total investment, plus approximately $10,000 working.
FINANCIAL ASSISTANCE: Financing is available for up to $27,000 of the initial $48,000.
TRAINING: Two weeks' training at company and two weeks at franchisee's location.
MANAGERIAL ASSISTANCE: Company support includes sales, marketing, and store preview procedures plus bulletins, local seminars, buying coordination, and so on.

REAL ESTATE

ACTION BROKERS CORPORATION
5001 West 80th Street
Bloomington, MN 55437
(612) 831–2262
Contact: Richard O. Watland

BUSINESS: Real estate sales offices.
FRANCHISES: 13 in Minnesota.
FOUNDED: 1975.
REQUIRED CAPITAL: $2,500.

FINANCIAL ASSISTANCE: None.
TRAINING: Prelicense classes and training classes.
MANAGERIAL ASSISTANCE: Assistance upon request.

BETHOM CORPORATION
d.b.a. Better Homes Realty
39 Quail Court
Suite 105
Walnut Creek, CA 94596
(415) 937–9601
Contact: Richard Killian

BUSINESS: Real estate sales offices.
FRANCHISES: 77 in California.
FOUNDED: 1969.
REQUIRED CAPITAL: $5,500.
FINANCIAL ASSISTANCE: None.
TRAINING: Management and salesperson orientation.
MANAGERIAL ASSISTANCE: Continued management assistance with ongoing educational seminars.

BETTER HOMES REALTY. See Bethom Corporation.

*CENTURY 21 REAL ESTATE CORPORATION
18872 MacArthur Boulevard
Irvine, CA 92715
(714) 752–7521
Contact: William McQuerry

BUSINESS: Real estate sales office.
FRANCHISES: 2,000 in 39 states.
FOUNDED: 1972.
REQUIRED CAPITAL: New worth of $10,000 for each franchise.
FINANCIAL ASSISTANCE. None.
TRAINING: Constant training for broker and sales associates in California.
MANAGERIAL ASSISTANCE: Management workshops where applicable.

*GALLERY OF HOMES, INC.
1001 International Blvd.
Atlanta, GA 30354
(404) 768–2460
Contact: Melvin J. Howell

BUSINESS: Service to real estate sales offices.
FRANCHISES: 743 in all states except Maine, plus six provinces of Canada.
FOUNDED: 1950.

* Asterisk denotes franchisor is a member of the International Franchise Association.

REQUIRED CAPITAL: An existing business plus $3,375 to $8,700 (varies by population of franchised area).

FINANCIAL ASSISTANCE: None.

TRAINING: One five-day orientation program and staff assistance and participation of new franchisee in local council of franchisees at no charge. Additional professional courses available for less than $300 each.

MANAGERIAL ASSISTANCE: Continuous company assistance upon request by toll-free telephone. Manuals are provided that cover general techniques, office layout, referrals and corporate business leads, supplies catalogs, image program, advertising format guide, and other material upon request as available; there are no additional charges for this material and assistance.

HERBERT HAWKINS COMPANY, INC.
5770 North Rosemead Boulevard
Temple City, CA 91780
(213) 287–9811
Contact: Preston Hawkins

BUSINESS: Real estate sales offices.

FRANCHISES: 80 in California.

FOUNDED: 1974.

REQUIRED CAPITAL: $4,500 for franchise plus office equipment and fixtures.

FINANCIAL ASSISTANCE: Franchise can be purchased on terms.

TRAINING: Continuous real estate training.

MANAGERIAL ASSISTANCE: Management training provided and continuous.

INTERNATIONAL REAL ESTATE NETWORK
18075 Ventura Boulevard
Encino, CA 91316
(213) 981–1155
Contact: C. J. Seibert, Jr.

BUSINESS: Real estate sales offices.

FRANCHISES: 850 in United States and Canada.

FOUNDED: 1974.

REQUIRED CAPITAL: Franchises are normally sold to established operating real estate companies. No capital required. Franchise membership fees range from $1,500 to $6,950.

FINANCIAL ASSISTANCE: None.

TRAINING: In-house video tape training program.

MANAGERIAL ASSISTANCE: Special assistance is offered by governing board.

RAM, INC., REALTORS
12901 Saratoga Avenue
Saratoga, CA 95070
(408) 446–9166
Contact: Clare P. Rooney

BUSINESS: Real estate sales offices.
FRANCHISES: 16 in California.
FOUNDED: 1966.
REQUIRED CAPITAL: Negotiable.
FINANCIAL ASSISTANCE: None.
TRAINING: Assist in setup procedures, accounting, training new sales personnel.
MANAGERIAL ASSISTANCE: Assistance provided at request of franchisee.

REALTY USA/INTERSTATE REFERRAL SERVICE, INC.
3855 Lucas & Hunt Road
St. Louis, MO 63121
(314) 389–1111
Contact: Thomas J. Malone

BUSINESS: Real estate sales offices.
FRANCHISES: 59 in 23 states.
FOUNDED: 1975.
REQUIRED CAPITAL: Initial franchise fee $2,990. Service fee, 1.5 percent of gross commissions.
FINANCIAL ASSISTANCE: None.
TRAINING: Twelve-week tape and workbook training program for licensed salespeople; one-day indoctrination meeting at franchisee's office and periodic review meetings for management and staff.
MANAGERIAL ASSISTANCE: Realty USA furnishes a policies and procedures manual, forms, and other materials; also assistance in advertising and personnel recruitment, evaluation, and training. Company representatives and in some areas field personnel provide consultation and assistance. Interstate Referral Service sponsors periodic meetings of Realty USA franchisees and Interstate members.

REALTY WORLD CORPORATION
1001 Connecticut Avenue
Washington, DC 20036
(208) 331–0007
Contact: William L. Janeski

BUSINESS: Real estate sales offices. There are two types of franchises available— one a master license for a large territory (such as a whole state) and the master licensee in turn franchises for the local real estate broker (full explanation upon request).
FRANCHISES: Over 400 in 22 states, District of Columbia, and Canada.
FOUNDED: 1974.
REQUIRED CAPITAL: Local franchise approximately $6,400.
FINANCIAL ASSISTANCE: None.
TRAINING: Master franchisee receives 30 days of training and instruction. For the local franchisee, training is ongoing.
MANAGERIAL ASSISTANCE: Continuous assistance as needed.

*RED CARPET CORPORATION OF AMERICA
1990 North California Boulevard
Suite 830
Walnut Creek, CA 94596
(415) 929–4550
Contact: Licensing manager

BUSINESS: Real estate sales offices.
FRANCHISES: 1,110 in 18 states.
FOUNDED: 1966.
REQUIRED CAPITAL: $7,900.
FINANCIAL ASSISTANCE: A total investment of $7,900 is required for initial franchise—reduced for subsequent franchises. Company will assist in financing the franchise fee.
TRAINING: Franchisee receives six-day seminar on office management and continued sales personnel training. Training tapes are also available to franchisees.
MANAGERIAL ASSISTANCE: Continuous assistance as needed.

RECREATION/ENTERTAINMENT/TRAVEL SERVICES/SUPPLIES

CORNER POCKETS OF AMERICA, INC.
134 Regal Street
Billings, MT 59102
(406) 248–8728
Contact: George Frank

BUSINESS: Billiard lounges featuring beverages and amusement games.
FRANCHISES: 60 in 15 states.
FOUNDED: 1972.
REQUIRED CAPITAL: $50,000 with satisfactory financial background.
FINANCIAL ASSISTANCE: None.
TRAINING: Two weeks' training at corporate office and on-the-job training at franchise location.
MANAGERIAL ASSISTANCE: Assistance is provided on a continuing basis. Intermittent billiard promotions, leagues, tournaments and exhibitions, and free pool clinics and instruction. Predesigned plans and specifications for standard building, assistance in site selection, construction, opening and grand opening program.

EMPRESS TRAVEL FRANCHISE CORPORATION
293 Madison Avenue
New York, NY 10017
(212) 697–9698
Contact: Jack Cygielman

BUSINESS: Travel agency.
FRANCHISES: 50 in New York, New Jersey, Connecticut, Pennsylvania, Maryland, Virginia, and Washington, D.C.

FOUNDED: 1958.

REQUIRED CAPITAL: $18,000 plus operating capital.

FINANCIAL ASSISTANCE: Provided to qualified applicants.

TRAINING: Training course for all new franchisees and their personnel at the company home office and on site at company offices, also at franchisee's location.

MANAGERIAL ASSISTANCE: Continual management service with advertising, complete manuals of operations, forms and directions, and so on. Management works closely with franchisees to help solve problems. Company sponsors meetings of franchisees and conducts marketing research.

FASCINATION, LTD.
1950 East Estes
Elk Grove, IL 60007
(312) 640–0770
Contact: Robert Anderson, Vice President

BUSINESS: Coin-operated video games in cocktail table format.

FRANCHISES: Over 500 in all states except Alaska.

FOUNDED: 1973.

REQUIRED CAPITAL: $2,500 to $100,000 and up, depending on whether franchisee works part-time or full-time. Average $10,000 to $15,000.

FINANCIAL ASSISTANCE: Company assists existing franchisee who wishes to expand; leasing, bank financing, and company financing are available based on credit experience. No part of investment is for fees; capital of franchisee is used 100 percent for hard merchandise. Company permits franchisee to use outside financing and assists in this area.

TRAINING: Training courses at the company manufacturing offices every Monday with the exception of holiday weekends. Field training in franchisee's home area also available. All training available to any franchisee on a continuing and need basis, with no cost to franchisee.

MANAGERIAL ASSISTANCE: Continuing and updated managerial and technical assistance program available to franchisees without additional cost. Company will arrange for locations, install equipment, train franchisee comprehensively on a continuing basis, and grant protected areas in cases which purchase 25 or more games with ongoing commitment.

GOLF PLAYERS, INC.
5954 Brainerd Road
Chattanooga, TN 37421
(615) 892–7264
Contact: Earl Magrath, President

BUSINESS: Miniature golf courses and go-kart tracks.

FRANCHISES: 25 in 10 states.

FOUNDED: 1964.

REQUIRED CAPITAL: $28,600 up plus construction cost.

FINANCIAL ASSISTANCE: Limited.

TRAINING: Training at company office and on the job. Continuing help by personal visits, newsletters, and phone calls. Operational manager's manual is provided.

MANAGERIAL ASSISTANCE: Engineering design and construction planning; continuing management service and advice.

LOMMA ENTERPRISES, INC.
Lomma Building
1120 South Washington Avenue
Scranton, PA 18503
(717) 346–5559
Contact: J. C. Rogari

BUSINESS: Miniature golf courses.

FRANCHISES: 2,100 in all 50 states.

FOUNDED: 1960.

REQUIRED CAPITAL: $5,000.

FINANCIAL ASSISTANCE: A minimum down payment required and the balance can be payable up to a two-year period.

TRAINING: Operational and promotional kit is provided.

MANAGERIAL ASSISTANCE: Manager's guide and periodic training seminars, along with national promotions and an international miniature golf tournament.

MISS AMERICAN TEEN-AGERS, INC.
P.O. Box 221
New Milford, NJ 07646
(201) 262–4111
Contact: Sol Abrams

BUSINESS: Pageant for girls aged 13 through 17, with national winner designated as "Miss American Teen-Ager."

FRANCHISES: Franchises are awarded for one-year periods in all states. Franchise holders are given first option for renewing in their areas for the following year.

FOUNDED: 1960.

REQUIRED CAPITAL: $750–$2,000 depending upon size of area desired.

FINANCIAL ASSISTANCE: None.

TRAINING: Operation manual and press kit provided. One-and-a-half-hour TV tape and 20-minute color film are also available. Personal consultation of company management available at all times.

MANAGERIAL ASSISTANCE: Company provides counseling and managerial services continuously.

*PLAYBOY CLUBS INTERNATIONAL, INC.
919 North Michigan Avenue
Chicago, IL 60611
(312) 751–8000
Contact: Karen Kress

BUSINESS: Entertainment facilities and hotels.

FRANCHISES: 7 in seven states.

* Asterisk denotes franchisor is a member of the International Franchise Association.

FOUNDED: 1960.
REQUIRED CAPITAL: Depends on location.
FINANCIAL ASSISTANCE: None.
TRAINING: Dependent upon the particular needs of each franchisee.
MANAGERIAL ASSISTANCE: Continuous assistance including food and beverage, personnel, operating procedures, publicity, and promotion assistance.

PUTT-PUTT GOLF COURSES OF AMERICA, INC.
P.O. Box 5237
Fayetteville, NC 28303
(919) 485–7131
Contact: Larry M. Lloyd, Sr.

BUSINESS: Miniature golf courses.
FRANCHISES: 779 in 42 states.
FOUNDED: 1954.
REQUIRED CAPITAL: $7,500.
FINANCIAL ASSISTANCE: Assistance in obtaining financing through banks and Small Business Administration is available.
TRAINING: One week annually at international convention. Five regional, two-day seminars each year from March 1 through June 1.
MANAGERIAL ASSISTANCE: Computer accounting and manager's manual. Promotional program provided including radio, TV, and newspaper advertising, and so on, for the duration of the length of the contract.

BATHIQUE INTERNATIONAL LTD.
1304 Long Pond Road
Rochester, NY 14626
(716) 225–4520
Contact: Don A. Seipel

BUSINESS: Bed and bath specialty shop.
FRANCHISES: 40 in 21 states.
FOUNDED: 1969.
REQUIRED CAPITAL: $30,000 ($15,000 cash) for nonmail. $60,000 ($30,000 cash) for mail locations.
FINANCIAL ASSISTANCE: None.
TRAINING: Three-week training conducted for new franchisees. Two individuals from each franchise participate in a one-week manager training program which includes classroom and on-the-job training. Two weeks of on-site training is provided by the company at the time the franchisee's shop opens.
MANAGERIAL ASSISTANCE: Company assists in areas such as sales, purchasing, advertising, and labor scheduling. Merchandise is recommended to franchisees after testing in company shop. Merchandise is bought directly from recommended suppliers. A continuous personnel training program is available. Annual and regional conferences are conducted.

BUNING THE FLORIST, INC.
144 East Las Olas Boulevard
Fort Lauderdale, FL 33301
(305) 467–1776
Contact: Nelson Bartfield

BUSINESS: Florist shops.
FRANCHISES: 15 in Florida.
FOUNDED: 1925.
REQUIRED CAPITAL: Total investment varies from $39,000 to $49,000.
FINANCIAL ASSISTANCE: Company will finance portion of fee to qualified applicant.
TRAINING: Four weeks of classroom training and two weeks on-the-job training.
MANAGERIAL ASSISTANCE: Company provides continual management services, accounting functions, advertising, and regular monthly profit and loss statements. Field supervisors available continuously.

CONROY'S INC.
10524 West Pico Boulevard
Los Angeles, CA 90064
(213) 870–5314
Contact: C. M. Conroy, President

BUSINESS: Plant and flower shops.
FRANCHISES: 11 in Southern California.
FOUNDED: 1974.
REQUIRED CAPITAL: Minimum $35,000.
FINANCIAL ASSISTANCE: Company may finance all or most of the capital requirements.
TRAINING: Up to six months' training for couples only. Training covers all phases of retail floristry including actual work in the main store unit, purchasing and merchandising, personnel management, and holiday preparation. Additional training and assistance is given as needed in franchisee's own unit.
MANAGERIAL ASSISTANCE: Company provides operating manual, advertising, and all accounting, and produces monthly profit and loss statements for each franchisee. Provides opportunities for mass buying for franchisees. Coordinates holiday purchasing and planning.

FAMOUS FRENCH GALLERIES, LTD.
Box 181
Saluda, VA 23149
(804) 758–2388
Contact: R. L. R. Smith

BUSINESS: Art gallery.
FRANCHISES: 47 in 16 states.
FOUNDED: 1964.
REQUIRED CAPITAL: Approximately $11,500.
FINANCIAL ASSISTANCE: None.

TRAINING: One-week free training at one of the company galleries. Transportation and lodging is at the franchisee's expense.

MANAGERIAL ASSISTANCE: For $200 per month, the franchisee uses company consulting services which includes the selection of the proper location, a representative to come out and hang the gallery and spend one week there in additional training. Service also includes continuing guidance and help 12 months from opening.

*FIREPLACE SHOPS, INC.
1600 Georgesville Road
Columbus, OH 43228
(614) 878–9331
Contact: Judy Boley

BUSINESS: Fireplaces and fireplace equipment stores.

FRANCHISES: 71 in 22 states.

FOUNDED: 1965.

REQUIRED CAPITAL: $25,000 with a total cost of $75,000 to $90,000.

FINANCIAL ASSISTANCE: Company will assist franchisees in securing their own bank loans, for payment of the purchase price.

TRAINING: Ten days of training at the company office, and one to two weeks of working with an existing store owner. A representative of the company will attend store opening and work with franchisee for first week. Continued assistance programs and seminars semiannually. Continuous training provided by updated manuals, bulletins, and on-the-spot counseling.

MANAGERIAL ASSISTANCE: Frequent visits to stores, training programs for new employees; central advertising and promotional services; merchandising committee consisting of successful franchisees; updated product and operating manuals; review of financial status and comparisons with stores.

FLOWERAMA OF AMERICA, INC.
3165 West Airline Highway
Waterloo, IA 50701
(319) 291–6004
Contact: Bryan Patzkowski

BUSINESS: Plant and flower stores in enclosed malls only.

FRANCHISES: 77 in 20 states.

FOUNDED: 1966.

REQUIRED CAPITAL: $12,000 to $25,000.

FINANCIAL ASSISTANCE: Company assists franchisee in obtaining financing from local bank. Supplies merchandise for resale on 30-day account basis.

TRAINING: Three days at company office and three days at shop location.

MANAGERIAL ASSISTANCE: Continual management service for the life of the franchise in such areas as bookkeeping, advertising, and inventory control. Complete manuals of operations, forms, and directions are provided. Company representatives are available to work closely with franchisees and visit stores regularly.

* Asterisk denotes franchisor is a member of the International Franchise Association.

*FLOWER WORLD OF AMERICA, INC.
1655 Imperial Way
Mid-Atlantic Park
West Deptford, NJ 08086
(609) 845–2426
Contact: Robert Sheets

BUSINESS: Flower, plant, and gift stores.
FRANCHISES: Over 200 in 40 states and Canada.
FOUNDED: 1959.
REQUIRED CAPITAL: $7,500.
FINANCIAL ASSISTANCE: None.
TRAINING: Three to six weeks' training consisting of bookkeeping, sales, and flower arrangement.
MANAGERIAL ASSISTANCE: Company assistance provided during the duration of the agreement both in sales, accounting, and designing.

GOLDEN DOLPHIN, INC.
29 East Rawls Road
Des Plaines, IL 60018
(312) 298–1460
Contact: Paul R. Paulson

BUSINESS: Bath shops.
FRANCHISES: 65 in 21 states.
FOUNDED: 1960.
REQUIRED CAPITAL: $25,000 to $50,000, including license fee and inventory.
FINANCIAL ASSISTANCE: The company provides assistance in the planning, fixturing, and initial setup of franchises. Training, operations manuals, and merchandising aids are available.
TRAINING: The company provides training, operation manuals, and merchandising aids.
MANAGERIAL ASSISTANCE: Company representatives provide regular assistance in merchandise only. Guides in the merchandising of color are provided on a continuing basis.

LAFAYETTE ELECTRONICS SALES, INC.
P.O. Box L
Syosset, NY 11791
(516) 921–7700
Contact: Stan Pohmer

BUSINESS: Consumer and hobby electronics.
FRANCHISES: 366 in all states.
FOUNDED: 1921.
REQUIRED CAPITAL: $50,000 to $75,000.
FINANCIAL ASSISTANCE: None.
TRAINING: On-the-job training in another franchisee-owned store is available,

but company prefers that prospective franchisees have retail electronics background.

MANAGERIAL ASSISTANCE: Uniform accounting system. Ongoing advertising program. Company merchandising specialists regularly visit stores.

LELLY'S DRIVE-IN PHOTOS, INC.
4641 State Road 84
Ft. Lauderdale, FL 33314
(305) 940–0160
Contact: Kenneth H. Lelly

BUSINESS: Photo developing and finishing store.
FRANCHISES: 11 in Florida.
FOUNDED: 1968.
REQUIRED CAPITAL: $15,000 to $24,000.
FINANCIAL ASSISTANCE: None.
TRAINING: Fifteen days on-the-job training in one of the operating stores.
MANAGERIAL ASSISTANCE: Company provides continuing management and technical assistance to franchisee.

MISS BOJANGLES, INC.
P.O. Box 14589
Baton Rouge, LA 70808
(504) 923–2571
Contact: Mike Stokes

BUSINESS: Costume jewelry store.
FRANCHISES: 39 in 19 states.
FOUNDED: 1975.
REQUIRED CAPITAL: $17,500 to $72,500 cash depending on size and type of location.
FINANCIAL ASSISTANCE: Bank financing available with 33 percent to 50 percent equity.
TRAINING: Continuous training available.
MANAGERIAL ASSISTANCE: Complete manual provided and company representative will assist two to four weeks after opening. Will also assist in hiring personnel. Regional managers visit franchisee every four to six weeks.

MISTER CLARK'S
5851 East 34th Street
Indianapolis, IN 46222
(317) 547–3444
Contact: Robert A. Lutey

BUSINESS: Appliance stores in Indiana only.
FRANCHISES: 10 in Indiana.

FOUNDED: 1968.
REQUIRED CAPITAL: Open.
FINANCIAL ASSISTANCE: None.
TRAINING: None.
MANAGERIAL ASSISTANCE: Group discussions and individual consultations.

NELSON'S PHOTOGRAPHY STUDIOS
41 Colonial Arcade
Cleveland, OH 44115
(216) 861–4570
Contact: Joseph G. Ballard

BUSINESS: Photography studio and store.
FRANCHISES: 9 in Ohio.
FOUNDED: 1969.
REQUIRED CAPITAL: $18,500 total.
FINANCIAL ASSISTANCE: The down payment of $10,000 pays for inventory and training. All equipment needed is included. Company will finance the balance to qualified applicant.
TRAINING: One-week training conducted at the company office school and on-site at company training store; two weeks at franchisee's outlet under the supervision of company supervisor.
MANAGERIAL ASSISTANCE: Company provides continual management service for the life of the franchise in such areas as bookkeeping, and advertising. Complete manuals of operations, forms, and directions are provided. District managers are available to work closely with franchisees and to visit stores regularly. Company sponsors meetings of franchisees and conducts marketing and product research, and supplies constantly new promotions.

OPEN BOOK MARKETING CORPORATION
2966 Biddle
Wyandotte, MI 48192
(313) 285–9533
Contact: David Sucher

BUSINESS: Book stores.
FRANCHISES: 19 in Michigan and Ohio.
FOUNDED: 1971.
REQUIRED CAPITAL: $20,000 with total cost of $35,000 to $60,000.
FINANCIAL ASSISTANCE: Company will assist in obtaining local bank financing.
TRAINING: One-week training is offered before store opening in an existing location. The second week is at the franchisee's location.
MANAGERIAL ASSISTANCE: Company provides site selection, lease negotiation, store layout, and stocking of the store. Company representatives provide continuous assistance for the life of the contract.

PAPERBACK BOOKSMITH
450 Summer Street
Boston, MA 02210
(617) 426–9010
Contact: Paul A. Supovitz

BUSINESS: Book and/or record stores.

FRANCHISES: 72 in 12 states.

FOUNDED: 1961.

REQUIRED CAPITAL: $30,000 to $35,000.

FINANCIAL ASSISTANCE: Company assists in obtaining local bank financing and provides credit with its subsidiary distribution company (Booksmith Distributing Corporation).

TRAINING: Three-week preopening training program at company expense, including in-store merchandising, methods of ordering, and financial controls.

MANAGERIAL ASSISTANCE: Company representatives assist owner in setting up and opening store and then make periodic visits to the stores to assist in merchandising and inventory control. Company maintains an experienced buying staff, merchandising department, in-house advertising, and public relations department and warehouse to provide backup support to store. Almost 100 percent of the store's inventory is returnable for credit.

SPORT SHACKS, INC.
Route 2, P.O. Box 349
Lindstrom, MN 55045
(612) 257–5737
Contact: Roger L. Adair

BUSINESS: Sporting goods stores and dealers.

FRANCHISES: 560 in United States.

FOUNDED: 1974.

REQUIRED CAPITAL: $1,500 to $5,000.

FINANCIAL ASSISTANCE: None.

TRAINING: None.

MANAGERIAL ASSISTANCE: None.

STEREO COMPONENT SYSTEMS, INC.
d.b.a. Tech Hifi
48 Teed Drive
Randolph, MA 02368
(617) 492–6446
Contact: Stephen M. Bahn

BUSINESS: Stores specializing in stereo high-fidelity components.

FRANCHISES: 7 in six states.

FOUNDED: 1967.

REQUIRED CAPITAL: $100,000.

FINANCIAL ASSISTANCE: A total investment of $100,000 is required. Company will assist franchisee in preparing financing proposals. Franchisee must have good credit standing and considerable net worth.

TRAINING: Four weeks' training including working experience in company-operated stores in Boston area. Additional training is provided at franchisee's location.

MANAGERIAL ASSISTANCE: Before store opening, company provides training, site selection, lease negotiation, store design, merchandise selection, and business management instruction and guidance. After store opening, franchisor provides continuing guidance in merchandise selection, advertising, bookkeeping, management planning, and visits stores regularly to assist in solving problems. Computerized budgeting and inventory analysis services provided.

*TEAM CENTRAL, INCORPORATED
720–29th Avenue Southeast
Minneapolis, MN 55414
(612) 331–8511
Contact: James H. Keefer, Vice President, Franchise Operations

BUSINESS: Electronics stores.

FRANCHISES: 90 in 16 states.

FOUNDED: 1946.

REQUIRED CAPITAL: Total investment of $70,000 to $160,000. Franchisees must have a substantial personal net worth.

FINANCIAL ASSISTANCE: Company will assist with bank presentation and lease negotiation.

TRAINING: Operating procedures, warranty, and sales training manuals provided. Prior to store opening a training period of up to one or two weeks is available with an existing franchise. Continued in-store training, management seminars, and sales training aids from company library available.

MANAGERIAL ASSISTANCE: Store setup including plans, drawings, and counseling, on fixturing and inventory provided. Company representatives available to set up and open store and to conduct in-store operational training. Two yearly conferences—one of which is a merchandising/trade show, the other a management seminar dealing with store operations. Continued assistance provided through updated manuals, bulletins, and in-store counseling.

TECH HIFI. See Stereo Component Systems, Inc.

THE TINDER BOX INTERNATIONAL, LTD.
P.O. Box 830
Santa Monica, CA 90406
(213) 829–4646
Contact: Lynda Bundrock

BUSINESS: Retail tobacco stores.

FRANCHISES: 165 in 35 states.

FOUNDED: 1928.

REQUIRED CAPITAL: $25,000 to $45,000.

FINANCIAL ASSISTANCE: Financial assistance available to qualified applicants or will assist franchisee in obtaining financing.

TRAINING: Nine days' training for franchisee and spouse at company headquarters. Company representative provided for first two weeks of operation at franchisee's own store.

MANAGERIAL ASSISTANCE: Advertising, retailing product counseling by phone or mail. Regular counselor—salesperson's visits to franchisee's operation. Franchisee may, but is not required to, buy merchandise from company.

*WICKS 'N' STICKS, INC.
6937 Flintlock
P.O. Box 40307
Houston, TX 77040
(713) 466–4125
Contact: Harold R. Otto

BUSINESS: Candle and candle-related items.

FRANCHISES: 86 in the United States.

FOUNDED: 1968.

REQUIRED CAPITAL: Total cost is approximately $102,500.

FINANCIAL ASSISTANCE: Financial assistance to qualified applicants, but only when franchising a company-owned unit.

TRAINING: One full week in Houston at company's expense. An operations manual, a simplified bookkeeping system, a price book which lists all vendors, all personnel, and payroll-related forms, procedures, and applicable state and federal procedures are supplied. Once the franchisee has taken possession of the store, district manager trains for a period of two weeks in that store. Continuous company support is provided.

MANAGERIAL ASSISTANCE: Company schedules franchisee meetings, normally in conjunction with major gift shows throughout the country, and has also provided franchise financial seminars. Company is in constant communication with franchisees, both by telephone and by letters, to inform them of new merchandising techniques and new products. District managers and corporate headquarters personnel are readily available to provide franchisees with assistance. District managers call on assigned franchised locations approximately once a month to assist these stores with any operational questions, color coordination, displays, and to present new lines of merchandise.

*WORLD BAZAAR
Division of Munford, Inc.
68 Brookwood Drive, Northeast
Atlanta, GA 30309
(404) 873–6641
Contact: J. S. Cooper, Jr.

BUSINESS: Store specializing in imported goods.

FRANCHISES: 65 in 21 states.

FOUNDED: 1969.

REQUIRED CAPITAL: $35,000 to $65,000.

FINANCIAL ASSISTANCE: Company finances 100 percent of the opening inventory at 9 percent.

TRAINING: Two weeks' training in existing stores and the company warehouse.

MANAGERIAL ASSISTANCE: Continuing assistance as needed.

DICTOGRAPH SECURITY SYSTEM
P.O. Box 96
Florham Park, NJ 07932
(201) 822–1400
Contact: Myles C. Goldberg, Vice President

BUSINESS: Automatic fire and security systems.

FRANCHISES: 171 in most states, and Canada.

FOUNDED: Parent company since 1902.

REQUIRED CAPITAL: Minimum $8,000 depending upon location. Inventory refundable on one-year money back guarantee.

FINANCIAL ASSISTANCE: Equipment financing available. Portion of lease incomes assigned to local distributors.

TRAINING: Two weeks of national academy training at company's international headquarters building. Training includes class and field instruction for proper guidance and assistance in sales, administration, installation, and service maintenance.

MANAGERIAL ASSISTANCE: The company is constantly developing new materials, manuals, and sales presentation literature for its distributors, as well as conducting regional seminars and international conventions following through with ongoing assistance.

THE NIGHT EYE CORPORATION
Route 6
P.O. Box 260A
Iowa City, IA 52240
(314) 351–5827
Contact: Elliott D. Full

BUSINESS: Automatic fire and security systems.

FRANCHISES: 52 in 12 states.

FOUNDED: 1961.

REQUIRED CAPITAL: Approximately $15,000.

FINANCIAL ASSISTANCE: None.

TRAINING: No assistance generally needed, but training provided.

MANAGERIAL ASSISTANCE: Upon purchase of franchise, company officer visits new franchise holder and instructs the franchisee in the operation of the system from a technical, managerial, and operational standpoint. A person with some electrical background is recommended as an installer.

TELCOA
16 Church Street
Greenwich, CT 06830
(203) 849–1847
Contact: Robert J. Dolin

BUSINESS: Automatic fire and security systems.
FRANCHISES: 8 in seven states.
FOUNDED: 1967.
REQUIRED CAPITAL: $20,000 is required for necessary inventory and working capital.
FINANCIAL ASSISTANCE: $15,000 in inventory can be financed by company sources or franchisee's own banking source. Credit depends on the franchisee's qualifications.
TRAINING: One-week training program with ongoing field training in sales, management, and technical assistance.
MANAGERIAL ASSISTANCE: Company provides assistance as needed.

*BUBBLE-UP COMPANY
2800 North Talman Avenue
Chicago, IL 60618
(312) 463–4608
Contact: Roy Gurvey

BUSINESS: Soft drink bottling.
FRANCHISES: 155 in all 50 states.
FOUNDED: 1939.
REQUIRED CAPITAL: Franchisee must be in the bottling business. No franchise fee.
FINANCIAL ASSISTANCE: Credit extended occasionally on the purchase of drink concentrate; also financing available for the purchase of returnable bottles.
TRAINING: Training is provided by company personnel relative to the sale, distribution of merchandise, and advertising during the term of the franchise agreement.
MANAGERIAL ASSISTANCE: Assistance rendered including accounting, production, sales and advertising, and technical assistance relative to laboratory techniques used in production. These services are provided regularly and at any other time that franchisee requests.

COCK 'N BULL, LIMITED
5664 West Raymond Street
Indianapolis, IN 46241
(317) 243–3521
Contact: Harold A. Bateman

BUSINESS: Soft drink bottling.
FRANCHISES: 8 in five states and Guam.

* Asterisk denotes franchisor is a member of the International Franchise Association.

FOUNDED: 1945.
REQUIRED CAPITAL: Franchisee must be in bottling business.
FINANCIAL ASSISTANCE: None.
TRAINING: Sales and technical training on a continuing basis.
MANAGERIAL ASSISTANCE: Ongoing assistance provided for length of franchise.

*DAD'S ROOT BEER COMPANY
2800 North Talman Avenue
Chicago, IL 60618
(312) 463–4600
Contact: Roy Gurvey

BUSINESS: Soft drink bottling.
FRANCHISES: 172 in all 50 states.
FOUNDED: 1938.
REQUIRED CAPITAL: Must be in the bottling business. No franchise fee.
FINANCIAL ASSISTANCE: Credit extended occasionally on the purchase of drink concentrate; also financing available for the purchase of returnable bottles.
TRAINING: Training is provided by company personnel relative to the sale, distribution of merchandise, and advertising during the term of the franchise agreement.
MANAGERIAL ASSISTANCE: Assistance rendered including accounting, production, sales and advertising, and technical assistance relative to laboratory techniques used in production. These services are provided regularly and at any other time that franchisee requests. Marketing costs are shared on a cooperative basis.

DOUBLE-COLA COMPANY
3350 Broad Street
Chattanooga, TN 37402
(615) 267–5691
Contact: Wayne R. Downey

BUSINESS: Soft drink bottling.
FRANCHISES: 125 throughout the United States.
FOUNDED: 1922.
REQUIRED CAPITAL: None.
FINANCIAL ASSISTANCE: Promotional allowances.
TRAINING: Field help given by company regional managers in sales, marketing, advertising, production, and so on.
MANAGERIAL ASSISTANCE: Continuous.

MOUNTAIN VALLEY SPRING COMPANY
150 Central Avenue
Hot Springs, AR 71901
(501) 623–6671
Contact: John G. Scott

BUSINESS: Distributing mineral water.
FRANCHISES: 120 in 42 states.

FOUNDED: 1871.
REQUIRED CAPITAL: None.
FINANCIAL ASSISTANCE: Advertising appropriation by parent body.
TRAINING: On-the-scene training, or at a convenient company operation. Annual three-day training refresher course at convention.
MANAGERIAL ASSISTANCE: No technical assistance needed. For managerial assistance given see "Training" above.

BLUE DOLPHIN POOLS, INC.
4013 Woodville Highway
P.O. Box 6326
Tallahassee, FL 32301
(904) 877–7134
Contact: Licensing Manager

BUSINESS: In-ground swimming pools and accessories, and industrial chemicals.
FRANCHISES: 50 in Florida, Georgia, Alabama, Texas, and Arkansas.
FOUNDED: 1968.
REQUIRED CAPITAL: $5,000 to $20,000, depending on location.
FINANCIAL ASSISTANCE: None.
TRAINING: Two weeks of training in Tallahassee. Constant contact through sales representatives.
MANAGERIAL ASSISTANCE: Seminars held quarterly on regional basis.

CASCADE INDUSTRIES, INC.
Talmadge Road
Edison, NJ 08817
(201) 287–1000
Contact: Ernest B. Zenckes

BUSINESS: Swimming pools.
FRANCHISES: 250 in 40 states.
FOUNDED: 1954.
REQUIRED CAPITAL: $1,500 deposit, returned on initial purchases.
FINANCIAL ASSISTANCE: None.
TRAINING: Continued guidance available. Construction and sales seminars once per year. Regular sales meetings. Local company representatives help dealers.
MANAGERIAL ASSISTANCE: See "Training" above.

LIFETIME POOLS, INC.
1819 H Street, N.W.
Washington, DC 20006
(202) 872–0914
Contact: Richard Micheel

BUSINESS: Swimming pools.
FRANCHISES: 3 in Virginia, District of Columbia, and Maryland.

FOUNDED: 1966.
REQUIRED CAPITAL: $5,000.
FINANCIAL ASSISTANCE: None.
TRAINING: One-week training in Washington, D.C., on the installation of a pool, and sales methods.
MANAGERIAL ASSISTANCE: Assistance is given as needed in the field.

SAN JUAN PRODUCTS, INC.
831 North East Northgate Way
Seattle, WA 98125
(206) 364–0900
Contact: Erv Parent

BUSINESS: Swimming pools, one-piece fiberglass.
FRANCHISES: 50 in 12 states.
FOUNDED: 1960.
REQUIRED CAPITAL: $10,000 to $20,000.
FINANCIAL ASSISTANCE: Provides training and equipment, worth approximately $4,300.
TRAINING: One to three weeks provided.
MANAGERIAL ASSISTANCE: Continual observation and systems provided.

TOOLS, HARDWARE

IMPERIAL HAMMER, INC.
9226 N. Second Street
Rockford, IL 61111
(815) 633–2122
Contact: John R. Sassaman

BUSINESS: Sales of industrial hammers and vice jaws.
FRANCHISES: 7 in seven states.
FOUNDED: 1957.
REQUIRED CAPITAL: $30,000 depending on size of territory.
FINANCIAL ASSISTANCE: Financial assistance is available to qualified individuals.
TRAINING: Two weeks in franchisor's plant and office to learn complete operation.
MANAGERIAL ASSISTANCE: Assistance available to help find location, assist, advise, and counsel at all times.

MAC TOOLS, INC.
P.O. Box 370
South Fayette Street
Wash Court House, OH 43160
(614) 335–4112
Contact: Tom Sizer

BUSINESS: Sales of mechanics' hand tools and shop equipment.
FRANCHISES: 1,300 throughout the United States and Canada.

FOUNDED: 1938.

REQUIRED CAPITAL: Over $20,000.

FINANCIAL ASSISTANCE: The $20,000 amount includes a basic starting inventory, initial payment on a lease truck, business supplies, and backup capital. All financing is arranged on a local level by the franchisee. There are no franchise fees and the original investment is protected by a buy-back agreement.

TRAINING: Each franchisee is assigned to a district manager who trains for two weeks, maintains monthly contact, and will aid in displaying the trucks, establishing bookkeeping systems, and technical knowledge.

MANAGERIAL ASSISTANCE: Assistance by district manager as needed.

*SNAP-ON TOOLS CORPORATION
2801–80th Street
Kenosha, WI 53140
(414) 654–8681
Contact: General Sales Manager

BUSINESS: Sales of hand tools and equipment to garages and service stations.

FRANCHISES: Over 2,200 in 50 states.

FOUNDED: 1920.

REQUIRED CAPITAL: $20,000 to $40,000.

FINANCIAL ASSISTANCE: Merchandise on consignment; financing for accounts receivable for customers who purchase on installment plan; finance plan to cover the purchase of equipment items, and so on.

TRAINING: Printed training material. Sales training meetings.

MANAGERIAL ASSISTANCE: Visits from field sales managers responsible for territory. Assistance afforded by branch managers who are sales administrators, and assistance and advice on credit from regional finance department manager.

VULCAN TOOLS
United-Greenfield Division of TRW, Inc.
2300 Kenmore Avenue
Buffalo, NY 14207
(716) 873–5150
Contact: Douglas H. Burdick

BUSINESS: Sales of mechanics' hand tools, shop supplies, and equipment.

FRANCHISES: 107 in 19 states, Puerto Rico, and Canada.

FOUNDED: 1960.

REQUIRED CAPITAL: Dealers: $2,000 minimum. Warehouse: $8,000 minimum.

FINANCIAL ASSISTANCE: Dealer financing: Dealer must own suitable vehicle and have cash investment of not less than $2,000 for inventory. Company will finance inventory up to $4,000 on long-term, no interest, repayment plan for a qualified person. Thirty-day financing for any sales made to established business houses. Assistance in locating finance company to purchase installment contracts. Warehouse financing: None.

TRAINING: Three days' training on use of catalog, sales book, reporting forms,

* Asterisk denotes franchisor is a member of the International Franchise Association.

truck display, and tool selection. One week's initial field training in dealer's own territory. Continuing sales and demonstration assistance offered on regular basis. Standard procedure manual furnished. Instruction booklets furnished on all equipment items.

MANAGERIAL ASSISTANCE: Complete training in all forms necessary for conducting business. Counseling on inventory and accounts receivable. Assistance in taking physical inventory at no charge. Regularly scheduled sales meetings and technical clinics. Technical bulletins furnished free of charge.

TRANSIT SERVICES

AERO MAYFLOWER TRANSIT COMPANY, INC.
Recruiting Section
Transportation Department
P.O. Box 107B
Indianapolis, IN 46206
(317) 299–1000
Contact: Allen Puckett

BUSINESS: Interstate movers.
FRANCHISES: 870 in every state and Canada.
FOUNDED: 1927.
REQUIRED CAPITAL: Franchisee either owns a truck tractor or has sufficient down payment for a new or used diesel tractor. If franchisee owns a tractor, minimum of $1,000 capital is needed. Down payment on new or used tractor varies from $4,500 to $6,500.
FINANCIAL ASSISTANCE: Company furnishes trailer and specialized moving equipment. Certain preparation of tractor, supplies, and insurance may be charged and payments made on a monthly basis.
TRAINING: Total training period approximately three weeks, including training and testing in driving techniques, complete laboratory furniture loading school, and classroom courses in administrative detail. Upon completion of training, driver certification as required by U.S. Department of Transportation is issued. Contract offered upon successful completion of training.
MANAGERIAL ASSISTANCE: Administrative counselors assist, advise, and counsel at all times.

VENDING

*FORD GUM & MACHINE CO., INC.
Division of Automatic Service Company
Newton & Hoag Streets
Akron, NY 14001
(716) 542–4561
Contact: John H. Fry, Executive Vice President

BUSINESS: Sales of chewing gum and candy through self-service vending machines.
FRANCHISES: 190 in all states, Canada, and Puerto Rico.

* Asterisk denotes franchisor is a member of the International Franchise Association.

FOUNDED: 1934.

REQUIRED CAPITAL: $25,000 minimum depending upon size of franchise.

FINANCIAL ASSISTANCE: Extended credit to franchisees for purchase of new or existing franchising territory and purchase of equipment and supplies.

TRAINING: Company plant training of three to five days for orientation and product manufacture, merchandising, record keeping, accounting, machine assembly, and vending route supervision. On-the-job training in machine and service operation in franchisee's area with complete supervision for two to four weeks.

MANAGERIAL ASSISTANCE: Company field staff for emergency assistance and/or recurring assistance when needed or desired.

CHEMICAL ENGINEERING CORPORATION
P.O. Box 246
Churubusco, IN 46723
(219) 693–2141
Contact: L. D. Gordon

BUSINESS: Sales, rentals, and servicing of water conditioning equipment.

FRANCHISES: 10 in Indiana, Ohio, Illinois, Florida, and Georgia.

FOUNDED: 1956.

REQUIRED CAPITAL: $5,000.

FINANCIAL ASSISTANCE: None.

TRAINING: Two weeks at company headquarters, and two weeks at business location. Training includes all phases of business including sales, accounting, and technical.

MANAGERIAL ASSISTANCE: Complete manuals of operations, all forms, and literature are provided. Periodic seminars are held covering both technical and selling activities. In-field assistance is available whenever required. Assistance in preparation of quotations for commercial and industrial water treatment equipment is also provided.

CULLIGAN INTERNATIONAL COMPANY
One Culligan Parkway
Northbrook, IL 60062
(312) 498–2000
Contact: Licensing manager

BUSINESS: Sales, rentals, and servicing of water conditioning equipment.

FRANCHISES: 910 in all states except Hawaii.

FOUNDED: 1938.

REQUIRED CAPITAL: $20,000 and up.

FINANCIAL ASSISTANCE: Company provides credit for qualified franchisees for purchase of equipment.

TRAINING: One-week training at established dealership and one-week training at Northbrook, Illinois, headquarters. Company provides management training, sales training, and technical training through frequent visits to franchisee's location.

MANAGERIAL ASSISTANCE: Company has continuing managerial and technical assistance to franchisee through traveling field sales managers, technical service engineers, district sales managers, and industrial managers as needed.

ECODYNE CORPORATION
The Lindsay Division
P.O. Box 43420
St. Paul, MN 55164
(612) 739-5330
Contact: Robert P. Gantzer, National Sales Manager

BUSINESS: Sales, rentals, and servicing of water conditioning equipment.

FRANCHISES: 600 in the United States.

FOUNDED: 1945.

REQUIRED CAPITAL: $10,000 and up.

FINANCIAL ASSISTANCE: Credit available to qualified applicants for equipment purchases; company-financed rental program.

TRAINING: Training is provided on all phases of a dealer's business, available both in St. Paul, and in the field.

MANAGERIAL ASSISTANCE: Continuous management, sales, and service assistance available through sales, service training, and marketing departments.

RAINSOFT WATER CONDITIONING COMPANY
1225 East Greenleaf Avenue
Elk Grove Village, IL 60007
(312) 437-9400
Contact: John Grayson

BUSINESS: Sales, rentals, and servicing of water conditioning equipment.

FRANCHISES: 200 in most states except Hawaii.

FOUNDED: 1953.

REQUIRED CAPITAL: $5,000 minimum.

FINANCIAL ASSISTANCE: Assists franchisee in obtaining financing. Rental financing to qualified dealers.

TRAINING: In-plant and field training in sales, service, and operation.

MANAGERIAL ASSISTANCE: Continuing contact for training and assistance through national and regional seminars, plus regular visits by regional field representatives.

SUPERIOR WATER CONDITIONERS
2015 South Calhoun Street
Fort Wayne, IN 46804
(219) 456-3596
Contact: Charles H. Sanderson

BUSINESS: Sales, rentals, and servicing of water conditioning equipment.

FRANCHISES: 10 in ten states.

FOUNDED: 1967.

REQUIRED CAPITAL: $5,000 minimum.

FINANCIAL ASSISTANCE: Total investment of $10,000 is required for inventory and needed supplies. Company will finance $5,000 for qualified applicants.

TRAINING: Factory training is provided covering installation. Field training is provided 30 days after franchisee has had basic instructions.

MANAGERIAL ASSISTANCE: Technical information is constantly being provided and a special telephone line is answered 24 hours a day, seven days a week for problem solving. An initial supply of manuals are furnished at no charge to the franchisee.

WATERCARE CORPORATION
1520 North 24th Street
Manitowoc, WI 54220
(414) 682–6823
Contact: William W. Granger

BUSINESS: Sales, rentals, and servicing of water conditioning equipment.

FRANCHISES: 82 in 21 states and Canada.

FOUNDED: 1948.

REQUIRED CAPITAL: $5,000.

FINANCIAL ASSISTANCE: After initial financing, company provides assistance on plant equipment and rental water conditioners.

TRAINING: Includes techniques of water conditioning, water analysis, sales and service of equipment, office procedures, management, all of which is done at home office and plant in Manitowoc, Wisconsin, and dealer-lab retail operation at Green Bay, Wisconsin. Time is approximately one week in Wisconsin and one week by dealer counselor at the franchisee's place of operation.

MANAGERIAL ASSISTANCE: Monthly call on franchisee by dealer counselor and semiannual area work seminars.

WATER PURIFICATION SYSTEMS, INC.
6502 N.W. 16th Street
Plantation, FL 33313
(305) 587–5581
Contact: Fred Mussler

BUSINESS: Residential water purification systems. Product attaches under the sink and to the ice maker in the consumer's home.

FRANCHISES: 34 in 16 states, and 5 foreign franchises.

FOUNDED: 1972.

REQUIRED CAPITAL: $25,000.

FINANCIAL ASSISTANCE: No charge for training and marketing programs, only the inventory.

TRAINING: Four days initially at the home office with periodic field training as requested.

MANAGERIAL ASSISTANCE: Company provides continual technical assistance with materials, new products, and government coordination. Complete manuals for instruction, advertising, and sales presentations are available. Company sponsors meetings in distributor's area.

WATER REFINING COMPANY
500 N. Verity Parkway
Middletown, OH 45042
(513) 423–9421
Contact: Charles Fleming

BUSINESS: Sales, rentals, and servicing of water conditioning equipment.
FRANCHISES: 900 in all 50 states.
FOUNDED: 1957.
REQUIRED CAPITAL: $5,000 up.
FINANCIAL ASSISTANCE: Total sales (marketing) , business, service, and so on.
TRAINING: Continuing.
MANAGERIAL ASSISTANCE: Continuing.

WHOLESALE AND SERVICE BUSINESSES—MISCELLANEOUS

AMERICAN HERITAGE AGENCY, INC.
104 Park Road
Hartford, CT 06119
(203) 233–6261
Contact: William Gellnas

BUSINESS: Wedding consulting business.
FRANCHISES: 4 in Connecticut.
FOUNDED: 1925.
REQUIRED CAPITAL: $10,000.
FINANCIAL ASSISTANCE: Financing of up to 50 percent of the franchise fee to qualified applicant.
TRAINING: Twelve days of formal classroom training and on-the-job training at established office; up to 30 days' training at franchisee's own office; periodic briefings and meetings.
MANAGERIAL ASSISTANCE: Company representative available to help in solving problems, expanding operations, and suggesting improvements.

THE ARMOLOY COMPANY
1405 First United Building
Fort Worth, TX 76102
(817) 332–4123
Contact: Gary L. Nickelson

BUSINESS: Electrodeposited chromium metal coating, for wear and corrosion protection of precision parts.
FRANCHISES: 9 in 8 states.

FOUNDED: 1958.

REQUIRED CAPITAL: $60,000 to $75,000 minimum.

FINANCIAL ASSISTANCE: None.

TRAINING: Two-week training period at company headquarters for key shop personnel. Continuing assistance in any phase of the business.

MANAGERIAL ASSISTANCE: Technical assistance is run by company quality control laboratory, and company provides any managerial help that is needed. Advertising, administrative, and sales help available.

BAR-MASTER INTERNATIONAL
2206 Beverly Boulevard
Los Angeles, CA 90057
(213) 385–0231
Contact: J. H. McMillen

BUSINESS: Sales and leasing of soft drink and liquor dispensers.

FRANCHISES: 55 in 27 states.

FOUNDED: 1952.

REQUIRED CAPITAL: $1,000 to $10,000, depending on area.

FINANCIAL ASSISTANCE: None.

TRAINING: Two weeks' training with technical support in the field.

MANAGERIAL ASSISTANCE: Ongoing assistance for life of franchise.

CONSUMER PRODUCTS OF AMERICA, INC.
10450 Southwest 187th Terrace
Miami, FL 33157
(305) 233–1946
Contact: M. Mattaway

BUSINESS: Rack merchandising in supermarkets, super-drugstores, and variety stores.

FRANCHISES: 4 in Florida, Texas, Louisiana, and New Jersey.

FOUNDED: 1965.

REQUIRED CAPITAL: $25,000 to $60,000.

FINANCIAL ASSISTANCE: None.

TRAINING: One to two weeks as required.

MANAGERIAL ASSISTANCE: Continuing.

MEISTERGRAM
310 Lakeside Avenue, West
Cleveland, OH 44113
(216) 621–8731
Contact: L. D. Katz

BUSINESS: Monogram embroidery equipment and supplies.

FRANCHISES: 500 in 48 states.

FOUNDED: 1931.

REQUIRED CAPITAL: $3,500.

FINANCIAL ASSISTANCE: The franchisee may pay half the amount and finance the rest over a period of 12 months.

TRAINING: Training available at franchise location.

MANAGERIAL ASSISTANCE: Factory-trained instructor installs machine on premises and teaches franchisee how to operate and maintain equipment and work with different materials and garments. Complete supplies and service available.

NADEAU LOOMS, INC.
725 Branch Avenue
Providence, RI 02904
(401) 331–4487
Contact: Elphege Nadeau

BUSINESS: Mind and body training systems involving handwoven fabrics, ready wound warps, and fillers.

FRANCHISES: 14 in New York, New Jersey, Florida, Illinois, and Pennsylvania.

FOUNDED: 1959.

REQUIRED CAPITAL: $5,300.

FINANCIAL ASSISTANCE: Financing available to qualified applicants.

TRAINING: One hundred hours of training.

MANAGERIAL ASSISTANCE: Continuous assistance.

NATIONWIDE EXTERMINATING
Division of Nationwide Chemical
P.O. Box 3027
Hamilton, OH 45013
(513) 895–2162
Contact: David M. Valentine, President

BUSINESS: Distribution of pest control products and service.

FRANCHISES: 40 in seven states, and 5 in Europe.

FOUNDED: 1968.

REQUIRED CAPITAL: Distributorship $4,000 minimum, service franchise only $400 per year.

FINANCIAL ASSISTANCE: None.

TRAINING: Two-week training course is suggested. For those not licensed in pest control, an intensive-training program is available for $100 per day.

MANAGERIAL ASSISTANCE: Continuous assistance.

NATIONWIDE CHEMICAL PRODUCTS, INC.
P.O. Box 3027
Hamilton, OH 45013
(513) 892–2102
Contact: David M. Valentine, President

BUSINESS: Manufacturer and custom packager of insecticides and rodenticides.

FRANCHISES: 40 in 7 states.

FOUNDED: 1968.
REQUIRED CAPITAL: $20,000.
FINANCIAL ASSISTANCE: None.
TRAINING: Two-week training program in Columbus, Ohio, at franchisee's expense.
MANAGERIAL ASSISTANCE: Continuous assistance.

NATIONWIDE FASTENER SYSTEMS, INC.
240 Laura Drive
Addison, IL 60101
(312) 543–3892
Contact: Frank Cavanaugh

BUSINESS: Sales of nuts and bolts from mobile warehouse.
FRANCHISES: 42 in ten states.
FOUNDED: 1969.
REQUIRED CAPITAL: $5,000.
FINANCIAL ASSISTANCE: Approximately 20 percent.
TRAINING: One week in company home office, plus one week in the field.
MANAGERIAL ASSISTANCE: Continuous backup through personal and telephone conferences, service equipment, manuals, and bookkeeping system.

PARKING COMPANY OF AMERICA
1515 Arapahoe Street
Denver, CO 80202
(303) 623–1217
Contact: Richard R. Chaves

BUSINESS: Self-service parking lots and garages.
FRANCHISES: 23 in 16 states.
FOUNDED: 1963.
REQUIRED CAPITAL: $100,000.
FINANCIAL ASSISTANCE: None.
TRAINING: Six months in Denver.
MANAGERIAL ASSISTANCE: Annual convention and seminars in Denver.

REDD PEST CONTROL COMPANY, INC.
4114 Northview Drive
Jackson, MS 39206
(601) 982–8315
Contact: Richard Redd

BUSINESS: Pest control and extermination service.
FRANCHISES: 6 in Tennessee, Louisiana, Mississippi, and Florida.
FOUNDED: 1946.
REQUIRED CAPITAL: $15,000 minimum.

FINANCIAL ASSISTANCE: Franchisee will be able to factor the accounts receivable to finance equipment and vehicles.

TRAINING: Three to six months depending on knowledge of franchisee.

MANAGERIAL ASSISTANCE: Extensive assistance for the first year; additional assistance thereafter, as required.

SELECTRA-DATE CORPORATION
2175 Lemoine Avenue
Ft. Lee, NJ 07024
(201) 461–8400
Contact: Robert Friedman

BUSINESS: Computer dating service.

FRANCHISES: 11 in 9 states.

FOUNDED: 1966.

REQUIRED CAPITAL: $7,500.

FINANCIAL ASSISTANCE: The total required investment for promotional material, initial advertising, franchise fee, and for forms and stationery is $10,000, of which company will finance $3,500 for qualified applicant. The franchisees should also have sufficient capital to adequately equip their offices and to see them through the first 30 days of operation.

TRAINING: Company trains each franchisee, on site, in all phases of the business during the first week of operation.

MANAGERIAL ASSISTANCE: Company furnishes continuing individual guidance.

*STRETCH & SEW, INC.
P.O. Box 185
Eugene, OR 97401
(503) 686–9961
Contact: H. B. Person

BUSINESS: Instructions in sewing with knits and sale of knit fabrics, patterns, and books.

FRANCHISES: 242 in the United States and Canada.

FOUNDED: 1969.

REQUIRED CAPITAL: Approximately $81,000.

FINANCIAL ASSISTANCE: None.

TRAINING: Management training for five days at company home office. Teacher training for the first three teachers of each franchise store.

MANAGERIAL ASSISTANCE: Provides continual management service for life of franchise agreement. Field Support Representatives available to assist franchisee. Annual convention and workshops available.

* Asterisk denotes franchisor is a member of the International Franchise Association.

TELOPHASE CORPORATION
7969 Engineer Road
San Diego, CA 92111
(714) 571–0507
Contact: Dr. Thomas B. Weber

BUSINESS: Cremation society with memberships available. It is the alternative to the mortuary-funeral-cemetery complex.
FRANCHISES: 5 in California, Washington, and Oregon.
FOUNDED: 1971.
REQUIRED CAPITAL: $15,000.
FINANCIAL ASSISTANCE: Assist franchisee in acquiring capital.
TRAINING: Two-week course of instruction.
MANAGERIAL ASSISTANCE: Continual, including legal, medical and health, funeral, and business.

TEPCO, INC.
2705 Industrial Lane
Garland, TX 75041
(214) 276–0591
Contact: Paul J. Thompson

BUSINESS: Manufacturers of electronic air cleaning and air pollution control equipment.
FRANCHISES: 70 in 45 states.
FOUNDED: 1969.
REQUIRED CAPITAL: $25,000.
FINANCIAL ASSISTANCE: None.
TRAINING: Three-day sessions of on-the-job training four times during the first year. Field training during the first 120 days. Training as required thereafter.
MANAGERIAL ASSISTANCE: Continuous managerial and technical assistance in sales, marketing, advertising, engineering, service, and maintenance.

THE UNEEDIT JEWELRY COMPANY
4420 Montana Avenue
El Paso, TX 79903
(915) 565–7063
Contact: Louis G. Glomb

BUSINESS: Sales of custom-designed hard enamel jewelry items to clubs, firms, associations, premium promoters, advertising agencies, churches, and so on.
FRANCHISES: 4 in Texas and New York.
FOUNDED: 1961.
REQUIRED CAPITAL: $500 for distributorship.
FINANCIAL ASSISTANCE: None.
TRAINING: Intensive eight-hour training course on site at the company training store.

MANAGERIAL ASSISTANCE: Company provides various lists of firms, advertising agencies, clubs, associations, and churches to be contacted in the franchisee's area.

UNITED AIR SPECIALISTS, INC.
6665 Creek Road
Cincinnati, OH 45242
(513) 891–0400
Contact: Thomas Fening

BUSINESS: Manufacture of commercial electronic air cleaners.

FRANCHISES: 51 in the United States and Canada.

FOUNDED: 1966.

REQUIRED CAPITAL: $6,500 secured by inventory. Additional $5,000 to $10,000 desirable.

FINANCIAL ASSISTANCE: Thirty-day terms on reorders.

TRAINING: Three days' training at company factory. Five days field training within first 45 days. Quarterly regional seminars. Annual sales meetings.

MANAGERIAL ASSISTANCE: Ongoing field and factory assistance provided by sales, marketing, and engineering.

section
5

U.S. Department
of Commerce

U.S. DEPARTMENT OF COMMERCE
14th Street between Constitution and E Street, N.W.
Washington, DC 20230
(202) 337-2000
Contact: Juanita M. Kreps, Secretary of Commerce

For information or guidance, telephone the Department of Commerce field office in your area. Most likely, they will be able to answer your questions on franchising. However, if they are not able to assist you, they will direct you to the proper person or office in Washington.

FIELD OFFICES

Alabama
Suite 200–201
908 South 20th Street
Birmingham, AL 35205
(205) 254–1331
Contact: Gayle C. Shelton, Jr.

Alaska
412 Hill Building
632 Sixth Avenue
Anchorage, AK 99501
(907) 265–5307
Contact: Sara L. Haslett

Arizona
508 Greater Arizona Savings Bldg.
112 North Central
Phoenix, AZ 85004
(602) 261–3285
Contact: Donald W. Fry

California
Eighth Floor
11777 San Vicente Boulevard
Los Angeles, CA 90049
(213) 824–7591
Contact: Eric C. Silberstein

Federal Building
Box 36013
450 Golden Gate Avenue
San Francisco, CA 94102
(415) 556–5860
Contact: Philip M. Creighton

Colorado
Room 161
New Customhouse
19th and Stout Streets
Denver, CO 80202
(303) 837–3246
Contact: Norman Lawson

Connecticut
Room 610-B
Federal Office Building
450 Main Street
Hartford, CT 06103
(203) 244–3530
Contact: Richard C. Kilbourn

Florida
Room 821
City National Bank Building
25 West Flagler Street
Miami, FL 33130
(305) 350–5267
Contact: Roger J. LaRoche

Georgia
Suite 600
1365 Peachtree Street, N.E.
Atlanta, GA 30309
(404) 526–2470
Contact: David S. Williamson

235 U.S. Courthouse & Post
Office Building
125–29 Bull Street
Savannah, GA 31402
(912) 232–4321
Contact: James W. McIntire

Hawaii
286 Alexander Young Building
1015 Bishop Street
Honolulu, HI 96813
(808) 546–8694
Contact: John S. Davies

Illinois
1406 Mid-Continental Plaza
Building
55 East Monroe Street
Chicago, IL 60603
(312) 353–4450
Contact: Gerald M. Marks

Indiana
357 U.S. Courthouse & Federal
Office Building
46 East Ohio Street
Indianapolis, IN 46204
(317) 269–6214
Contact: Mel R. Sherar

Iowa
609 Federal Building
210 Walnut Street
Des Moines, IA 50309
(515) 284–4222
Contact: Jesse N. Durden

Louisiana
432 International Trade Mart
No. 2 Canal Street
New Orleans, LA 70130
(504) 589–6546
Contact: Edwin A. Leland, Jr.

Maryland
415 U.S. Customhouse
Gay and Lombard Streets
Baltimore, MD 21202
(301) 962–3560
Contact: Carroll F. Hopkins

Massachusetts
10th Floor
441 Stuart Street
Boston, MA 02116
(617) 223–2312
Contact: Francis J. O'Connor

Michigan
445 Federal Building
Detroit, MI 48226
(313) 226–6088
Contact: William L. Welch

Minnesota
218 Federal Building
110 South Fourth Street
Minneapolis, MN 55401
(612) 725–2133
Contact: Glenn A. Matson

Missouri
120 South Central Avenue
St. Louis, MO 63105
(314) 425–3302
Contact: Donald R. Loso

Nebraska
1815 Capitol Avenue
Omaha, NB 68102
(402) 221–3665
Contact: George H. Payne

Nevada
2028 Federal Building
300 Booth Street
Reno, NV 89502
(702) 784–5203
Contact: Joseph J. Jeremy

New Jersey
4th Floor Gateway Building
Newark, NJ 07102
(201) 645–6214
Contact: Clifford R. Lincoln

New Mexico
U.S. Courthouse—Room 316
Albuquerque, NM 87101
(505) 766–2386
Contact: William E. Dwyer

New York
1312 Federal Building
111 West Huron Street
Buffalo, NY 14202
(716) 842–3208
Contact: Robert F. Magee

37th Floor
Federal Office Building
26 Federal Plaza
Foley Square
New York, NY 10007
(212) 264–0634
Contact: Arthur C. Rutzen

North Carolina
203 Federal Building
West Market Street
P.O. Box 1950
Greensboro, NC 27402
(919) 275–9111
Contact: Joel B. New

Ohio
8028 Federal Office Building
550 Main Street
Cincinnati, OH 45202
(513) 684–2944
Contact: Gordon B. Thomas

Room 600
666 Euclid Avenue
Cleveland, OH 44114
(216) 522–4750
Contact: Charles B. Stebbins

Oregon
521 Pittock Block
921 S.W. Washington Street
Portland, OR 97205
(503) 221–3001
Contact: Lloyd R. Porter

Pennsylvania
9448 Federal Building
600 Arch Street
Philadelphia, PA 19106
(215) 597–2850
Contact: Patrick P. McCabe

2002 Federal Building
1000 Liberty Avenue
Pittsburgh, PA 15222
(412) 644–2850
Contact: William M. Bradley

Puerto Rico
Room 100
Post Office Building
San Juan, PR 00902
(809) 723–4640
Contact: Enrique Vilella

South Carolina
2611 Forest Drive
Forest Center
Columbia, SC 29204
(803) 765–5345
Contact: Philip A. Ouzts

Tennessee
Room 710
147 Jefferson Avenue
Memphis, TN 38103
(901) 534–3213
Contact: Bradford H. Rice

Texas
Room 7A5
1100 Commerce Street
Dallas, TX 75202
(214) 749–1515
Contact: C. Carmon Stiles

1017 Old Federal Building
201 Fannin Street
Houston, TX 77002
(713) 226–4231
Contact: Felicito C. Guerrero

Utah
1203 Federal Building
125 South State Street
Salt Lake City, UT 84138
(801) 524–5116
Contact: George M. Blessing, Jr.

Virginia
8010 Federal Building
400 North 8th Street
Richmond, VA 23240
(804) 782–2246
Contact: Director

Washington
Room 706
Lake Union Building
1700 Westlake Avenue North
Seattle, WA 98109
(206) 442–5615
Contact: Judson S. Wonderly

West Virginia
3000 New Federal Office Building
500 Quarrier Street
Charleston, WV 25301
(304) 343–6181, Ext. 375
Contact: Roger L. Fortner

Wisconsin
Federal Bldg.—U.S. Courthouse
517 East Wisconsin Avenue
Milwaukee, WI 53202
(414) 224–3473
Contact: Russel H. Leitch

Wyoming
6022 O'Mahoney Federal Center
2120 Capitol Avenue
Cheyenne, WY 82001
(307) 778–2220, Ext. 2151
Contact: Lowell O. Burns

section
6

Small Business
Administration

The Small Business Administration (SBA) renders assistance in various ways to those persons planning to enter business as well as to those already in business. This assistance includes counseling and possible financial aid.

Counseling may be by SBA specialists or retired executives under the Service Corps of Retired Executives (SCORE) program, and could include various seminars or courses, or a combination of services including reference publications.

Financial assistance may take the form of loans or the participation in, or guarantee of, loans made by financial institutions. Such assistance can be given only to those eligible applicants who are unable to provide the money from their own resources and cannot obtain it on reasonable terms from banks, franchisors, or other usual business sources.

The Small Business Administration financial support under its own legislation can provide up to $350,000 with the usual maximum maturity of six years for working capital and up to ten years for fixtures and equipment. Under some circumstances, portions of a loan involving construction can qualify for longer terms up to 15 years. For those who qualify, loans made under Title IV of the Economic Opportunity Act can be up to $25,000 and the maturity can be up to 10 years for working capital and 15 years for fixed assets.

A list follows of Small Business Administration field offices where more detailed information regarding the various services available can be obtained.

REGION 1
(Connecticut, Maine, Massachusetts, New Hampshire, Rhode Island, Vermont)

150 Causeway Street
10th Floor
Boston, MA 02203
(617) 223-2100

District Offices

Federal Bldg.
450 Main Street
Room 710
Hartford, CT 06103
(203) 244-2000

Federal Bldg.
40 Western Ave.
Room 512
Augusta, ME 04330
(207) 622-6171

302 High Street
Holyoke, MA 01040
(413) 536–8770

55 Pleasant Street
Room 213
Concord, NH 03301
(603) 224–4041

57 Eddy Street
Room 710
Providence, RI 02903
(401) 528–1000

REGION 2
(New Jersey, New York, Puerto Rico, Virgin Islands)

26 Federal Plaza
Room 3930
New York, NY 10007
(212) 264–1468

District Offices

970 Broad Street
Room 1635
Newark, NJ 07102
(201) 645–3581

99 Washington Avenue
Twin Towers Bldg.
Room 922
Albany, NY 12210
(518) 472–4411

111 West Huron Street
Room 1311
Federal Bldg.
Buffalo, NY 14202
(716) 842–3311

180 State Street
Room 412
Elmira, NY 14904
(607) 734–1571

Federal Building
100 State Street
Rochester, NY 14604
(716) 263–5700

Hunter Plaza
Fayette and Salina Streets
Room 308
Syracuse, NY 13202
(315) 473–3350

225 Ponce De Leon Avenue
Hato Rey, PR 00919
(809) 763–6363

REGION 3
(Delaware, District of Columbia, Maryland, Pennsylvania, Virginia, West Virginia)

231 St. Asaphs Road
Bala Cynwyd, PA 19004
(215) 597–3311

District Offices

1030 15th Street, N.W.
2d Floor
Washington, DC 20417
(202) 382–3525

844 King Street
Federal Bldg.
Room 5207
Wilmington, DE 19801
(302) 571–6294

7800 York Road
Towson, MD 21204
(301) 962–3311

1500 North 2nd Street
Harrisburg, PA 17108
(717) 782–3840

Federal Bldg.
1000 Liberty Avenue
Room 1401
Pittsburgh, PA 15222
(412) 644–2728

20 N. Pennsylvania Avenue
Wilkes-Barre, PA 18702
(717) 825–6811

109 North 3d Street
Room 301
Lowndes Bldg.
Clarksburg, WV 26301
(304) 623–3461

Federal Bldg.
400 North 8th Street
Room 3015
Richmond, VA 23240
(703) 782–2618

REGION 4
(Alabama, Florida, Georgia, Kentucky, Mississippi, North Carolina, South Carolina, Tennessee)

1401 Peachtree Street, N.E.
Room 441
Atlanta, GA 30309
(404) 526–0111

District Offices

908 South 20th Street
Room 202
Birmingham, AL 35205
(205) 254–1000

Federal Bldg.
400 West Bay Street
Room 261
Jacksonville, FL 32202
(904) 791–2011

2222 Ponce de Leon Blvd.
5th Floor
Miami, FL 33184
(305) 350–5011

1802 N. Trask Street
Suite 203
Tampa, FL 33607
(813) 228–2594

Federal Bldg.
600 Federal Plaza
Room 188
Louisville, KY 40202
(502) 582–5971

111 Fred Haise Blvd.
Gulf Nat. Life Ins. Bldg.
2d Floor
Biloxi, MS
(601) 863–1972

Petroleum Bldg.
Suite 690
200 Pascagoula Street
Jackson, MS 39201
(601) 969–4371

Addison Bldg.
230 S. Tryon Street
Charlotte, NC 28202
(704) 372–0711

215 South Evans Street
Greenville, NC 27834
(919) 752–3798

1801 Assembly Street
Room 117
Columbia, SC 29201
(803) 765–5376

502 South Gay Street
Room 307
Fidelity Bankers Bldg.
Knoxville, TN 37902
(615) 637–9300

Federal Bldg.
167 North Main Street
Room 211
Memphis, TN 38103
(901) 534–3011

REGION 5

(Illinois, Indiana, Michigan, Minnesota, Ohio, Wisconsin)

Federal Bldg.
219 South Dearborn Street
Room 437
Chicago, IL 60604
(312) 353–4400

District Offices

502 East Monroe Street
Ridgely Bldg.
Room 816
Springfield, IL 62701
(217) 525–4416

575 N. Pennsylvania Avenue
Century Bldg.
Indianapolis, IN 46204
(317) 269–7272

1249 Washington Blvd.
Room 1200
Book Bldg.
Detroit, MI 48226
(313) 226–6075

201 McClellan Street
Marquette, MI 49855
(906) 225–1108

12 South 6th Street
Plymouth Bldg.
Minneapolis, MN 55402
(612) 725–2362

Federal Bldg.
550 Main Street
Cincinnati, OH 45202
(513) 684–2814

1240 East 9th Street
Room 5524
Cleveland, OH 44199
(216) 522–4180

34 North High Street
Columbus, OH 43215
(614) 469–6860

500 South Barstown Street
Room 16
Federal Office Bldg. &
   U.S. Courthouse
Eau Claire, WI 54701
(715) 834–9012

122 West Washington Avenue
Room 713
Madison, WI 53703
(608) 252–5261

735 West Wisconsin Avenue
Room 905
Continental Bank & Trust Co.
Milwaukee, WI 53233
(414) 244–3941

REGION 6
(Arkansas, Louisiana, New Mexico, Oklahoma, Texas)

1720 Regal Row
Regal Park Office Bldg.
Dallas, TX 75235
(214) 749–1011

District Offices

611 Gaines Street
Suite 900
Little Rock, AR 72201
(501) 740–5011

Plaza Tower
17th Floor
1001 Howard Avenue
New Orleans, LA 70113
(504) 682–2611

5000 Marble Avenue, N.E.
Patio Plaza Bldg.
Albuquerque, NM 87110
(505) 474–5511

50 Penn Place
Suite 840
Oklahoma City, OK 73118
(405) 736–4011

727 E. Durango
Room A-513
San Antonio, TX 78206
(512) 730–5511

3105 Leopard Street
Corpus Christi, TX 78408
(512) 734–3011

1100 Commerce Street
Room 300
Dallas, TX 75202
(214) 749–1991

109 North Oregon Street
Suite 416
First National Bldg.
El Paso, TX 79901
(915) 572–7200

219 East Jackson Street
Harlingen, TX 78550
(512) 734–3011

One Allen Center
500 Dallas
Houston, TX 77002
(713) 527–4011

1205 Texas Avenue
Lubbock, TX 79408
(806) 738–7011

505 East Travis Street
Room 201
Travis Terrace Bldg.
Marshall, TX 75670
(318) 749–1011

REGION 7
(Iowa, Kansas, Missouri, Nebraska)

911 Walnut Street
24th Floor
Kansas City, MO 64106
(816) 374–7212

District Offices

New Federal Bldg.
210 Walnut Street
Room 749
Des Moines, IA 50309
(515) 284–4000

110 East Waterman
Wichita, KS 67202
(316) 267–6311

Suite 2500 Mercantile Tower
St. Louis, MO 63101
(314) 279–4110

Federal Bldg.
215 North 17th Street
Room 7419
Omaha, NE 68102
(402) 221–1221

REGION 8
(Colorado, Montana, North Dakota, South Dakota, Utah, Wyoming)

1405 Curtis Street
Denver, CO 80202
(303) 327–0111

District Offices

618 Helena Avenue
Helena, MT 59601
(406) 588–5011

Federal Bldg.
653 2d Avenue, North
Room 218
Fargo, ND 58102
(701) 783–5771

515 9th Street
Federal Bldg.
Rapid City, SD 57701
(605) 782–7000

National Bank Bldg.
8th and Maine Avenue
Room 402
Sioux Falls, SD 57102
(605) 782–4980

Federal Bldg.
125 South State Street
Room 2237
Salt Lake City, UT 84111
(801) 588–5500

REGION 9
(Arizona, California, Hawaii, Nevada, Pacific Islands)

Federal Bldg.
450 Golden Gate Avenue
San Francisco, CA 94102
(415) 556–9000

District Offices

112 North Central Avenue
Phoenix, AZ 85004
(602) 261–3900

Federal Bldg.
1130 O Street
Room 4015
Fresno, CA 93721
(209) 487–5000

350 S. Figuero Street
Los Angeles, CA 90071
(213) 688–2000

110 West C Street
San Diego, CA 92101
(714) 293–5000

149 Bethel Street
Room 402
Honolulu, HI 96813
(808) 546–8950

301 E. Stewart
Las Vegas, NV 89121
(702) 385–6011

REGION 10
(Alaska, Idaho, Oregon, Washington)

710 2d Avenue
5th Floor
Dexter Horton Bldg.
Seattle, WA 98104
(206) 442–0111

District Offices

1016 West 6th Avenue
Suite 200
Anchorage Legal Center
Anchorage, AK 99501
(907) 272–5561

501½ 2d Avenue
Fairbanks, AK 99701
(907) 452–1951

216 North 8th Street
Room 408
Boise, ID 83701
(208) 342–2711

921 Southwest Washington Street
Portland, OR 97205
(503) 221–2000

Court House Bldg.
Room 651
Spokane, WA 99210
(509) 456–0111

section
7

Bibliography

Advice for Persons Who Are Considering an Investment in a Franchise Business. Federal Trade Commission, Consumer Bulletin No. 4. Superintendent of Documents, U.S. Government Printing Office, Washington, DC 20402. 1970. 12 pp. 10 cents.

Discusses the selection of a franchise and what steps you can take to protect yourself as a prospective franchisee.

Anti-Trust Problems in Franchising. The Conference Board Record, 845 Third Ave., New York, NY 10022. July 1970. pp. 56–60. Reprint. $1.

A commentary on recent court decisions.

Are You Ready for Franchising? A. L. Tunick. Small Business Administration, Washington, DC 20416. (Small Marketers Aids No. 115, October 1965). Reprinted January 1974. 4 pp. Free.

Defines and discusses the franchise system of distribution in connection with the advantages, disadvantages, and investment requirements of a successful franchise operation.

Business Building Ideas for Franchises and Small Business. Med Serif. Pilot Industries, Inc., 347 Fifth Ave., New York, NY 10016. 1970. 48 pp. $2.

Presents helpful ideas and suggestions on the promotional aspects of establishing a new business.

Checklist for Going into Business. Small Business Administration, Washington, DC 20416. (Small Marketers Aids No. 71, revised August 1970). 12 pp. Free.

Checklist designed to help the prospective franchisees decide whether they are qualified or have considered the various phases of going into business for themselves.

Continental Franchise Review. P.O. Box 6360, Denver, CO 80206. Biweekly, $75 annual subscription.

Eight-page analytical newsletter to keep both franchisors and franchisees informed and current on important topics.

The Economic Effects of Franchising. Select Committee on Small Business, U.S. Senate. U.S. Government Printing Office, Washington, DC 20402. 1971. 354 pp. $1.50. SN 5270–1172.

Report includes economic effects of franchising in fast-food, convenience grocery, and laundry-dry cleaning.

Expanding Sales through Franchising. Al Lapin, Jr. Small Business Administration, Washington, DC 20416. (Management Aids for Small Manufacturers No. 182, March 1966). Reprinted June 1974. 4 pp. Free.

Discussion of the advertising techniques and promotional guidance required to increase sales and accelerate the growth of small companies through the franchise system of distribution.

Federal Assistance Programs for Minority Business Enterprise. Office of Minority Business Enterprise, U.S. Department of Commerce, Washington, DC 20230. 1969. 141 pp. Free.

Special catalog of selected, relevant federal programs designed to assist minority entrepreneurs and minority group members interested in new business opportunities, and supporting organizations and groups. Includes detailed description of each program, arranged by agency eligibility requirements, operational procedures, and sources of program information.

Financial Security and Independence through a Small Business Franchise. Donald J. Scherer. Pilot Industries, 347 Fifth Ave., New York, NY 10016. Revised 1973. 48 pp. $2.

Guide describing the management requirements, basic record-keeping methods, proper financial arrangements, and income potential to be derived from the establishment and operation of a franchise business with limited investment.

"Financing Franchise Systems and the Franchising Game Is Basic Operations." *The Cornell Hotel and Restaurant Administration Quarterly,* School of Hotel Administration, Cornell University, Ithaca, NY 14850. August 1971. pp. 17–32. $1 a reprint.

Outlines alternatives available to franchisors, financial climate for franchising, and financial checklist for franchisors. Discusses treatment of franchise fee and use of the names of celebrities for franchisor operations.

"Franchise: An Alternative to Independent Operation." Gary M. Munsinger, *Arizona Review,* Division of Economic and Business Research, College of Business and Public Administration, University of Arizona, Tucson, AZ 85721. Vol. 16, November 1967. pp. 10–14. 50 cents.

Details the major pitfalls facing the small business executive. Discusses the four basic types of franchise operations and the components of the franchise package, and weighs the strengths and weaknesses of franchising as an alternative to individually owned small businesses.

A Franchise Contract. Jerrold G. Van Cise, International Franchise Association, 7315 Wisconsin Ave., Suite 600W, Bethesda, MD 20014. 1975. $2 for IFA members, $4 for nonmembers.

A legal examination of the proper elements of a contract to protect franchisor and franchisee.

Franchise Index/Profile. Small Business Administration, U.S. Government Printing Office, Washington, DC 20402. 1973. pp. 56. 65 cents. SN 4500–00125.

A franchise evaluation process covering the franchise in general, the franchise company, finance and legal, training, marketing, and home office support.

Franchise Investigation: A Contract Negotiation, 1967. Harry Gross and Robert S. Levy. Pilot Industries, Inc., 347 Fifth Ave., New York, NY 10016. 1967. 48 pp. $2.

Explains how to select, analyze, and investigate a franchise and then what to look for when negotiating the franchise contract.

Franchise Laws, Regulations and Rulings. IFA Members: first set free, additional sets $50 per set, including update service for 1976. $400 per set for nonmembers, including update service for 1976.

Two-volume loose-leaf set contains every state franchise law regulating franchising and licensed distribution generally (except for regulations pertaining to specific industries such as gasoline, beer, and automobile dealerships), the Alberta law, the Uniform Franchise Offering Circular, names and addresses of administrators, tables of fees, renewal dates, and advertising regulations.

Franchise Operations and Antitrust. Donald N. Thompson. D. C. Heath and Co., 125 Spring St., Lexington, MA 02173. 1971. 190 pp. $12.50.

A comprehensive coverage of franchising and antitrust laws and regulations. Analyzes legislation and regulation of the franchising system with an overview of the nature of franchising.

Franchised Distribution. The Conference Board, 845 Third Ave., New York, NY 10022. 1971. 122 pp. $17.50.

This report examines the evolution and structure of franchising, and the organization and management of franchised distribution systems. Tables and exhibits are used extensively.

"Franchises—One Way to a Business of Your Own." *Changing Times,* Reprint Service, 1729 N St., N.W., Washington, DC 20006. July 1974. pp. 41–44.

Pitfalls to guard against. How to size up a franchise. Realistic appraisal of what you could expect of a typical, sound franchised business.

"Franchising." Leonard L. Berry, et al. *Journal of Small Business Management,* Bureau of Business Research, West Virginia University, Vol. 11. April 1973. 47 pp. Available from Adolph Rebensburg, General Secretary, NCSBMD, UW-Extension, 600 Kilbourn Ave., Milwaukee, WI 53203. $1.25.

Many facets of franchising are discussed, including realistic planning for the franchisee's prebreak-even operations, the franchising industry as perceived by small business. Guidelines to the potential franchisee are provided.

Franchising. Gladys Glickman. Matthew Bender & Co., Inc., 235 East 45th St., New York, NY 10017. 1976 revision. $33.50.

A legal look at franchising—for both the franchisor and the franchisee, including franchise relationships, legal and business problems, and development of the franchise-distribution agreement with legal citations footnoted. Also covers the legal, tax, and estate planning problems facing the franchisee.

Franchising: Its Nature Scope, Advantages, and Development. Charles L. Vaughn, D. C. Heath and Company, 125 Spring St., Lexington, MA 02173. 1974. 208 pp. $12.

A comprehensive overview of the nature, scope, and history of franchising as well as practical advice and information to students of marketing, potential franchisors and franchisees, and large companies contemplating entering the field. Notes, tables, figures, index, bibliography, and appendixes.

"Franchising—Recent Trends." Alfred R. Oxenfeldt, et al., eds. *Journal of Retailing,* New York University, 202 Tisch Hall, Washington Square, New York, NY 10003. 1973. 124 pp. $5.

Selected articles provide information on recent trends in franchising. Topics include a perspective on franchising, sources of revenue to the franchisors and their strategic implications, franchise operations and antitrust law, the fast-food franchise, the trend toward company-oriented units in franchise chains, blacks in franchising, and so on.

This book shows, step by step, the procedures to follow to franchise a business. The information given is not theoretical. Actual franchise operations were started and successfully marketed using the methods.

Franchising: Report of Ad Hoc Committee on Franchising. FTC Legal and Publications Office, Room 130, Washington, DC 20580. June 2, 1969. 37 pp. Free.

Report includes franchise problems, selection of the franchisee, buying and selling restrictions, and conclusions and recommendations.

Franchising & Antitrust (Complete Transcript Set). Four volumes, 1973 through 1976. IFA members $62.50; nonmembers $125,000.

Franchising & Antitrust (1973). IFA members $15.00; nonmembers $30.00. Official transcript of the proceedings of IFA's 6th annual Legal and Government Affairs Symposium. Topic: "The Antitrust Problems and Solutions of Distribution through Franchised Outlets and/or Company-Owned Outlets."

Franchising & Antitrust (1974). IFA members $17.50; nonmembers $35.00. Official transcript of the proceedings of IFA's 7th annual Legal and Government Affairs Symposium. Topic: "The Practical Application of Antitrust Laws to Franchised Distribution: Comments, Cases, Litigation, Regulation."

Franchising & Antitrust (1975). IFA members $20.00; nonmembers $40.00. Official transcript of the proceedings of IFA's 8th annual Legal and Government Affairs Symposium. Topic: "Growing with Antitrust: Practical Advice on Adapting Successfully to Antitrust Limitations on Franchising and Licensed Distribution."

Franchising & Antitrust (1976). IFA members $25.00; nonmembers $50.00. Official transcript of the proceedings of IFA's 9th annual Legal and Government Affairs Symposium. Topic: "Operating in the Franchise Relationship."

"Franchising—Some Hurdles Ahead." E. Patrick McGuire. *The Conference Board Record,* 845 Third Ave., New York, NY 10022. Vol. VII. July 1970. pp. 54–56. Reprint $1.

This article presents preliminary results of one phase of a study which reveals that many franchising executives foresee some serious obstacles to the continued growth of their organizations.

"Franchising Realities & Remedies." Harold Brown. *New York Law Journal,* 258 Broadway, New York, NY 10007. Summer 1972. $20.

Outlines sound courses of action franchisees may consider and sound principles against which franchisors must examine their operations if their enterprises are to avoid destruction through legal attacks.

Guidelines for More Effective Planning and Management of Franchise Systems. Robert J. Mockler and Harrison Easop. Publishing Services Division, School of Business Administration, Georgia State University, University Plaza, Atlanta, GA 30303. May 1968. Research paper No. 42. 60 pp. $3.

Research paper on the factors that contribute to successful management of a franchise system of marketing.

Handbook for Small Business. Senate Select Committee on Small Business and House Select Committee on Small Business. U.S. Government Printing Office, Washington, DC 20402. 3d edition, 1969. 200 pp. $1.75.

A survey of small business programs of the federal government includes special sections on business development, buying from the government, complaints against unfair business practices, disaster and emergency assistance, international commerce, management assistance, research, patents, technical information and technology, selling to the government, and taxes.

How to Franchise Your Business. Mack A. Lewis. Pilot Industries, Inc., 347 Fifth Ave., New York, NY 10016. 1974. 48 pp. $2.50.

A Guide to Franchises. National Federation of Independent Business. 150 W. 20th Ave., San Mateo, CA 94403. 8 pp. Free.

Important points to bear in mind when investigating franchise agreements.

How to Get Started in Your Own Franchised Business: Short-cut to Profit and Independence. David D. Seltz. Farnsworth Publishing Co., Inc., 78 Randall Ave., Rockville Centre, NY 11570. 1967. 197 pp. $3.95.

Guidebook to selecting and starting a franchise business. Explains how to finance and evaluate a franchise, how to get off to a prosperous start and to continue to grow. Lists with their addresses, 450 specific franchise opportunities.

How to Organize and Operate a Small Business. Baumback, et al. Prentice-Hall, Englewood Cliffs, NJ 07632. 1973. 5th ed. 612 pp. $11.95. (013–425736–7)

Role of small business in the economy. Buying a going concern. Justifying a new business. Acquiring a franchise. Financing and organizing the business, and so on.

International Franchise Association Membership Roster. International Franchise Association, 7315 Wisconsin Ave., Suite 600W, Bethesda, MD 20014. Free on request.

Listing of members, associate members, and companies with subsidiaries. (IFA members are marked with an asterisk in this book.)

Investigate before Investing: Guidance for Prospective Franchisees. Jerome L. Fels and Luis G. Rudnick. International Franchise Association, 7315 Wisconsin Ave., Suite 600W, Bethesda, MD 20014. Rev. 1974. 32 pp. $2.

Explains how to investigate and evaluate franchise offerings before investing.

"A Model for Determining Cash Balance Requirements in the Franchise Operation." Marvin A. Jolson and Takao Hoshi, *Atlanta Economic Review,* Publishing Services Division, School of Business Administration, Georgia State University, University Plaza, Atlanta, GA 30303. September 1971. Reprints $2.

An analysis of inadequacy of capital, constant sales, and linearly increasing sales.

"The Nature of Franchising: Part I—Its History and Part II—The Legal Difficulties." Wayne Lucas and B. J. Linder. *Atlanta Economic Review,* Publishing Services Division, School of Business Administration, Georgia State University, University Plaza, Atlanta, GA 30303. October–November 1969. $2.75.

History of franchising and its economic advantages and disadvantages. Legal difficulties in monopolization, restraint of trade, price fixing, and tying or requirement restrictions.

Pilot's Question and Answer Guide to Successful Franchising. Pilot Industries, Inc., 347 Fifth Ave., New York, NY 10016. 1969. 32 pp. $1.

Discussion of the franchise system with question and answer guide and checklist.

The Realities of Franchising. Harold Brown, et al. Financial Publishing Company, 82 Brookline Ave., Boston, MA 02215. 1970. 198 pp. $22.50.

Explores in depth the development of a franchise operation, the degree of control franchisors can assert to protect their interests, and the remedies of the franchisees for abuse. Court decisions and pending legislation are reviewed and analyzed.

Starting a Business after 50. Samuel Small. Pilot Industries, Inc., 347 Fifth Ave., New York, NY 10016. 1974. 48 pp. $2.

Information on how to establish a small business, a franchise business, and a business at home. Includes a list of over 175 franchise opportunities.

"State Franchising Regulations." E. Patrick McGuire. *The Conference Board*

Record, 845 Third Ave., New York, NY 10022. Vol. VII. October 1970. pp. 29–32. Reprint $1.

Summarizes the responses of 38 state attorneys general about the status of franchising regulation in their states.

"The Trend toward Company-Operated Units in Franchise Chains." Shelby D. Hunt. *Journal of Retailing.* New York University, 202 Tisch Hall, Washington St., New York, NY 10003. Vol. 49. Summer 1973. pp. 3–12. $2.

The issue of whether successful franchise systems would ultimately become wholly owned chains has been questioned. Presented here are data for a recently completed study on the economic effects of franchising. The study focuses on franchising in the areas of fast-food, convenience grocery, and laundry/dry cleaning.

A Woman's Guide to Her Own Franchised Business. Anne Small and Robert S. Levy. Pilot Industries, Inc., 347 Fifth Ave., New York, NY 10016. 47 pp. $2.

Explains the opportunities that have been created for women and how to take advantage of them. Includes a listing of over 150 franchise opportunities.

The Vaughn Report on Franchising of Fast Food Restaurants. Charles L. Vaughn. Farnsworth Publishing Company, Inc., 78 Randall Ave., Rockville Centre, NY 11570. 1970. 74 pp. $25.

A report and analysis of in-depth interviews with franchise executives covering: general characteristics of franchisor firms, recruiting, selecting and training policies and practices, financing of franchisees, real estate, consumer marketing, and franchisee relations.

index

A

A-1 Personnel Franchise Systems, Inc., 95
A-Tech, Inc., 81
A&W International, Inc., 130
Aamco Automatic Transmissions, Inc., 36
Abbey Carpet Company, 175
ABC Maintenance Development Corporation, 186
ABC Mobile Systems, 36
Acme Personnel Service, 96
Across the Street Restaurants of America, Inc., 130
Action Brokers Corporation, 204
Adia-Partime Services, 96
Aero Mayflower Transit Company, Inc., 226
Aid Auto Stores, Inc., 36
Ajax Rent A Car Company, 54
Ald, Inc.; *see* Cook Machinery Company
The All American Burger, Inc., 130
American Drapery Consultants, Inc.; *see* Decorating Den
American Heritage Agency, Inc., 230
American Laundry Machinery; *see* Martin Sales (Martinizing)
American Pre-Schools, Inc., 90
American Travel Inns, 193
Americlean National Service Corporation, 186
Amfood Industry Inc., 131
Amity Inc., 176
Angelina's Pizza, Inc., 131
Angelo's Italian Restaurants of Illinois, Inc., 131
Apparelmaster, Inc., 109
Arman's Systems, Inc., 132
Armico Business Services, 60

The Armoloy Company, 230
Armstrong Building Maintenance Company, 187
Athlete's Foot Marketing Associates, Inc., 76
Arthur Treacher's Fish & Chips, Inc., 132
ATV-Auto, Truck and Van, 37
Audit Controls, Inc., 60
Automatic Service Company; *see* Ford Gum & Machine Co., Inc.
Automation Equipment, Inc., 37

B

Baby-Tenda Corporation, 75
Bailey Employment System, Inc., 97
Baker & Baker Employment Service, Inc., 97
Bar-Master International, 231
The Barbers, Hairstyling for Men and Women, Inc., 57
Barbizon Schools of Modeling, 90
Barnhill's Ice Cream Parlor and Restaurant, 120
Baskin-Robbins, Inc., 120
Bathique International Ltd., 211
Beef-A-Roo, Inc., 132
Ben Franklin, 170
Bernardi Bros., Inc., 38
Bethom Corporation, 205
Better Homes Realty; *see* Bethom Corporation
Big B Franchise Inc., 182
Big Daddy's Restaurants, 133
Big Red Q Quickprint Centers, 201
Binex-Automated Business Systems, Inc., 61
Black Angus Systems, Inc., 133
Blimpie International, Ltd., 133
H&R Block, Inc., 61
Blue Dolphin Pools, Inc., 223
Bonanza International, Inc., 134
Bou-Faro Company, 38
Boy Blue Stores, Inc., 134
BQF Steakhouses, 135
Bresler's 33 Flavors, Inc., 121
Browns Chicken, 135
Bubble-Up Company, 221
Budget Rent A Car Corporation of America, 55
Buning The Florist, Inc., 212
Burger Chef Systems, Inc., 135
Burger King Corporation, 136
Burger Queen Enterprises, Inc., 136
Burger Train Systems, Inc., 137
Business Consultant of America, 62
Business Exchange, Inc., 62
Business Men's Clearing House, Inc., 98
Business & Professional Consultants, Inc., 98
Butler Learning Systems, 90

C

Calico Cottage Candies, Inc., 121
Captain D's, 137
Car-Matic System, 38
Car-X Service Systems, Inc., 39
Care/Sentry Drug Centers, 88
Career Employment Services, Inc., 99
Carpeteria, Inc., 176
Carvel Corporation, 121
Cascade Industries, Inc., 223
Casey Jones Junction, Inc., 137
Cassano's Inc., 138
Castro Convertibles, 176
Central Organization Inc.; *see* Coast to Coast Stores
Century 21 Real Estate Corporation, 205
Cheese Shop International, Inc., 114
Chem-Clean Furniture Restoration Center, 177
Chem-Mark International, Inc., 187
Chemical Engineering Corporation, 227
Chicasea, Inc., 138
Chicken Delight, 139
Chicken Unlimited Family Restaurants, 139
El Chico Corporation, 143
The Circle K Corporation, 114
City Products Corporation; *see* Ben Franklin
A Cleaner World, 181
Coast to Coast Stores, 171
Cock 'N Bull, Limited, 221
Coit Drapery & Carpet Cleaners, Inc., 182
Collex, Inc., 39
Commercial Services Company, 62
Commissary Corporation; *see* Dairy Isle & 3 in 1 Restaurants
Comprehensive Accounting Service Company, 63
Comprehensive Business Service Company, 63
Computer Capital Corporation, 64
Conroy's Inc., 212
Consumer Products of America, Inc., 231
Contacts Influential, 64
Convenient Food Mart, Inc., 115
Convenient Industries of America, Inc., 115
Cook Machinery Company, 40, 182
Corner Pockets of America, Inc., 208
Cottman Transmission Systems, Inc., 40
Country Kitchen International, Inc., 140
Country Style Donuts, 111
Courtesy Interstate Corporation, 122
Cozzoli Corporations, 140
Craig Food Industries, 140

Craig's, Inc., Candy & Ice Cream Shops, 122
Credit Service Company, 65
Crossland Furniture Restoration Studios, 177
Culligan International Company, 227

D

Dad's Root Beer Company, 222
Dairy Cheer Stores, 141
Dairy Isle & 3 in 1 Restaurants, 122
Dairy Sweet Company, 141
Davis Paint Company, 199
Decorating Den, 177
Delhi Chemicals, Inc., 178
Delko Transmissions Truck, Inc., 40
Dicker Stack-Sack International, 81
Dickies Fish & Chips, 142
Dictograph Security System, 220
Diet Control Centers, Inc., 172
The Diet Workshop, 172
Dino's Inc., 142
Dog N Suds Restaurants, 142
Doktor Pet Centers, Inc., 200
Dollar Rent-A-Car-Systems, Inc., 55
Domesticare, Inc., 188
Domino's Pizza, Inc., 143
Donutland, Inc., 112
Dootson Driving School, 91
Double-Cola Company, 222
Dr. Personnel, Inc., 99
Downtowner/Rountowner Motor Inns, 193
Drive Line Service, Inc., 41
Dunhill Personel System, Inc., 99
Dunkin' Donuts of America, Inc., 112
Duraclean International, 188
Dutch Girl Continental Cleaners, 183

E

E-Z Keep Systems, 65
Ecodyne Corporation, 228
Econo-Car International, Inc., 55
Econo-Travel Motor Hotel Corp., 194
Edie Adam's Cut & Curl, 58
Eldorado Stone Corporation, 82
Ells Personnel Systems, Inc., 100
Employers Overload Company, 100
Empress Travel Franchise Corporation, 208
Endrust Corporation, 41
Energy Saving International, Inc., 41
Engineering Corporation of America, 101

262

F

Family Inns of America, Inc., 194
Famous French Galleries, Ltd., 212
Famous Recipe Fried Chicken, Inc., 143
Fascination, Ltd., 209
Fast Foods, Inc., 144
FDI, Inc.; *see* Rayco
Fedder Computer Systems, 66
Financial Computer Corporation; *see* Fedder Computer Systems
Fireplace Shops, Inc., 213
The Firestone Tire and Rubber Company, 42
Flower World of America, Inc., 214
Flowerama of America, Inc., 213
Ford Gum & Machine Co., Inc., 226
Formal Wear Service, 76
F-O-R-T-U-N-E Franchise Corporation, 101
G. Fried Carpetland, Incorporated, 178
Frostie Enterprises; *see* Stewart's Drive-Ins
Frostop Corporation, 144

G

Gail Industries, 42
Gallery of Homes, Inc., 205
Gamble Stores; *see* Gamble–Skogmo, Inc.
Gamble–Skogmo, Inc., 171
General Business Services, Inc., 66
General Energy Devices, Inc., 82
General Franchising Corporation, 127
General Sewer Service, Inc., 188
Getting to Know You International, Ltd., 66
Gigantic Cleaners & Laundry, Inc., 183
Gilbert Lane Personnel Service, 102
Gingiss International, Inc., 76
Gloria Stevens Figure Salons, 173
Golden Chicken Franchises, 145
Golden Dolphin, Inc., 214
Golden Skillet Companies, 145
Golf Players, Inc., 209
B. F. Goodrich Tire Company, 43
The Goodyear Tire and Rubber Company, 43
Greentree Enterprises, Inc., 146
Guarantee Carpet Cleaning & Dye Company, 178

H

Happy Inns of America, Inc., 194
Happy Joe's Pizza & Ice Cream Parlors, 146
The Happy Steak, Inc., 147
Hardee's Food Systems, Inc., 147
Harper Method Incorporated, 58

Hazlert Ent., Inc., Main Street Original Ice Cream Parlors, 123
Heavenly Fried Chicken, Inc., 147
Heel 'N Toe, Inc., 77
Herbert Hawkins Company, Inc., 206
Hertz Corporation, 56
Hickory Farms of Ohio, Inc., 116
High Performance Auto Parts; *see* Service Center
Holiday Inns, Inc., 195
Homewood Industries, Inc., 82
Horizons of America; *see* Business Consultant of America

I–J

Imperial Hammer, Inc., 224
Incotax Systems, Inc., 67
Insta-Tune, Inc., 44
Insty-Prints, Inc., 201
Intercontinental Coffee Service, Inc., 123
International Dairy Queen, Inc., 148
International House of Pancakes, 127
International Multifoods Corporation; *see* Mister Donut of America, Inc.
International Real Estate Network, 206
International Travel Training Courses, Inc., 91
Interstate Automatic Transmission Co., Inc., 44
Jack the Stripper, 179
Jellystone Campgrounds Ltd., 73
Jerrico, Inc.; *see* Jerry's Restaurants *and* Long John Silver's Inc.
Jerry's Restaurants, 148
Jewel Companies, Inc.; *see* White Hen Pantry
Jiffy Drive-Ins; *see* Fast Foods, Inc.
Jilene, Inc., 77
Jitney-Jingle, Inc., 116
John Robert Powers Finishing & Modeling School, 92
Jreck Enterprises, Inc., 149
Juice Factory; *see* Greentree Enterprises Inc.
Just Pants, 78

K

Kamp Dakota, Inc., 74
Kampgrounds of America, Inc., 74
Karmelkorn Shoppes, Inc., 124
KFC Corporation, 149
King Bear Enterprises, Inc., 44
Knapp Shoe Company, 78
Kopy Kat, Inc., 202
Kwik Kar Wash, 45
Kwik-Kopy Corporation, 202

L

Lady Madonna Management Corp., 79
Lafayette Electronics Sales, Inc., 214

Lawn-A-Mat Chemical and Equipment Corporation, 184
Lawn Doctor Incorporated, 184
Lawn King, Inc., 185
Lawn Medic Inc., 185
Lee Myles Associates Corporation, 45
Lee's Bars 'N Stools 'N Dinettes; *see* Lee's Purchasing, Inc.
Lee's Purchasing, Inc., 179
Leisure Learning Centers, Inc., 92
Lelly's Drive-In Photos, Inc., 215
Lien Chemical Company, 189
Lifetime Pools, Inc., 223
Lil' Duffer of America, Inc., 150
Li'l Shopper, Inc., 116
Little Caesar Enterprises, Inc., 150
Lomma Enterprises, Inc., 210
London Fish 'N Chips, Ltd., 150
Long John Silver's Inc., 151
Losurdo Foods, Inc., 151
Love's Enterprises, Inc., 151
Lum's Restaurant Corporation, 152

M

Maaco Enterprises, Inc., 46
Mac Cleen's, Inc., 46
Mac Tools, Inc., 224
McDonald's Corporation; *see* McDonald's System, Inc.
McDonald's System, Inc., 153
McGraw-Edison Company; *see* Martin Sales (Martinizing)
MACLevy Products Corporation, 173
Magic Mirror Beauty Salons, Inc., 58
Maid Rite Products, Inc., 152
Main Street Original Ice Cream Parlors; *see* Hazlert Ent., Inc.
Majik Market, 117
Malco Products, Inc., 46
Management Recruiters International, Inc.; *see* Sales Consultants International
Manpower, Inc., 103
Marcoin, Inc., 67
Martin Sales (Martinizing), 183
Mary Belle Restaurants, 128
Mary Carter Industries, Inc., 199
Mary Moppet's Day Care Schools, Inc., 93
Masonry Systems International, Inc., 83
Master Hosts Inns, 195
Medi-Fax, Inc., 68
Medicine Shoppes International, Inc., 88
Medipower, 174
Meineke Discount Muffler Shops, Inc., 47
Meistergram, 231
Messina Meat Products, Inc.; *see* Red Devil
Midas-International Corp., 47

Mind Power, Inc., 93
Minute Man of America, Inc., 153
Miracle Auto Painting, 47
Miss America Teen-Agers Inc., 210
Miss Bojangles, Inc., 215
Mister Clark's, 215
Mister Donut of America, Inc., 113
Mister S'Getti Restaurant, 153
Mister Softee, Inc., 124
Mode O'Day Company, 79
Modern Bridal Shoppes, Inc., 79
Mom's Pizza, Inc., 154
Morrison, Inc., 195
Mountain Valley Spring Company, 222
Mr. Dunderbak, Inc., 154
Mr. Rooter Corporation, 189
Mr. Steak, Inc., 155
Multiple Allied Services, Inc.; *see* Miracle Auto Painting
Munford, Inc.; *see* Majik Market *and* World Bazaar
Music Dynamics, 94
Muzak, 68

N

Nadeau Looms, Inc., 232
Nathan's Famous, Inc., 155
National Auto Glass Company, Inc., 48
National Auto Service Centers, 48
National Automotive Industries, Inc., 48
National Homeowners Service Association, Inc., 69
National Surface Cleaning Corporation, 189
National Teacher Placement Bureau, Inc., 103
National Tire Wholesale, Inc., 49
Nationwide Chemical; *see* Nationwide Exterminating
Nationwide Chemical Products, Inc., 232
Nationwide Exterminating, 232
Nationwide Fastner Systems, Inc., 233
Nationwide Income Tax Service Company, 69
Nelson's Photography Studios, 216
New England Log Homes, Inc., 83
Nickerson Farms Franchising Company, 156
The Night Eye Corporation, 220
Noble Roman's Inc., 156
Norrell Temporary Services, Inc., 103

O

The Olsten Corporation, 104
Open Book Marketing Corporation, 216
Open Pantry Marts, Inc., 117
Orange Julius of America, 156
Otasco, 49

P

Pacific Tastee Freez, Inc., 157
Pail-O-Chicken, Inc., 157
Paintmaster Auto/Truck Paint Centers, 50
Paintmaster Systems Corporation; *see* Paintmaster Auto/Truck Paint Centers
Paperback Booksmith, 217
Pappy's Enterprises, Inc., 157
Parking Company of America, 233
Parts, Inc., 50
Parts Industries Corp.; *see* Parts, Inc.
Pasquale Food Company, Inc., 158
Passport Inns of America, Inc.; *see* Downtowner/Rowntowner Motor Inns
Patricia International, Inc., 94
Paul W. Davis Systems, Inc., 83
Pauline's Sportswear, Inc., 80
Payless Car Rental System, Inc., 56
The Peddler, Inc., 158
Pedigree Industries, Inc.; *see* Pedigree Pet Centers
Pedigree Pet Centers, 200
Pedro's Food Systems, Inc., 158
Peneprime International, Inc., 84
Penn Jersey Auto Stores, Inc., 50
Perma-Stone Company, 84
The Permentry Company, 85
Personnel Pool of America, Inc., 104
The Pewter Mug, 159
Pewter Pot Management Corporation, 159
Pioneer Take Out Corporation, 160
The Pizza Inn, Inc., 160
Pizza-Q Enterprises, Inc., 161
Place Mart Franchising Corp., 105
Playboy Clubs International, Inc., 210
Polock Johnny's Inc., 161
Poly-Oleum Corporation, 51
Ponderosa System, Inc., 161
Porcelain Patch & Glaze Company of America, 85
Porcelite Enterprises, Inc., 85
Port-O-Let Company, Inc., 190
Positions, Inc., International, 105
Postal Instant Press (PIP), 203
Pre-Schools, Inc., 95
Princeton Air Research Park; *see* Systemedics, Inc.
The Printing Place, Inc., 202
Putt-Putt Golf Courses of America, Inc., 211

Q

Quality Care Inc., 174
Quality Inns International, Inc., 196
Quick Print, Inc., 204
Quick Stop Markets, Inc., 118

R

Rainsoft Water Conditioning Company, 228
Ram, Inc., Realtors, 206
Ramada Inns, Inc., 196
Rasco Stores; *see* Gamble–Skogmo, Inc.
Rayco, 51
RCI, Inc., 175
Reaban's, Inc., 162
Red Wing Shoe Company, 80
Realty USA/Interstate Referral Service, Inc., 207
Realty World Corporation, 207
The Red Barn System, Inc., 162
Red Carpet Inns of America; *see* Master Hosts Inns
Red Devil, 163
Redd Pest Control Company, Inc., 233
Regal 8 Inns, 197
Reliable Business Systems, Inc., 69
Retail Recruiters International, Inc., 105
Rexall Drug Company, 88
Richard P. Rita Personnel System, Inc., 106
Robo-Wash, Inc., 52
Rodeway Inns of America, 197
Roffler Industries, Inc., 59
Roto-Rooter Corporation, 190
The Round Table Franchise Corporation, 163
Roxbury of America, Inc.; *see* Uncle Johns Family Restaurants
Rug Crafters, 180
Rustique Brik International, 86

S

S-H-S International, 106
Safari Campgrounds, 75
Safeguard Business Systems, 70
Sales Consultants International, 107
Sally Wallace Brides Shop, Inc., 80
San Juan Products, Inc., 224
The Schneider-Hill-Spangler Network: *see* S-H-S International
Selectra-Date Corporation, 234
Sermac, 190
Service Center, 52
Servicemaster Industries, Inc., 191; *see also* Sermac
Servomation Corporation; *see* The Red Barn System, Inc.
Servpro Industries, Inc., 191
7–Eleven; *see* The Southland Corporation
Shakey's Incorporated, 163
Shawnee Steps of America, Inc., 86
Sheraton Inns, Inc., 197
Siesta Sleep Shop, Inc., 180
Sir Beef Limited, 164

Sir Speedy Instant Printing Centers, 204
Sizzler Family Steak Houses, 164
Small Business Advisors, Inc.; *see* Whitehill Systems
Snap-On Tools Corporation, 225
Snelling & Snelling, Inc., 107
The Sobriety Sarsaparilla and Sandwich Shoppe Franchise Corporation, 125
The Southland Corporation, 118
Sparkle Wash, Inc., 192
Speer Personnel Consultants, 108
Sport Shacks, Inc., 217
Spring Crest Company, 180
Staff Builders International, Inc., 108
Staff Builders Medical Services, 174
Steamatic Incorporated, 181
Stereo Component Systems, Inc., 217
Stewart's Drive-Ins, 165
Stillman & Dolan, Inc., 70
Stretch & Sew, Inc., 234
Stuckey's, Inc., 165
Suburban Lawn Services, 185
Subway, 165
Success Motivation Institute, Inc., 71
Super 8 Motels, Inc., 198
Superior Water Conditioners, 228
Surfa-Shield Corporation, 86
Swensen's Ice Cream Company, 125
Swift Dairy & Poultry Company, 126
Swiss Colony Stores, Inc., 119
Syd Simons Cosmetics, Inc., 89
Systemedics, Inc., 71

T

Taco Hut, 166
Taco John's; *see* Woodson-Holmes Enterprises, Inc.
Taco Time International, Inc., 166
Tastee Donuts, Inc., 113
Tastee Freez Big T Family Restaurant Systems, 167
Tastee Freez International, Inc.; *see* Tastee Freez Big T Family Restaurant Systems
Tax Man, Inc., 71
Tax Offices of America, 72
Taylor Rental Corporation, 109
Team Central, Incorporated, 218
Tech Hifi; *see* Stereo Component Systems, Inc.
Telcoa, 221
Telecake International, 119
Telecheck Services, Inc., 72
Telophase Corporation, 235
Tepco, Inc., 235
Thetford Corporation; *see* Port-O-Let Company, Inc.
Thrifty Rent-A-Car System, 57

Timberlodge, Inc., 87
Time Tool and Equipment Rentals, Inc., 110
The Tinder Box International, Ltd., 218
Tippy's Taco House, Inc., 167
Travelodge International, Inc., 198
Treadway Inns Corporation, 198
TRW, Inc.; *see* Vulcan Tools
Tuff-Kote Dinol, Inc., 52
Turf-O-Matic, Inc., 186

U

Uncle Johns Family Restaurants, 128
The UNEEDIT Jewelry Company, 235
Uniforce Temporaries, 109
Union Chemical Company, Inc.; *see* Chem-Clean Furniture Restoration Center
Union Prescription Centers, Inc., 89
United Air Specialists, Inc., 236
United Rent-All, Inc., 110
United Safari International, Inc.; *see* Safari Campgrounds
Up-Grade Tutoring Service, Inc., 95
U.S. Rooter Corporation, 192

V

Vail Spring Works, Inc.; *see* Car-Matic System
Van's Belgian Waffles, Inc., 128
Village Inn Pancake House, Inc., 129
Von Schrader Manufacturing Company, 193
Vulcan Tools, 225

W

Waffle King of America, Inc., 129
Walt's Roast Beef, Inc., 167
Water Purification Systems, Inc., 229
Water Refining Company, 230
Watercare Corporation, 227
Wendy's International, Inc.; *see* Wendy's Old Fashioned Hamburgers
Wendy's Old Fashioned Hamburgers, 168
Western Auto Supply Company, 53
Western Metro Guard Dogs, Inc., 200
White Hen Pantry, 119
White Stores, Inc., 53
Whitehill Systems, 73
Wicks'N'Sticks, Inc., 219
Wiener King Corporation, 168
Der Wienerschnitzel International, Inc., 141
Wife Saver Franchises and Supply, 169
Williams, Edwin K., & Company; *see* E-Z Keep Systems
Winkys Drive-In Restaurants, Inc., 169
Winslow Manufacturing, Inc., 59
Woodson-Holmes Enterprises, Inc., 169

Woody's Little Italy Restaurants, 170
World Bazaar, 219

Z

Zell-Aire Corporation, 87
Ziebart Rustproofing Company, 54
Zip'z, 126